–TWENTY-THIRD CENTURY

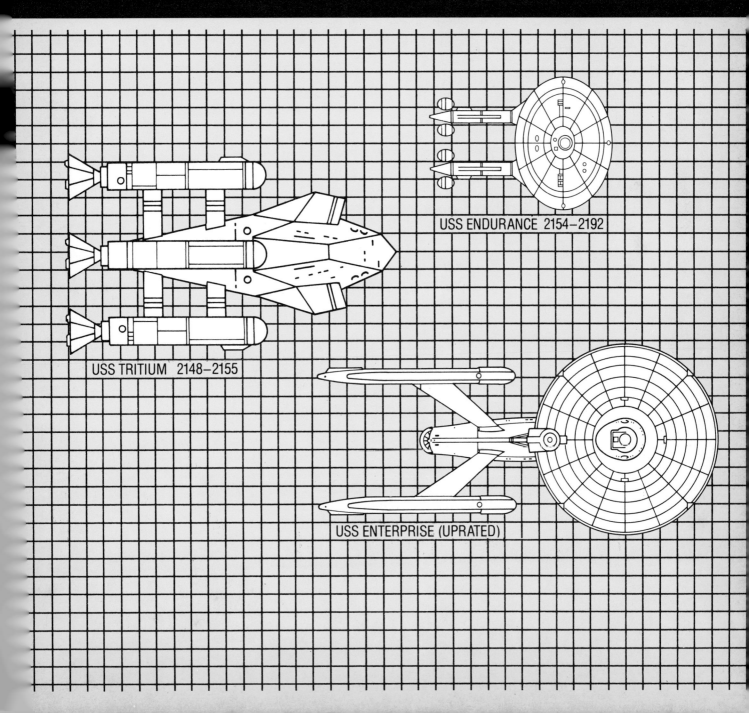

USS ENDURANCE 2154–2192

USS TRITIUM 2148–2155

USS ENTERPRISE (UPRATED)

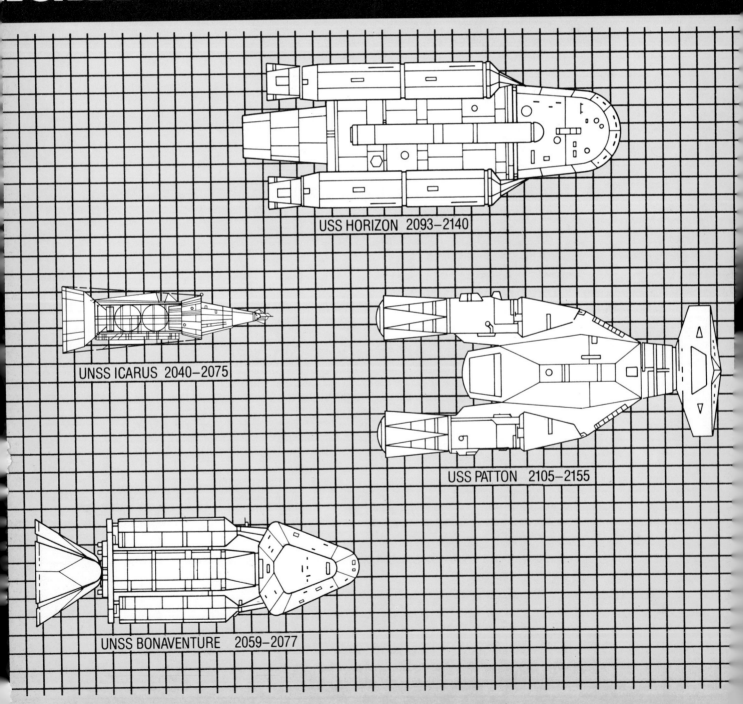

USS HORIZON 2093-2140

UNSS ICARUS 2040-2075

USS PATTON 2105-2155

UNSS BONAVENTURE 2059-2077

THE EVOLUTION OF SPACEFL

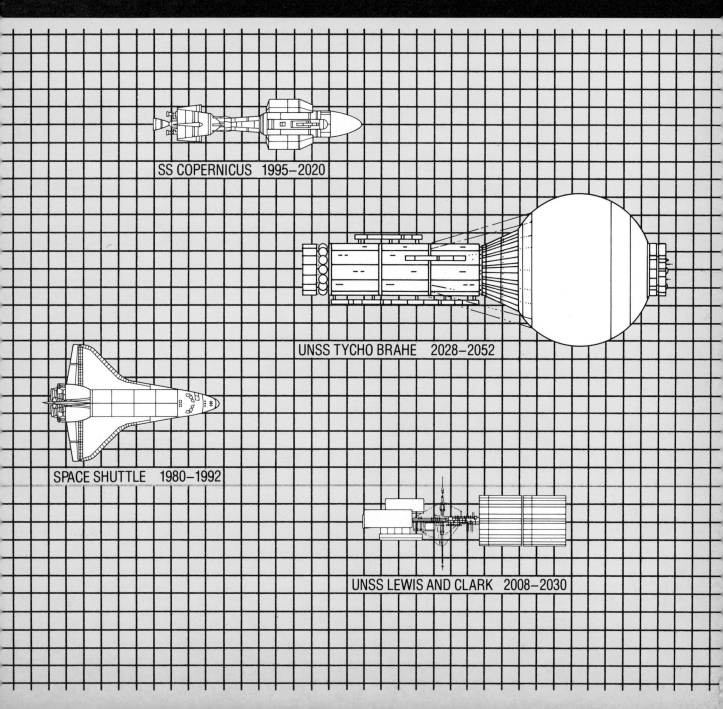

SS COPERNICUS 1995–2020

UNSS TYCHO BRAHE 2028–2052

SPACE SHUTTLE 1980–1992

UNSS LEWIS AND CLARK 2008–2030

STAR TREK®
SPACEFLIGHT CHRONOLOGY

Dedication
For Debbie and Sherri who are the joy and hope of the future.

Acknowledgments
A book of this nature can hardly be the result of the authors' efforts alone. In particular we wish to acknowledge the considerable assistance accorded us by Timothy Downey in preparing the manuscript. And Rick Sternbach, a masterful illustrator with an exceptional knowledge and understanding of spaceship technology.

There are a special group of people we would like to acknowledge for their helpful thoughts and enthusiastic spirit and who exemplify an optimistic future. Susan Sackett for her enthusiasm; Jesco Von Puttkamer for his vision; Ron Busch for believing; Karen Weitzman for her editorial assistance and understanding and Gene Roddenberry for creating the world of Star Trek.

ART DIRECTION: Corinne Felder

STAR TREK®
SPACEFLIGHT CHRONOLOGY

by Stan Goldstein and Fred Goldstein
Illustrated by Rick Sternbach

A WALLABY BOOK

PUBLISHED BY POCKET BOOKS NEW YORK

CONTENTS

INTRODUCTION

The faculty of Star Fleet Academy, the Editors, is proud and privileged to have had the opportunity to develop the forthcoming series of spaceflight chronology books.

The publication of this edition, The Earth, represents the first part of this ambitious project to provide Star Fleet Academy Cadets with a concise, illustrated history of their home planet's spaceflight evolution and development.

Henceforth, freshman Cadets of planet Earth, and eventually all freshman Cadets from Vulcan, Rigel, Alpha Centauri, Tellar and Andor, will be required to read the chronology of their home planet's spaceflight history.

But it is important to note when the United Federation of Planets was formed in 2087, man's space progress was equal to, and in some cases beyond, the other founding members. From mutual discussion and agreement it was decided the Federation would look to Earth technology for leadership in this area.

In addition, this is, of course, a concise history, to be used in conjunction with other basic spaceflight texts. The serious student of starship history should augment the foundation he receives from these pages with reference to the standard ENCYCLOPEDIA OF SPACEFLIGHT, edited by April and April. Also, the definitive index of all ships, past and present, STAR FLEET'S SHIPS OF THE GALAXY, can complement the illustrations in this volume.

This Chronology is divided into ten chapters. The first traces the beginning of space exploration back on Earth in the twentieth century, from 1957 to 2000 (Since this volume concerns only the Sol Star System, stardates have not been necessary; instead, Earth's standard dating system, the Gregorian, provides the units of chronology for this book.) The next eight examine the following two centuries in twenty-five-year segments, and the final chapter not only runs to the present time, but offers speculations of the future of spaceflight and its ancillary fields.

These opinions were solicited by Star Fleet Command and made available to Star Fleet Academy from the leading experts in their fields. The vital role they've served in strategic planning has, till now, justified their Code Orange Secret classification. However, the Editors feel that just as this Chronology anchors the Cadet to his past, so too should it point the future officer to the future.

Chapters 1 through 9 begin with an overview of the main historical, and scientific highlights of the period, followed by a four-page comprehensive illustrated ships chronology, major representative ships pages with detailed specifications, a minor representative ships and probes page with abbreviated specifications, a stellar explorations page of the era, and concludes with six pages of official logs. Chapter 10 contains, in addition to the previously mentioned speculations, an overview, major ship pages, a glossary and two ship summary pages which provide a comparison of ship evolution through the centuries.

A word about the format. The twentieth century did not have any centralized archive system to draw upon, so the Editors have researched the major reporting media of the time and developed stories on the first historic spaceflight events as they might have appeared in the twentieth century. The next two centuries' major events are illuminated by excerpting the appropriate Ship's Log entry, providing the unique perspective of the active participants. Space is explored by individual people, no matter what their affiliation, and the sum of their personal dramas and crises and breakthroughs is what makes up history. This Chronology should prove that truth.

So, Cadets, welcome to the history of Earth spaceflight. It has been an illustrious, galaxy-changing 258 years, filled with extraordinary achievement, darkened by great tragedy. The future should hold equal marvels and perils, and the future will be made by you, the readers of this Chronology. Learn the past to make the future.

Brigham Wu, Commandant
Star Fleet Academy 2215

20th
CENTURY

OVERVIEW

It is no doubt hard for star-bred cadets to imagine that only a little over two and a half centuries ago, space was still a dream for the people of Earth. But it was a dream as old as mankind, like the ancient myth of Icarus flying to the sun. Since the first man scanned with wonder the mysteries of the nighttime sky, the stars have beckoned, and he longed to respond. The opportunity came a little past midway into the twentieth century.

The Space Age began in 1957 with the launching of the satellite SPUTNIK 1 by Russia, and was followed very shortly thereafter by EXPLORER 1, sent up by the United States. These were the two major space faring nations at that time. Before the century was out, the Earth had been orbited extensively, its moon settled, and the initial exploration of planets in our home Solar System (Sol) had begun.

Of course, spaceflight did not just become an instant reality. For a half century before, such individual pioneers as Konstantin Tsiolkovsky in Russia, Robert Goddard in the United States, and Hermann Oberth in Germany painstakingly worked out the fundamental principles of guided rocketry and interplanetary travel.

Though often scorned as impractical dreamers, these brilliant scientists helped create the theory and technology from which all subsequent spaceflight grew. Without them there would have been no SPUTNIK or APOLLO 11 or DY-100. These men are honored as the fathers of spaceflight. The late twentieth century was a rapidly changing, turbulent time for mankind, marked by global tensions, social unrest, and unprecedented breakthroughs in science and technology. It was a time of great transitions: from an industrial to a nuclear and solar age; from a world of splintered, mutually hostile nation-states to the beginnings of cooperative, autonomous regions working in harmony and mutually beneficial competition; from an Earth-centered mankind to a space pioneering race reaching towards the stars.

The first full decade of the space age saw the United States pledge itself to putting a man on the moon. This ten-year-long national goal was achieved in 1969, when APOLLO 11 touched down on the Sea of Tranquility. Hundreds of millions of people from around the world watched their television screens as Earthmen stood, for the first time, on the surface of another celestial body.

But the excitement, interest and adventure of space which prevailed during the 1960's diminshed in the 70's. There were five other moon landings and SKYLAB, a research station, was put into orbit, but the overall attitude was one of apathy. People became very vocal about allocating funds for an accelerated space program when there were so many problems to solve closer to home.

One of these problems, ever increasing energy needs, endured throughout the 1970's and 80's. Back then, there were no matter/antimatter reactors, no ion power generators, practically no safe nuclear processes. Most industry utilized the inefficient burning of fossil fuels like coal or oil. Though many of the people of Earth believed their future was beyond their planet, to explore this possibility with greater support first required the ability to satisfy this fundamental problem.

The long-awaited solution to this problem began in the early 1990's, with the construction of the first orbiting Solar Power Satellite, which began transmitting energy to meet the world's pressing demands. With humanity now on the path to solving its energy needs, man could at last set his sights beyond his world to the neighboring planets and to the unknown galaxy beyond.

The abundance of cheap energy began the worldwide eradication of poverty. The Gross World Product (GWP) accelerated to sufficient levels to sustain most of the world's peoples. Futurologists of the time had predicted that the increased affluence would flatten the population curve to acceptable levels of growth. Concurrently, the excesses of the industrial age—pollution, ravaged landscapes, urban decay—started to be corrected using the nearly unlimited influx of energy resources.

Earth's gravest crisis in this period resulted not from any natural catastrophe or traditional political tension, but from biology, the then-revolutionary field of genetic engineering. The Eugenic Wars, Earth's last major conflict, were waged over this new-found ability to manipulate human genes, making it possible to wipe out most birth defects and organic diseases, such as diabetes. However, some leaders, like the infamous Khan Noonian Singh, also saw it as an opportunity to produce a genetically perfect master race. The 1990's witnessed an intense struggle between these would-be supermen and those who understood that humanity wasn't defined by some preselected string of genes. Fortunately, the latter prevailed, and today we still possess the incredible diversity that is perhaps the greatest hallmark of man.

A lasting testament to the global cooperation that prevailed in the aftermath of the Eugenic Wars was the construction of the Goddard Moonbase, mankind's first permanent landbased station away from Earth. An impressive product of international design and manufacture, this first of the many moonbases served as an invaluable resource depot for orbital space industrialization and as a center for space research. The original Moonbase survives today as an historic monument to early space exploration.

In retrospect, it is not surprising that mankind's ethical coming of age, the elimination of war, poverty and pollution, the beginning of true worldwide cooperation, the recognition of the supreme virtue of individuality coincided with the dawn of the space age. Before the most pressing problems on Earth were solved, space exploration could be little more than a ray of hopeful light cutting through the darkness of human despair. But it was just this ray, and the discoveries that resulted from the first space efforts, that helped mankind see its way to a new age of harmony and growth. By the beginning of the twenty-first century man was truly ready to go where no man had gone before.

SPACEFLIGHT CHRONOLOGY

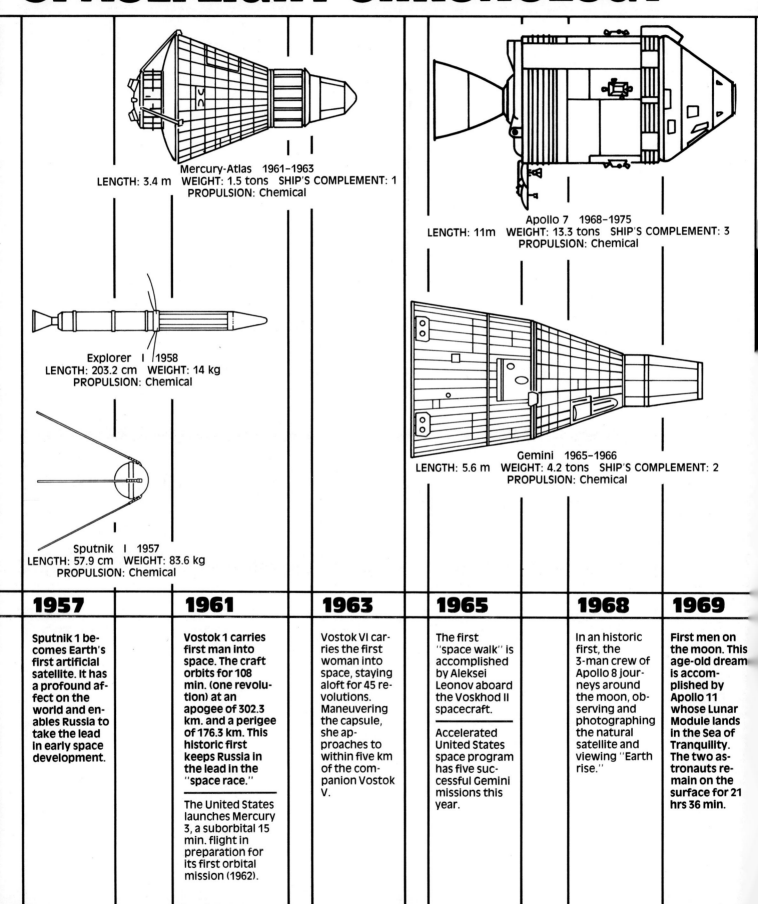

Mercury-Atlas 1961–1963
LENGTH: 3.4 m   WEIGHT: 1.5 tons   SHIP'S COMPLEMENT: 1
PROPULSION: Chemical

Apollo 7   1968–1975
LENGTH: 11m   WEIGHT: 13.3 tons   SHIP'S COMPLEMENT: 3
PROPULSION: Chemical

Explorer I   1958
LENGTH: 203.2 cm   WEIGHT: 14 kg
PROPULSION: Chemical

Gemini 1965–1966
LENGTH: 5.6 m   WEIGHT: 4.2 tons   SHIP'S COMPLEMENT: 2
PROPULSION: Chemical

Sputnik I   1957
LENGTH: 57.9 cm   WEIGHT: 83.6 kg
PROPULSION: Chemical

1957	**1961**	**1963**	**1965**	**1968**	**1969**
Sputnik 1 becomes Earth's first artificial satellite. It has a profound affect on the world and enables Russia to take the lead in early space development.	Vostok 1 carries first man into space. The craft orbits for 108 min. (one revolution) at an apogee of 302.3 km. and a perigee of 176.3 km. This historic first keeps Russia in the lead in the "space race."	Vostok VI carries the first woman into space, staying aloft for 45 revolutions. Maneuvering the capsule, she approaches to within five km of the companion Vostok V.	The first "space walk" is accomplished by Aleksei Leonov aboard the Voskhod II spacecraft.	In an historic first, the 3-man crew of Apollo 8 journeys around the moon, observing and photographing the natural satellite and viewing "Earth rise."	First men on the moon. This age-old dream is accomplished by Apollo 11 whose Lunar Module lands in the Sea of Tranquility. The two astronauts remain on the surface for 21 hrs 36 min.
	The United States launches Mercury 3, a suborbital 15 min. flight in preparation for its first orbital mission (1962).		Accelerated United States space program has five successful Gemini missions this year.		

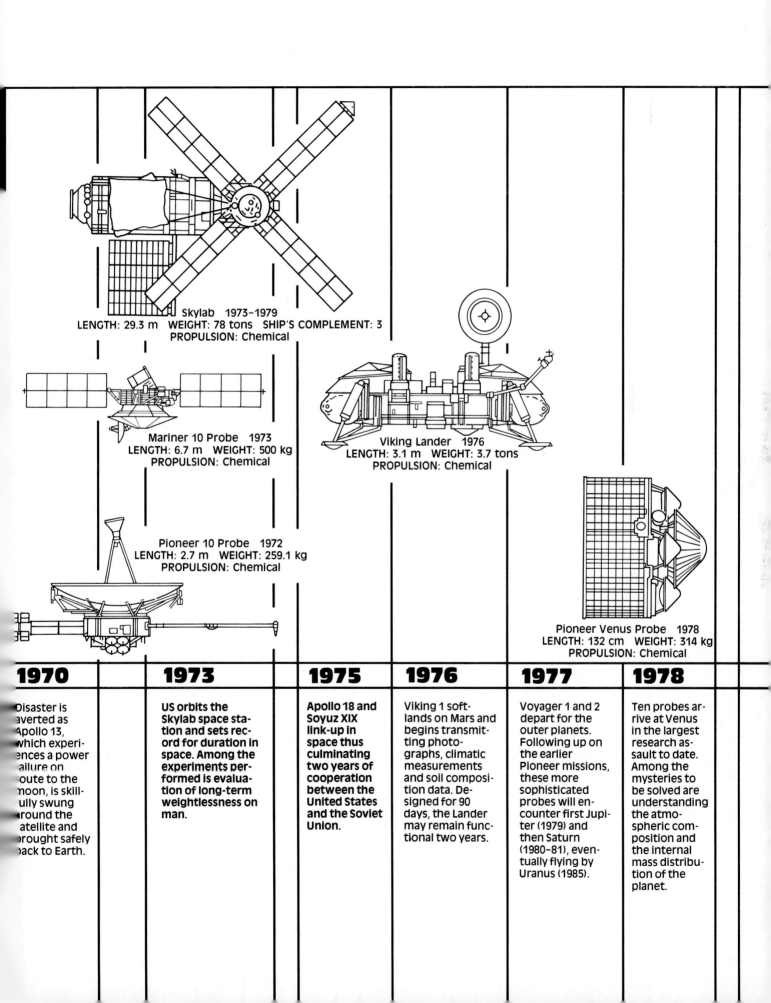

Skylab   1973–1979
LENGTH: 29.3 m   WEIGHT: 78 tons   SHIP'S COMPLEMENT: 3
PROPULSION: Chemical

Mariner 10 Probe   1973
LENGTH: 6.7 m   WEIGHT: 500 kg
PROPULSION: Chemical

Viking Lander   1976
LENGTH: 3.1 m   WEIGHT: 3.7 tons
PROPULSION: Chemical

Pioneer 10 Probe   1972
LENGTH: 2.7 m   WEIGHT: 259.1 kg
PROPULSION: Chemical

Pioneer Venus Probe   1978
LENGTH: 132 cm   WEIGHT: 314 kg
PROPULSION: Chemical

1970

Disaster is averted as Apollo 13, which experiences a power failure on route to the moon, is skillfully swung around the satellite and brought safely back to Earth.

1973

US orbits the Skylab space station and sets record for duration in space. Among the experiments performed is evaluation of long-term weightlessness on man.

1975

Apollo 18 and Soyuz XIX link-up in space thus culminating two years of cooperation between the United States and the Soviet Union.

1976

Viking 1 softlands on Mars and begins transmitting photographs, climatic measurements and soil composition data. Designed for 90 days, the Lander may remain functional two years.

1977

Voyager 1 and 2 depart for the outer planets. Following up on the earlier Pioneer missions, these more sophisticated probes will encounter first Jupiter (1979) and then Saturn (1980–81), eventually flying by Uranus (1985).

1978

Ten probes arrive at Venus in the largest research assault to date. Among the mysteries to be solved are understanding the atmospheric composition and the internal mass distribution of the planet.

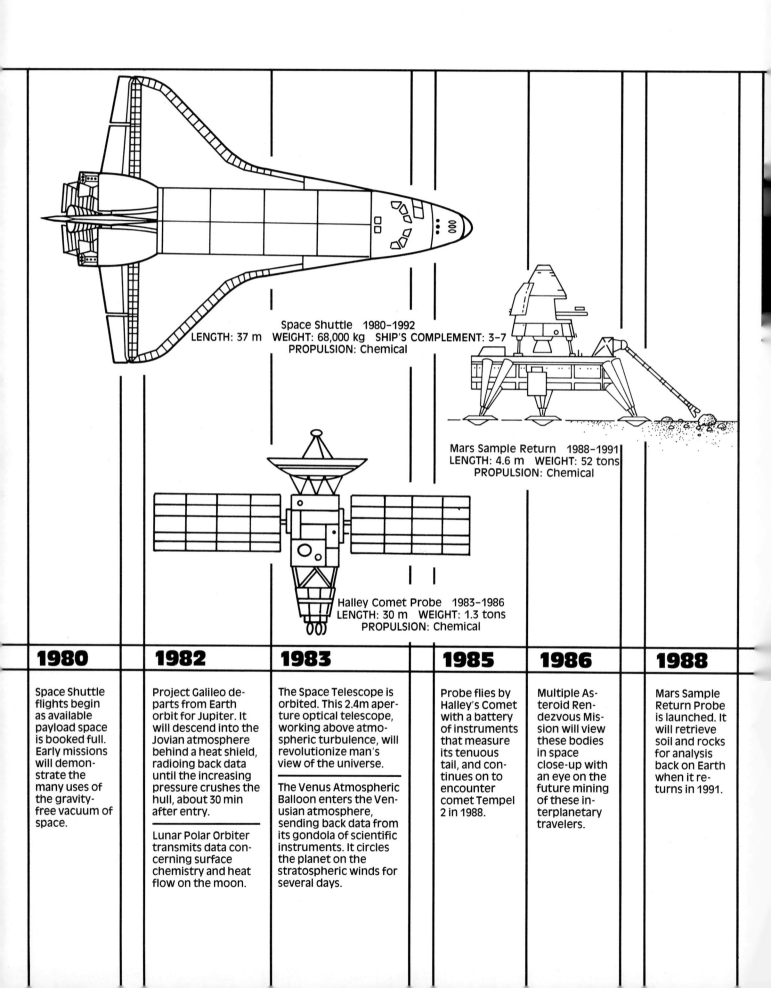

Space Shuttle   1980–1992
LENGTH: 37 m   WEIGHT: 68,000 kg   SHIP'S COMPLEMENT: 3–7
PROPULSION: Chemical

Mars Sample Return   1988–1991
LENGTH: 4.6 m   WEIGHT: 52 tons
PROPULSION: Chemical

Halley Comet Probe   1983–1986
LENGTH: 30 m   WEIGHT: 1.3 tons
PROPULSION: Chemical

1980	1982	1983	1985	1986	1988
Space Shuttle flights begin as available payload space is booked full. Early missions will demonstrate the many uses of the gravity-free vacuum of space.	Project Galileo departs from Earth orbit for Jupiter. It will descend into the Jovian atmosphere behind a heat shield, radioing back data until the increasing pressure crushes the hull, about 30 min after entry. Lunar Polar Orbiter transmits data concerning surface chemistry and heat flow on the moon.	The Space Telescope is orbited. This 2.4m aperture optical telescope, working above atmospheric turbulence, will revolutionize man's view of the universe. The Venus Atmospheric Balloon enters the Venusian atmosphere, sending back data from its gondola of scientific instruments. It circles the planet on the stratospheric winds for several days.	Probe flies by Halley's Comet with a battery of instruments that measure its tenuous tail, and continues on to encounter comet Tempel 2 in 1988.	Multiple Asteroid Rendezvous Mission will view these bodies in space close-up with an eye on the future mining of these interplanetary travelers.	Mars Sample Return Probe is launched. It will retrieve soil and rocks for analysis back on Earth when it returns in 1991.

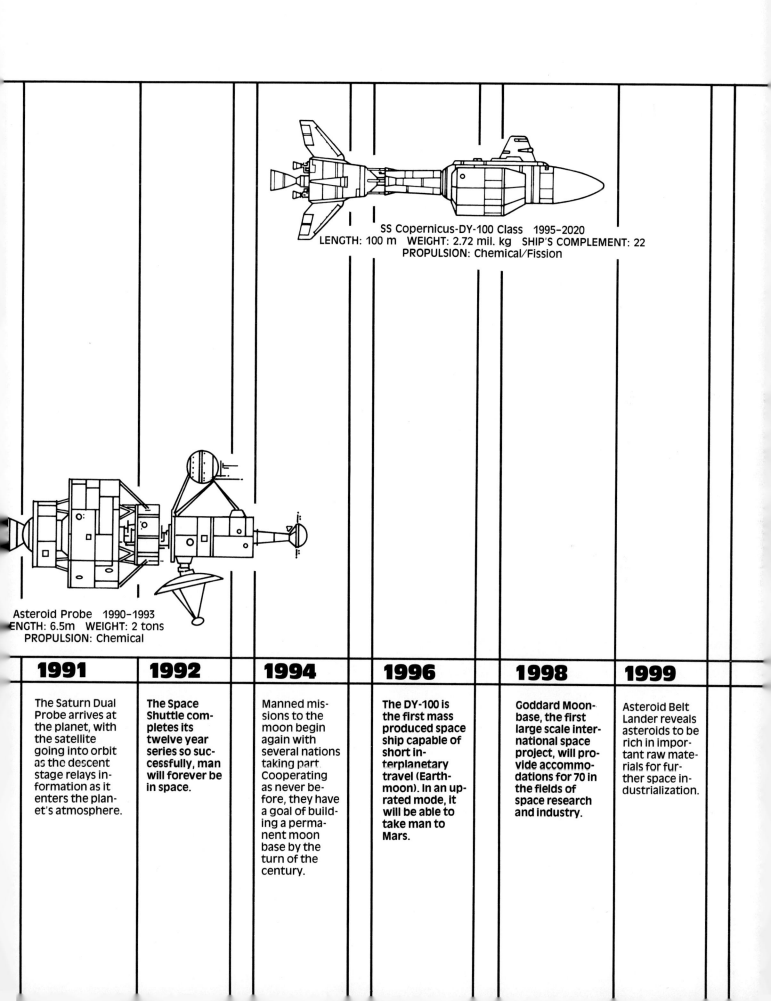

SS Copernicus-DY-100 Class   1995–2020
LENGTH: 100 m   WEIGHT: 2.72 mil. kg   SHIP'S COMPLEMENT: 22
PROPULSION: Chemical/Fission

Asteroid Probe   1990–1993
ENGTH: 6.5m   WEIGHT: 2 tons
PROPULSION: Chemical

1991	**1992**	**1994**	**1996**	**1998**	**1999**
The Saturn Dual Probe arrives at the planet, with the satellite going into orbit as the descent stage relays information as it enters the planet's atmosphere.	The Space Shuttle completes its twelve year series so successfully, man will forever be in space.	Manned missions to the moon begin again with several nations taking part. Cooperating as never before, they have a goal of building a permanent moon base by the turn of the century.	The DY-100 is the first mass produced space ship capable of short interplanetary travel (Earth-moon). In an up-rated mode, it will be able to take man to Mars.	Goddard Moonbase, the first large scale international space project, will provide accommodations for 70 in the fields of space research and industry.	Asteroid Belt Lander reveals asteroids to be rich in important raw materials for further space industrialization.

SHIPS

VOSTOK I

Vostok I carried the first man in space, the Russian Yuri Gagarin. Making a single revolution of the Earth in a little under two hours, the Vostok's successful launch and recovery kept the U.S.S.R. in the early lead of the "space-race," the 20th century period marked by strong competition between nation-states to develop spaceflight capacity.

Specifications

Length	6.7 m
Diameter	4.3 m
Mass	4734.5 kg
Apogee	302.3 km
Perigee	176.3 km
Orbital Period	108 min
No. of Revolutions	1
Scientific Experiments	Conducted radio and television communication with Earth.

Voyage Duration Capability	Capsule has life support and power supply system effective for 12 day orbital flight.

APOLLO 11

The famous Apollo 11 took the first earthmen to the moon, the fulfillment of a millennia-old dream. With one astronaut (Collins) remaining in the orbiting Command Module, the other two members (Armstrong and Aldrin) landed in the Lunar Module on the moon's dusty surface, spending over 21 hours conducting experiments and taking exploratory moon walks.

Specifications

Command Module	
Length	3.23 m
Diameter	3.91 m
Mass	5545 kg
Service Module	
Length	7.54 m
Diameter	3.91 m
Mass	24,000 kg
Lunar Module (Overall)	
Length	6.99 m
Diameter	9.45 m
Mass	15,091 kg
Total Mass (Command, Service, Lunar)	44,636 kg

Performance

Mission Duration	195 hrs 18 min
Lunar Orbits	31
LM on moon	21 hrs 36 min
Maximum Distance	402,576 km

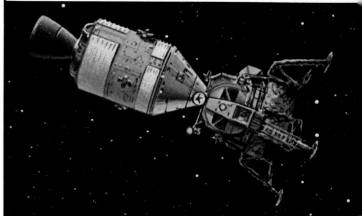

SOYUZ

This Russian-built spaceship was part of the longest Earth-orbiting series in early spaceflight history. A large amount of the experimentation necessary for space exploration was conducted on board the numerous Soyuz ships, and Soyuz IX linked up with the American Apollo 18 in an historic first. Soyuz IX held the early record for longest flight duration (425 hrs.).

Specifications

Length	8.7 m
Diameter	7.3 m
Mass	6690 kg
Apogee	224 km
Perigee	204 km
Orbital Period	106 min
No. of Revolutions	64
Duration	94 hrs 51 min

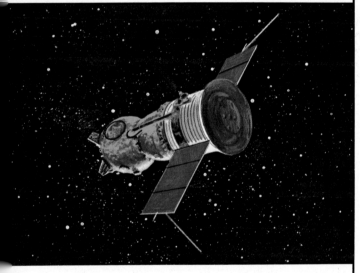

SPACE SHUTTLE

This historic twelve-year series truly put man into space to stay. The prototypes carried on the reusable shuttle laid the groundwork for space industry, and its work on the orbital Solar Power Satellites helped make space-generated energy a reality. Experiments conducted within its modular Spacelab provided invaluable data concerning long-term space radiation and the nature of the Earth's upper atmosphere:

Specifications

Length	37 m
Wingspan	24 m
Mass (Empty)	68,000 kg
Payload Bay	18.3 m x 4.6 m diameter
External Tank—length	47 m
Crew	Up to seven (Commander Pilot, Mission Specialist, 1-5 Payload Specialists)
Payload mass	29,500 kg

Performance

Mission duration	7-30 days
Number of missions per Orbiter	about 50
Thrust	11.6 nextons
Maximum altitude	1000 km
Fuel Capacity	703,000 kg liquid oxygen and hydrogen
Crossrange Capability	2035 km
Landing Speed	335 km/hr

SS COPERNICUS DY-100 CLASS

1995-2020

The *DY-100* was the first mass-produced interplanetary ship. With its interchangeable cargo/fuel/passenger modules and its engine pack of chemical boosters for Earth-escape and fission engine for short Earth-Moon transfer, the *DY-100* proved a most versatile carrier. Rigged for duration travel, it was the first manned ship to Mars and was used as the sleeper ship for the exodus of Khan Noonian Singh's "supermen."

Specifications

Length	100 m
Beam	23.37 m
Draught	34.9 m to fin tips
Mass	2.72 million kg
Living Units ⎫	Interchangeable modules
Fuel Units ⎬	each 27 m X 5.5 m X 6.57 m
Cargo Units ⎭	(795 cu m usable volume)
Engine Section (Combination Chemical/Fission)	Diameter - 6.13 m Length - 19 m
Command Con	12.3 m X 7.4 m X 4.9 m

Ship's Complement

Officers (Captain, Lieutenant)	2
Passengers — depending upon mission	0-20
Maximum passenger complement	22

Performance

Range: Standard	900,000 km
Maximum	387 million km (refitted for duration travel)
Cruising Velocity	55,000 km/hr
Maximum Velocity	80,000 km/hr
Earth-Escape Velocity:	38,000 km/hr
Typical Voyage Duration (Earth-Moon)	9.2 hr

Maximum Voyage (With Supply Stops)	934 days (Earth-Mars-Asteropolis-Mars-Earth)
Thrust - Chemical	4.2 million kg (700,000 kg each)
Fission	68,000 kg average thrust

Systems Overview

Navigation	Optical Tracker-Controlled Inertial Guidance
Communications	Laser Radiotelemetry
Computer	Standard Program-dependent Digital memory
Life Support: Gravity	No internal Control
Atmosphere	34.7% O_2; 11% humidity

Engineering and Science

- 6 Rocketol Chemical Boost Engines for Earth-escape and planet-capture
- 1 Amjet Hydrogen Fission Thruster for interplanetary transfer
- Emergency Chemical Retrorocket in detachable Primary Life Support Module
- Fuel: Chemical — liquid hydrogen (with liquid oxygen oxidizer)
  Fission — processed plutonium pellets
- Instrument Nosecone with Interplanetary sensor capability and experimental package compartment

Improvements and Innovations

- First mass-produced circumlunar ships
- Chemical/fission configuration allowed for both Earth lift-off and pioneer interplanetary flight
- Retrofins for take-off stability and upper atmosphere maneuvering
- Interchangeable modules permitted wide diversity of mission profiles, from routine circumlunar transport to long duration travel

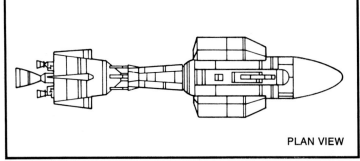

PLAN VIEW

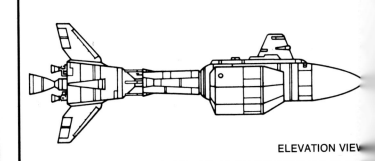

ELEVATION VIEW

SPUTNIK I   1957

The birth of the Earth's space age began in 1957 with the launching, by the Soviet Union, of a sphere shaped, artificial satellite with the capability to orbit the globe once every ninety-six minutes. Throughout the world people listened with wonder to the electronic voice from space as *Sputnik* achieved the first step on the long voyage to Earth's exploration of its Solar System and the galactic community beyond.

Specifications

Diameter	57.9 cm
Mass	83.6 kg
Apogee	901.8 km
Perigee	201.3 km
Velocity	29,995 km/hr
Orbital Period	96 min
Orbital Life	3 months

Scientific Experiments
Studied density and temperature of upper atmosphere. Studied the concentration of electrons in the ionosphere.

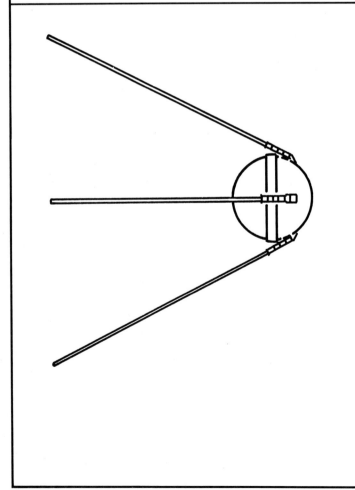

SKYLAB   1973–1979

The United States placed its first space station in Earth orbit in 1973. The station provided a suitable environment to study the effects of long-term weightlessness on man. Within its first year in orbit, three crews completed long duration missions, including one of 84 days, a record to that date, working in space without any ill effects. These missions provided the knowledge, confidence and impetus for the early interplanetary space exploration programs.

Specifications

Length	29.3 m
Diameter	7.2 m
Mass	70,900 kg
Apogee	444 km
Perigee	345 km
Orbital Period	102 min

Performance

Skylab 2	
Duration	672 hrs 49 min
Revolutions	404
Skylab 3	
Duration	1345 hrs 22 min
Revolutions	817
Skylab 4	
Duration	2017 hrs 17 min
Revolutions	1214

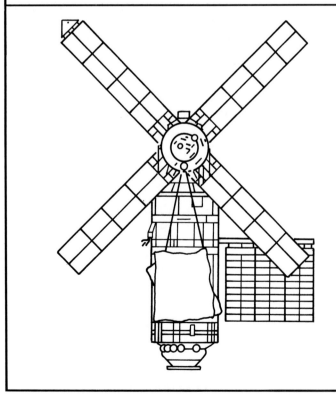

SOL SYSTEM EXPLORATIONS

Moon

The single celestial companion of planet Earth, the moon has played a vital part in Earth history, both physically and spiritually. A lifeless world devoid of atmosphere, the moon has stood as a gateway for mankind's outward progress, and the first manned landing by astronauts in *Apollo 11* was perhaps the most significant milestone in early space exploration.

The first Moon missions

Apollo 11—1969	Man walks on his first celestial body, the Moon.
Apollo 12—1969	Second Moon mission lands in the Sea of Storms.
Apollo 14—1971	Fra Mauro is the landing site for this mission.
Apollo 15—1971	Astronauts in Lunar Module land in Hadley Rille area.
Apollo 16—1972	Over 71 hours on Lunar surface.
Apollo 17—1972	Last two astronauts spend a record 75 hours on the moon and return with 113.6 kg of Lunar material.

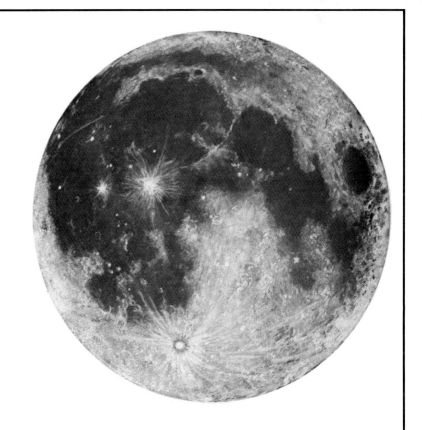

From the Earth to the moon—and back.

In the 20th century, there was but one Sol-System destination; the Earth's moon. Primative spaceflight capability prevented any further explorations although man arrived on the moon as early as 1969. The remainder of the century was devoted to many unmanned interplanetary probe series launched by several nations of the time, and the beginnings of Earth orbiting industry.

The early years of manned moon missions (1969-72), involved one country, the United States. Journeys in the 1990's were more international in scope as several spacefaring countries conducted experiments leading toward the construction of the Goddard Moonbase, completed in 1998.

As the century ended, mining activity was begun at various locations initiated by the demand for raw materials from Earth orbiting industry.

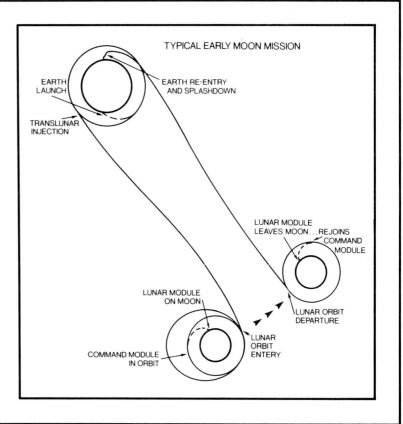

TYPICAL EARLY MOON MISSION

EARTH LAUNCH

EARTH RE-ENTRY AND SPLASHDOWN

TRANSLUNAR INJECTION

LUNAR MODULE LEAVES MOON...REJOINS COMMAND MODULE

LUNAR MODULE ON MOON

LUNAR ORBIT DEPARTURE

COMMAND MODULE IN ORBIT

LUNAR ORBIT ENTERY

LAUNCHING OF FIRST EARTH SATELLITE
(Based on TASS news release)

1957

In the exploratory spirit of this International Geophysical Year, the first artificial satellite of the Earth was successfully launched today, October 4, by the Union of Soviet Socialist Republics. This successful launching of *Sputnik 1* represents the culmination of years of tireless research by the worker-scientists of the Republic and proves that the free and conscious labor of the people can turn even the most daring of man's dreams into reality.

According to first reports, the propulsion rocket performed flawlessly in achieving the required orbital velocity of 8000m/sec. The satellite is presently describing an elliptical trajectory around the globe which will enable it to pass over the capital city of Moscow twice tomorrow, at 1:46 A.M. and 6:42 A.M.

Sputnik 1 is of spherical design, fifty-eight centimeters in diameter, and weighing 83.6 kilograms. It will travel at altitudes of up to 900 kilometers and calculations indicate it should remain in orbit three months, after which it will burn up like a meteor as it reenters the denser layers of the atmosphere.

The possibility of cosmic flight with rockets was first theoretically substantiated in Russia by the aeronautical visionary Konstantin Tsiolkovsky. Today, the work this great man of the nineteenth century inaugurated has become a reality through the efforts of great men of the twentieth century.

UNITED STATES ENTERS SPACE RACE
America launches Explorer 1
(Based on <u>New York Times</u> report of Jan. 31)

1958

President Eisenhower announced today the United States Army has successfully placed a scientific satellite into orbit around the Earth. "This launching is part of our country's participation in the International Geophysical Year," the President stated, further promising, "All information received from this satellite will promptly be made available to the scientific community of the world."

The Soviet Union, the first to orbit an artificial satellite, has come under criticism for the secrecy surrounding its space program. With America's entry into what some are already calling a space race, the president hoped the flow of scientific knowledge could proceed unimpeded by political considerations. Following up on that, the vice-president hailed the *Explorer 1* launching as a victory for the United States' peace policy.

The thirty-one pound satellite was put into orbit by a modified seventy-foot-tall *Jupiter-C* rocket. The rocket, developed jointly by the Army Ballistic Missile Agency (ABMA) in Huntsville, Alabama, and the Jet Propulsion Laboratory of California, was in three stages, the first using liquid propellant with the upper stages solid propellant.

As firing time neared at Cape Canaveral, an anxious silence fell over the crowd gathered there to witness the historic event. Just a few weeks ago, America's first attempt to launch a satellite failed as the rocket blew up on ignition. This time, blast-off was heralded by a billowing orange cloud of fire that thrust from the base of the rocket in all directions. As the spectators held their collective breath, the *Jupiter-C*, which rose painfully slowly at first as it cleared its launch pad, quickly picked up speed and shot into the nighttime sky. The people spontaneously cheered as America entered the race for space and mankind began a new dawn of exploration.

LOGS

FIRST MAN IN SPACE
Soviet Cosmonaut orbits Earth
(Based on official Soviet radio announcement of April, 12)

1961

... We interrupt our regularly scheduled programming for a momentous message to the peoples of the Republic ...

The Union of Soviet Socialist Republics announced this morning it has successfully put the first man into orbit around the Earth. The name of this Cosmonaut is Major Yuri Gagarin. He was launched in a sputnik named *Vostok 1*.

His sputnik revolved once around the Earth at a minimum altitude of 176 kilometers and a maximum of 302 kilometers. The weight of the space capsule was 4734 kilograms and the flight lasted 108 minutes.

Major Gagarin proclaimed upon returning, "Please report to the Party and the People that the landing was normal. I feel well and have no injuries or bruises." Major Gagarin, who is twenty-seven years old and married, is an industrial technician. He received extensive pre-flight training in preparation for this historic flight, training that he himself will now give to future cosmonauts.

Premier Khrushchev has hailed this great feat as another first for the Soviet Union and invites all Soviet citizens to take Communist pride in this achievement. The space race, he declared, is yet another example of the historic Marxist-Leninist dialectic which will see the honest workers triumphant over the capitalist oppressors ...

... That concludes our special report. We now return to regular programming.

PREFACE

The first decades of man's spaceflight were yet disorganized times, marked by rapid breakthroughs and heady competition among participating nation-states. However, unlike the Logs, which have been faithfully kept since the inauguration of the United Space Initiative, no comprehensive information retrieval system existed back then. Announcements of space events were apt to appear in any number of media: radio, video, daily newspapers, and periodic journals of popular or scientific appeal. In addition, reporting was often tinged with propaganda for the particular nation-state responsible for the event.

To give the flavor of those rawboned, vibrant first years of space exploration, the Editors have reconstructed announcements of the major events as they might have appeared in the twentieth century media. The remainder of this history, from 2003 to the present era, will employ the standardized Log format that is the norm for Federation Spaceflight Chronology.

FIRST INTERNATIONAL OUTER SPACE TREATY SIGNED
(From the United Nations Bulletin)

1967

The General Assembly of the United Nations has, after two years of consideration, signed the Treaty of Principles Governing the Activities of States in the Exploration and Use of Outer Space; also known as the Outer Space Treaty.

This document is the first to address the global implications of spaceflight by stressing both the peaceful exploration of space and the need to extend the rule of law into the skies. The Treaty states: "The exploration and use of outer space, including the moon and other celestial bodies, shall be carried out for the benefit, and in the interest of, all mankind."

The Outer Space Treaty limits countries exclusively to peaceful activities in space and specifically prohibits the use of nuclear or other arms. To guarantee this, an "oversight provision" allows any country access to another's installations to assure concordance with the military ban.

Of the many legal aspects covered in the Treaty, liability for damages resulting from space accidents and the need to avoid harmful contamination, or other adverse changes, to the terrestrial environment could prove to be two of the most important.

Finally, to imbue the spirit of international cooperation such humane considerations as, "Astronauts of one nation shall render all possible assistance to astronauts of another nation," are liberally found throughout the document.

Diplomatic sources agree the 1967 Outer Space Treaty represents the first important international step in the exploration of space and will, in years to come, be a model for all future international agreements.

FIRST MAN ON THE MOON
(Based on New York Times report of July, 21)

1969

Today, two American astronauts of *Apollo II* navigated their gawky lunar module onto the powdery surface of the Sea of Tranquility, fulfilling a decade-long national goal and a timeless dream of mankind. Man had made it to the moon. The following transcript between the Lunar lander *Eagle* and NASA officials at the Houston, Texas ground control records the historic moment:

Eagle: Houston, Tranquility Base here. The *Eagle* has landed.

Houston: Roger, Tranquility, we copy you on the ground. You've got a bunch of guys about to turn blue. We're breathing again. Thanks a lot.

Tranquility Base: Thank you.

Houston: You're looking good here.

Tranquility Base: A very smooth touchdown.

Columbia (the Command Module orbiting moon): How do you read me?

Houston: *Columbia*, he has landed Tranquility Base. *Eagle* is at Tranquility.

Columbia: Yeah, I heard the whole thing.

Houston: Well, it's a good show.

Columbia: Fantastic.

Tranquility Base: I'll second that.

Six and a half hours later, with his landing companion, Edwin "Buzz" Aldrin looking on, the Apollo Commander, Neil A. Armstrong, left the fragile security of Tranquility Base and became the first man to step foot on Earth's celestial partner.

"That's one small step for a man, one giant leap for mankind," declared Mr. Armstrong, in words that will probably be remembered for centuries.

The President of the United States called the astronauts at Tranquility Base to convey his country's profound gratitude for their courageous feat. "Because of what you have done, the heavens have become a part of man's world," he said. "For one priceless moment, the whole history of man, all the people of this Earth are truly one."

The two astronauts will conduct experiments and take samples of the moon crust back with them, which should provide invaluable insights into our celestial neighbor.

U.S. PUTS SPACE STATION INTO ORBIT
Skylab will be the astronauts home away from home.
(Based on <u>Newsweek</u> magazine report)

1973

Another era in space exploration began this week when Skylab was launched from Cape Kennedy, Florida. This orbiting research station will provide a semi-permanent home for astronauts studying outer space, themselves and our world.

By previous standards, Skylab has an almost opulent amount of accommodation for the three astronauts to live and work in. Made from a converted Saturn booster shell, the main workshop area is forty-eight feet long and 21.5 feet in diameter. It is divided into two decks, one serving as a laboratory for experimentation and the other as the crew's living quarters. In addition, there's an airlock module for space walks and a multiple docking adaptor to link the station with the Command Module for transportation to and from Earth. Three man crews will be rotated on a continuing basis, the length of residence increasing with each stay.

Skylab will serve several purposes. It will provide the first suitable environment to study the effects of long-term weightlessness on man, information which is vitally important for further space exploration. Its sophisticated cameras will furnish us with high-resolution pictures to be used for mineral exploration, crop surveying, oceanography, better land-use management and cartography. The data gathered from these photographs alone should economically justify Skylab's expense. In addition, a whole range of corollary scientific experiments is planned in such areas as astrophysics, botany and metals processing.

Skylab will give us more understanding of our world than ever before, and, the hope is, more understanding of the peoples who inhabit it.

US-USSR LINK-UP IN SPACE
Apollo-Soyuz fly first joint mission
(Based on <u>Time</u> magazine report)

1975

The air-lock opened and U.S. Astronaut Thomas Stafford stared across the docking module at his green-suited Soviet counterpart Aleksei Leonov. The men grinned at one another and each extended his hand in a gesture of profound significance for mankind. The link-up had worked!

This historic handclasp was the culmination of two years of cooperative effort between the United States and the Soviet Union. The astronauts and cosmonauts had exchanged visits, studied each other's equipment and language, and thoroughly geared themselves for the difficult challenge of linking up spacecraft of different nations in Earth orbit.

Finally this week the Soviet Soyuz was launched from the Baikonur Cosmodrome. Seven and one-half hours later, halfway around the world at Cape Kennedy, a Saturn booster propelled the last of the Apollo Series capsules into orbit. What followed was forty-four hours of complex maneuvering as the vessels precisely aligned their trajectories.

"Please do not forget about your breaking engines," joked Cosmonaut Leonov, as the crafts neared. The cheerful commander of the Soyuz crew, and first man to walk in space, proved a most able ambassador of high-flying détente with his steady stream of Russian humor.

The American Commander Stafford assured him he wouldn't, as the Apollo edged closer and closer, painstakingly slow, until the docking latches locked with a sturdy click. Then Stafford climbed into the docking module and shook hands with his fellow sky-pilot. After eighteen years of fierce, at times even hostile competition, cooperation had finally made its way into the space age.

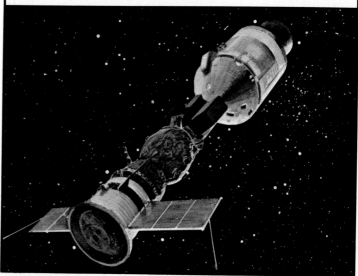

SPACE SHUTTLE ENDS ITS HISTORIC SERIES
(Based on NASA News Release)

1992

This week, the Space Shuttle made the last of its 553 flights, thus bringing to a close the most significant space effort so far in human history. And the Earth will never be the same.

Begun at the start of the 1980's, the twelve year series used two generations of reuseable Shuttle Orbiters to launch men and materials into space. The early shuttle flights were oriented primarily toward experimentation and demonstration of the possible uses of the gravity-free vacuum of space. Later missions were directed more towards economically fruitful applications.

Looking specifically at some of its achievements, early shuttle flights were responsible for *Spacelab,* designed and built by the European Space Agency, a complete scientific laboratory that fit into the spacious 18.29 m by 4.25 m cargo hold. This small space station made significant discoveries about long-term space radiation and the nature of the Earth's upper atmosphere. In addition, the series of orbiting optical and radio telescopes, unimpeded by the atmosphere's blanket, have been sending back invaluable astronomical data for a decade with more benefits from the series still to come. And for the first time, colleges and universities, corporations and even individuals, were able to put into orbit various satellites of space-worthy merit.

Later in the series, the shuttle carried prototypes for what should someday be major space industries in such areas as contamination-free pharmaceuticals, perfect lens manufacturing, and a revolutionary new generation of electronic microcircuits. In fact, the satellite-city, which is currently under design consideration, will be constructed to accommodate these budding space industries.

But the major credit attributable to the shuttle is the growing space industry which will dramatically raise the Gross World Product. The first Orbital Solar-Power Satellite has begun to tap the virtually unlimited free energy of the sun. Solar cell banks, over fifty kilometers in area, convert sunlight into five gigawatts (billion watts) of electrical energy, which is then beamed to Earth via coherent microwave laser transmission to receiving stations on the planet surface. As more satellites are built, and the new generation of greater efficiency solar cells is brought on-line, much of the world's industrial power will be generated by this network of nonpolluting space platforms.

With the advent of the new high-performance chemical boosters, whose waste products are water and carbon dioxide, another generation of Earth-to-orbit Space Ferries has risen to fill the place being vacated by the Space Shuttle. But the people of Earth will always be grateful for the Space Shuttle because it made them believe in space as a practical reality.

MYSTERY SHIP LEAVES SOLAR SYSTEM
(Based on United News Service report)

1996

n an apparent postscript to the recently ended Eugenic Wars, radar experts at NASA's Johnson Space Center in Houston, Texas, reported today a rocket was launched from Khanton, the capital of Khan Noonian Singh's collapsed empire. After several revolutions of the Earth, the spacecraft accelerated out of orbit along a trajectory that NASA scientists calculate will take the unknown ship out of the Solar System. The purpose of this flight, its destination, or whether it is manned or unmanned, remain mysteries as of this time. However, it is certain on its present course and speed, no human could live long enough to reach any stellar destination.

GODDARD MOONBASE OPERATIONAL
(Based on <u>London Times</u> report)

1998

United Nations Representatives of the nine major spacefaring nations met a half million kilometers from their home countries today to witness an historic first: the opening of man's first interplanetary permanent research station, the Goddard Moonbase.

Encased in three double-skinned geodesic domes, which were built with the combined efforts of American, European and Soviet engineers, the Moonbase provides generous living quarters for up to seventy persons, a comprehensive research and astronautics area, and a dome to be used for space industries. The base is completely self-contained, generating its own electricity and water supply, and recycling its air and wastes with near total efficiency.

From the very beginning, an important use for the Goddard Moonbase will be as a resource depot for Earth orbital space construction due to the moon's favorable low gravity launch requirements. The mining of titanium and other metals, and the manufacture of struts and girders within the space industries dome, will make space construction economically attractive for many Earth companies. What's more, the base will provide support and transportation services for men and materials at similarly attractive costs.

But perhaps the most significant aspect of the Goddard Moonbase is its true international nature. The recent Eugenic Wars have shown the necessity for peaceful cooperation among all nations, and the Moonbase stands as a vivid testament to the potential of global participation. As Secretary General Sevron said in his dedication, "Each time we on Earth look up at the moon, we can think of this base as a symbol of harmony and cooperation, of something higher than our own parochial concerns. The Goddard Moonbase is a sign post to the future. Let us all heed it."

21st CENTURY

OVERVIEW

Many of the foundations of spaceflight had been established by the beginning of the twenty-first century: earth-to-orbit transportation, interorbital transfer, space habitation, space construction, space industrialization, autonomous onboard navigation, laser communication, the basics of space medicine. Yet man's space efforts still lacked a worldwide consensus in spite of the enormous impact space exploration had so far produced. A global commitment was missing—until 2003. That year, the United Nations passed the historic United Space Initiative.

This was official recognition of a trend that had been steadily growing since the APOLLO-SOYUZ linkup. Cooperation among space nations had been increasing, and politically, the planet was moving closer to a one-world concept. Also, the Eugenic Wars were a recent reminder that the welfare of man required worldwide harmony. With the passing of the United Space Initiative, Earthmen pledged themselves irreversibly to exploration of the heavens.

The blueprints for man's space efforts can be found in this extraordinary document: the creation of a solar fleet, centralized research activities, joint settlement of the other planets, star probes, and the setting up of a Chronological Space Log (from which all entries in this Chronology have been taken).

One of the first results of this new initiative was the establishment of a permanent base on Mars. Started as a research station, it quickly grew into a space settlement and eventually established planet autonomy. Marsbase experiments yielded invaluable data about mechanics, environments and extraterrestrial geologies paving the way for all future space sciences. But most importantly, in 2021, it was discovered that the dust storms that ravaged Mars contained the planet's first evidence of life. Silicone fossil fragments of creatures with entirely different molecular structure than any life on Earth were the first proof that man was no longer alone, nor ever had been.

The exploration of man's home Solar System continued outward during this period with an extensive survey of the largest planet, Jupiter. Over ten times the size of Earth and 300 times more massive, this huge hydrogen and helium formed world had been a source of astronomical fascination for hundreds of years, ever since the first telescopes discovered a vast surface marking that became known as the Red Spot of Jupiter. Researchers stationed on the Jovian moon Ganymede sent probes into the Red Spot seeking its origin and cause. From the data returned, it was shown to be a permanent hurricane sustained by the magnetic configuration of the underlying mantle of liquid metallic hydrogen.

Closer to home, moonbases began springing up at strategic points including the far side, which was primarily used for radio astronomy research. It was there that one of the greatest events in history took place: the birth of the first spacechild. This world shaking milestone was yet another step toward the stars for mankind.

The area of space manufacturing had proven its economic competitiveness and functional desirability, and L-5 industrial complexes, such as Tsiolkovskygrad, began producing revolutionary new products in earnest; superconductive electronics for a new generation of microcomputers, perfect optical lenses, pure vaccines, and new metal composites for deep space construction, to name just a few. Asteroid mining began first with Earth-approaching asteroids, followed by mining colonies located in the asteroid belt between Mars and Jupiter which provided unlimited raw materials for industry in space and on Earth itself.

It was also during this era that space tourism has its origins, first with visits by families to space construction workers, followed by an increasing stream of curious citizens eager to experience the ineffable beauty of space.

Others saw space as a new beginning, a limitless frontier that would give their dreams a chance the Earth no longer could. Groups of like-minded people banded together to create L-5 and asteroid colonies to house their vision of the perfect society. Since the demand for deep space labor was desperate, the United Nations encouraged these space age pilgrims with the "Space Homesteading Act of 2014," and our present pluralistic space society owes much to this initial openness to all varieties of people.

As civilization expanded further into the Solar System, the need for more advanced propulsion became painfully evident. The messy chemical rockets of the twentieth century could not traverse the planetary void within acceptable time limits. Meeting this challenge, fission propulsion was perfected, harnessing the explosive releases of nuclear energy to propel rockets with a high enough thrust and impulse to span solar distances.

The Earth-Saturn Probe was the era's most important mission because of the discovery of extraterrestrial evidence, in the form of mining and excavating scars, on two moons. (To this day, who they were remains a mystery.) The era's greatest tragedy was the unfortunate loss of the UNSS COURAGEOUS, which lead to the raising of design and safety standards for all forthcoming ships.

But man was not content to remain restricted to his home Solar System. The Stellar Series of unmanned probes were sent on data-collecting missions to the nearest stars to our sun (Alpha Centauri, Barnard's Star, Sirius), one of which, the U THANT, detected for the first time the presence of appreciable amounts of antimatter in the interstellar void. This resource was later exploited for the fuel needed for matter/antimatter propulsion.

Toward the end of this era, a new generation of ships, the DY-500 series, journeyed well into the extra-solar void beyond Pluto, familiarizing crews with extended voyages of up to three years. But it would be almost two decades of tireless experimentation before science supplied the answers needed for even rudimentary interstellar travel to the stars.

SPACEFLIGHT CHRONOLOGY

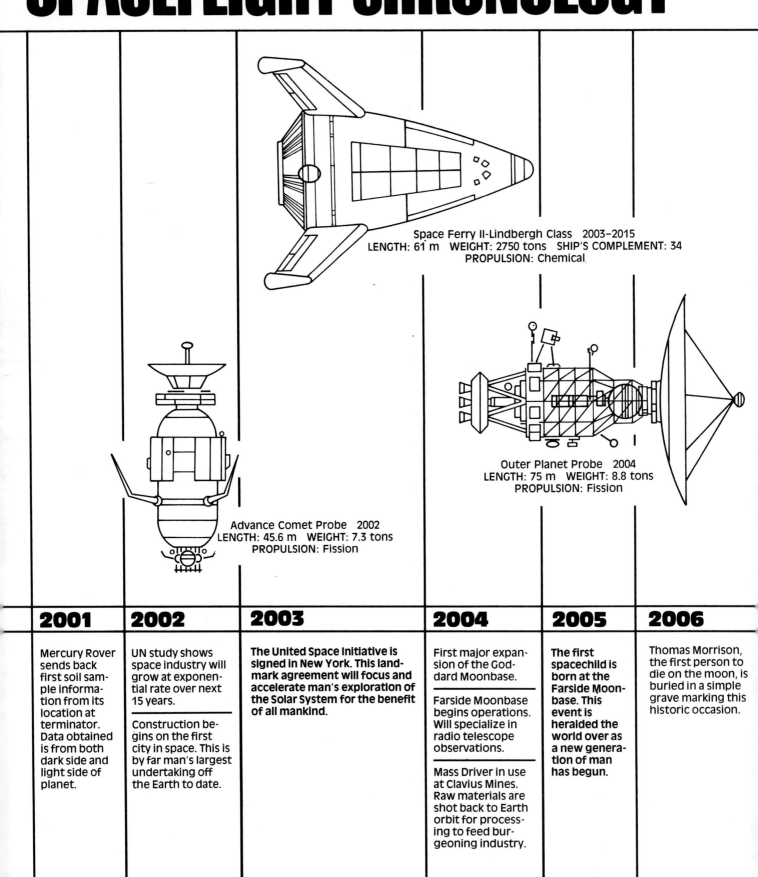

Space Ferry II-Lindbergh Class   2003–2015
LENGTH: 61 m   WEIGHT: 2750 tons   SHIP'S COMPLEMENT: 34
PROPULSION: Chemical

Outer Planet Probe   2004
LENGTH: 75 m   WEIGHT: 8.8 tons
PROPULSION: Fission

Advance Comet Probe   2002
LENGTH: 45.6 m   WEIGHT: 7.3 tons
PROPULSION: Fission

2001	**2002**	**2003**	**2004**	**2005**	**2006**
Mercury Rover sends back first soil sample information from its location at terminator. Data obtained is from both dark side and light side of planet.	UN study shows space industry will grow at exponential rate over next 15 years. Construction begins on the first city in space. This is by far man's largest undertaking off the Earth to date.	**The United Space Initiative is signed in New York. This landmark agreement will focus and accelerate man's exploration of the Solar System for the benefit of all mankind.**	First major expansion of the Goddard Moonbase. Farside Moonbase begins operations. Will specialize in radio telescope observations. Mass Driver in use at Clavius Mines. Raw materials are shot back to Earth orbit for processing to feed burgeoning industry.	**The first spacechild is born at the Farside Moonbase. This event is heralded the world over as a new generation of man has begun.**	Thomas Morrison, the first person to die on the moon, is buried in a simple grave marking this historic occasion.

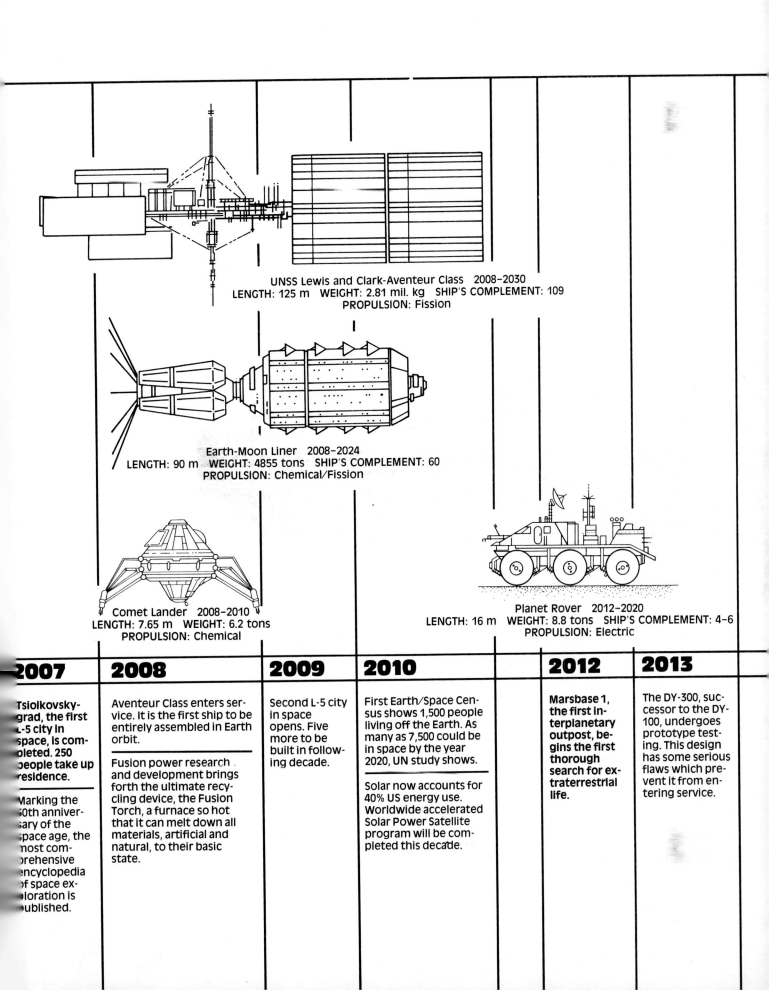

UNSS Lewis and Clark-Aventeur Class   2008–2030
LENGTH: 125 m   WEIGHT: 2.81 mil. kg   SHIP'S COMPLEMENT: 109
PROPULSION: Fission

Earth-Moon Liner   2008–2024
LENGTH: 90 m   WEIGHT: 4855 tons   SHIP'S COMPLEMENT: 60
PROPULSION: Chemical/Fission

Comet Lander   2008–2010
LENGTH: 7.65 m   WEIGHT: 6.2 tons
PROPULSION: Chemical

Planet Rover   2012-2020
LENGTH: 16 m   WEIGHT: 8.8 tons   SHIP'S COMPLEMENT: 4–6
PROPULSION: Electric

2007	**2008**	**2009**	**2010**	**2012**	**2013**
Tsiolkovsky-grad, the first L-5 city in space, is completed. 250 people take up residence. Marking the 50th anniversary of the space age, the most comprehensive encyclopedia of space exploration is published.	Aventeur Class enters service. It is the first ship to be entirely assembled in Earth orbit. Fusion power research and development brings forth the ultimate recycling device, the Fusion Torch, a furnace so hot that it can melt down all materials, artificial and natural, to their basic state.	Second L-5 city in space opens. Five more to be built in following decade.	First Earth/Space Census shows 1,500 people living off the Earth. As many as 7,500 could be in space by the year 2020, UN study shows. Solar now accounts for 40% US energy use. Worldwide accelerated Solar Power Satellite program will be completed this decade.	Marsbase 1, the first interplanetary outpost, begins the first thorough search for extraterrestrial life.	The DY-300, successor to the DY-100, undergoes prototype testing. This design has some serious flaws which prevent it from entering service.

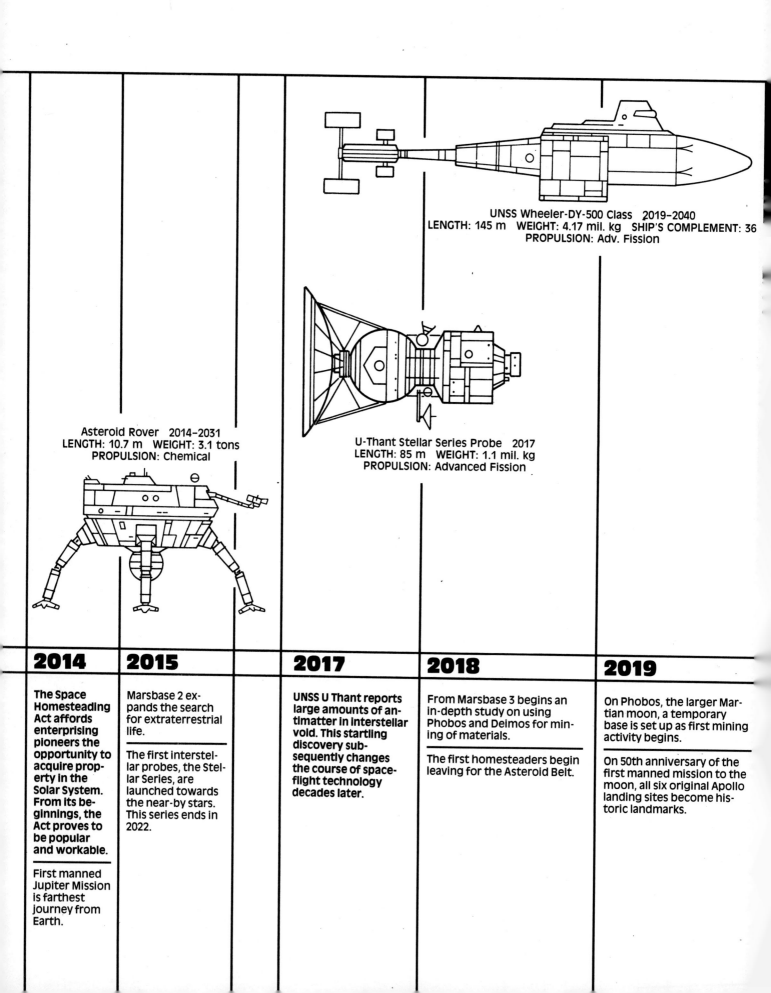

UNSS Wheeler-DY-500 Class 2019–2040
LENGTH: 145 m   WEIGHT: 4.17 mil. kg   SHIP'S COMPLEMENT: 36
PROPULSION: Adv. Fission

U-Thant Stellar Series Probe 2017
LENGTH: 85 m   WEIGHT: 1.1 mil. kg
PROPULSION: Advanced Fission

Asteroid Rover 2014–2031
LENGTH: 10.7 m   WEIGHT: 3.1 tons
PROPULSION: Chemical

2014	**2015**		**2017**	**2018**	**2019**
The Space Homesteading Act affords enterprising pioneers the opportunity to acquire property in the Solar System. From its beginnings, the Act proves to be popular and workable.	Marsbase 2 expands the search for extraterrestrial life.		UNSS U Thant reports large amounts of antimatter in interstellar void. This startling discovery subsequently changes the course of spaceflight technology decades later.	From Marsbase 3 begins an in-depth study on using Phobos and Deimos for mining of materials.	On Phobos, the larger Martian moon, a temporary base is set up as first mining activity begins.
First manned Jupiter Mission is farthest journey from Earth.	The first interstellar probes, the Stellar Series, are launched towards the near-by stars. This series ends in 2022.			The first homesteaders begin leaving for the Asteroid Belt.	On 50th anniversary of the first manned mission to the moon, all six original Apollo landing sites become historic landmarks.

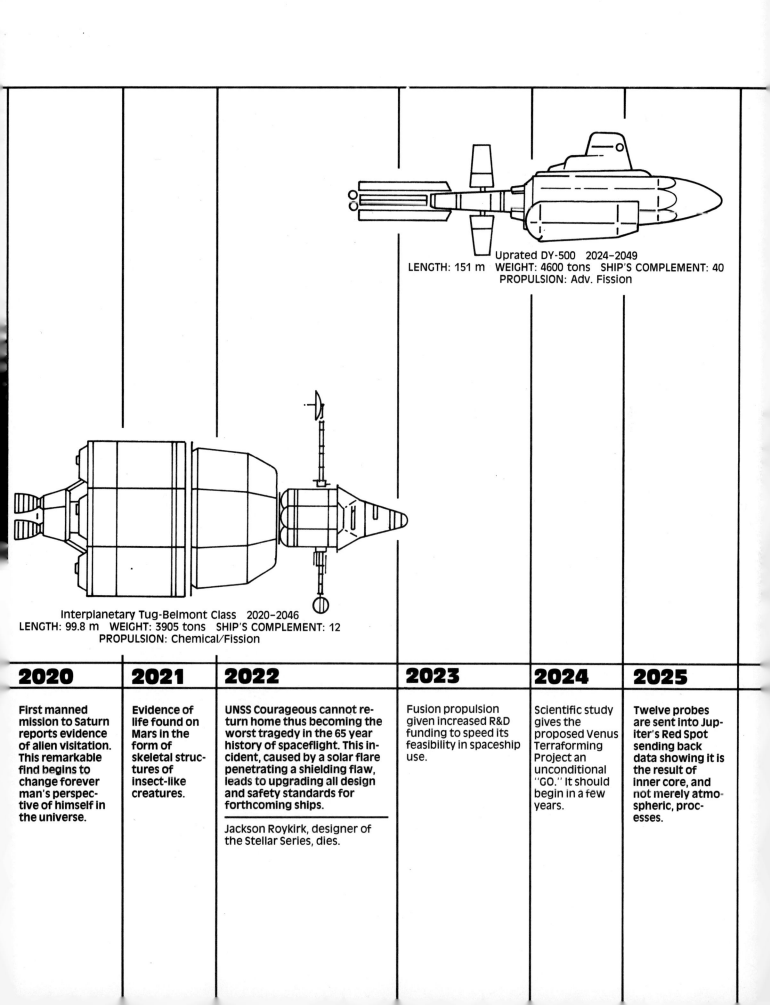

Uprated DY-500   2024–2049
LENGTH: 151 m   WEIGHT: 4600 tons   SHIP'S COMPLEMENT: 40
PROPULSION: Adv. Fission

Interplanetary Tug-Belmont Class   2020–2046
LENGTH: 99.8 m   WEIGHT: 3905 tons   SHIP'S COMPLEMENT: 12
PROPULSION: Chemical/Fission

2020

First manned mission to Saturn reports evidence of alien visitation. This remarkable find begins to change forever man's perspective of himself in the universe.

2021

Evidence of life found on Mars in the form of skeletal structures of insect-like creatures.

2022

UNSS Courageous cannot return home thus becoming the worst tragedy in the 65 year history of spaceflight. This incident, caused by a solar flare penetrating a shielding flaw, leads to upgrading all design and safety standards for forthcoming ships.

Jackson Roykirk, designer of the Stellar Series, dies.

2023

Fusion propulsion given increased R&D funding to speed its feasibility in spaceship use.

2024

Scientific study gives the proposed Venus Terraforming Project an unconditional "GO." It should begin in a few years.

2025

Twelve probes are sent into Jupiter's Red Spot sending back data showing it is the result of inner core, and not merely atmospheric, processes.

UNSS LEWIS AND CLARK
AVENTEUR CLASS
2008-2030

This was the first ship whose final assembly was completed entirely in Earth orbit. Advanced fission propulsion and capacious cargo modules made this an invaluable vessel for early interplanetary flight, and in fact the *Lewis and Clark* was the first manned ship to Jupiter. Under the command of Colonel Shaun Christopher, later Chief of Staff of UNSF, it took part in the historic Earth-Saturn probe of 2020.

Specifications

Length	125 m
Beam	28.5 m
Draught	28.5 m
Antennae Span	59.3 m
Mass	2.81 million kg
Heat Radiators	each 2 m X 8.7 m
Carrier Modules	up to 12, each with 1140 cu m usable volume
Front Command Sensors (not visible here)	80 sq m area of command monitors

Ship's Complement

Officers (Captain, Lieutenant, Ensign)	3
Crew	12
Passenger Capacity	94
Standard Ship's Complement	109

Performance

Range - Standard	150 million km (Earth - Mars)
Maximum	2.57 billion km (Earth - Saturn)
Cruising Velocity	700,550 km/hr
Typical Voyage Duration	5 - 6 days (Earth - Mars)
	39.5 days (Earth - Jupiter)
	81 days (Earth - Saturn)
Thrust	135,000 kg per fission engine

Systems Overview

Navigation	Gamma ray tracker-controlled Inertial Guidance
Communication	Laser Radiotelemetry
Computer	Multiscan Digital Memory
Life Support: Gravity	0.2 g
Atmosphere	28.7% O_2; 11% humidity
Sustenance Duration	288 days @ ship's complement of 15

Engineering and Science

- 6 Amjet-II Fission Engines with common exhaust
- 1 Emergency Retrorocket in detachable Primary Life Support Module. Fuel: liquid hydrogen
- Command Sensors could, orbitally or approaching, monitor many relevant planetary parameters (precise mass, inner core temperature, chemical composition of crust and atmosphere, etc.)
- Heat radiators provided great improvement in fission engine performance
- Interchangeable Carrier Modules locked around central Engineering and Command Core

Improvements and Innovations

- Lattice-sliced radiator ribs had 10 times greater radiant capacity than previous heat radiators
- Most powerful on-board radio transmitter/receiver to date
- Exhaust vent lined with near-perfect thermo-forged insulation tiles
- Clean Fission Engines doubled the efficiency of early-fission power packs
- Because of large cargo volume, Aventeur Class were first ships used for export from Asteroid Belt
- Ship could maintain sustained .2 g thrust, necessary for crew health on long-duration flight

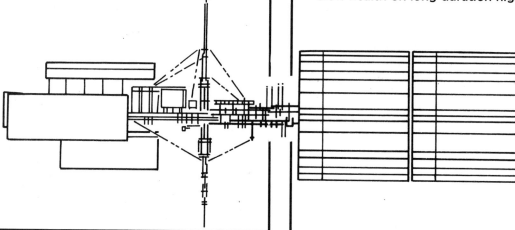

UNSS WHEELER DY-500 CLASS

2019-2055

While the *Aventeur* class was fulfilling its commissioned lifespan, the earlier *DY-100* series underwent extensive design and performance upgrading to become the *DY-500* series. It's almost pure fission engine plant produced a clean gas exhaust, which in turn powered an advanced Magnetohydrodynamic (MHD) generator for on-board electricity. This class was particularly popular for travel to and within the Asteroid Belt. The loss of a *DY-500*, the UNSS *Courageous*, was also the worst space tragedy in the first 65 years of spaceflight.

Specifications

Length	145 m
Beam	33 m
Draught	47 m
Mass	4.17 million kg
Cargo Modules	each 19.8 m X 10.7 m (2900 cu m usable volume)
Engine Section (advanced fission)	Diameter - 8.2 m length - 24.7 m
Fuel Tanks (6)	each 33 m X 8.5 m X 4.2 m
Command Con	12.35 m X 16.5 m X 5 m
Living Unit (2 Decks)	36.25 m X 20.6 m X 17 m
Sensor nosecone	Maximum diameter - 20.6 m length - 24.7 m

Ship's Complement

Officers (Captain, Lieutenant, Engineering)	3
Crew/Passengers	33
Standard Ship's Complement	36

Performance

Range - Standard	600 million km
Maximum	1.15 billion km
Cruising Velocity	135,000 km/hr
Typical Voyage Duration	185 days (Earth-Asteropolis)
Thrust	33,000 kg per fission engine

Systems Overview

Navigation	Interplanetary Triangulation (3-body) Guidance
Communication	Laser Radiotelemetry
On-Board Power	Magnetohydrodynamic Electric Generator
Computer	Elementary Independent Thought Processing Digital
Life Support: Gravity	.2 g internally sustained
Atmosphere	25% O_2, 9% humidity
Sustenance Duration	424 day's at standard ship's complement of 36

Engineering and Science

- 5 Amjet Fission Thrusters in Quincaux configuration
- Nosecone detachable with Emergency Life Support capability and Amjet II thruster for propulsion. Fuel: liquid hydrogen
- 3 sets of heat radiators for greater engine efficiency
- Forward MHD-powered sweeps for cleaning Asteroid Belt debris

Improvements and Innovations

- Amjet V Thrusters most efficient engines of the 21st century
- Magnetohydrodynamic (MHD) generator provided all on-board power
- First of its class of programmed spaceship to be equipped with elementary independent thought computers
- Quincaux engine configuration provided excellent maneuvering capability so important for Asteroid Belt navigation
- Extremely durable construction permitted high tonnage transport and long operational lifespan
- First class of ships outfitted with forward sweeps

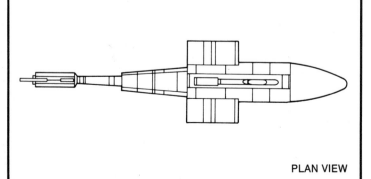

PLAN VIEW

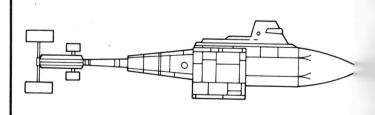

ELEVATION VIEW

SPACE FERRY CLASS LINDBERGH   2003-2015

The Space Ferry took over the Shuttle series as the primary surface-to-orbit craft. Early versions were equipped with booster rockets, much like the Shuttle, but advances in early-21st century technology eliminated the need for them. The Space Ferry played a vital role in the completion of the Orbital Power Satellite network that guaranteed energy-independence for Earth and also in the construction of orbiting satellite-cities.

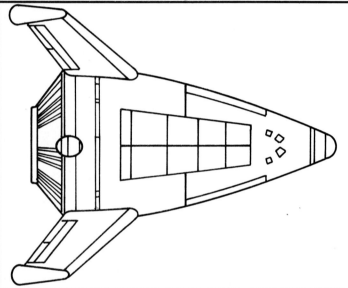

Specifications

Length	61 m
Beam	51 m to fintips
Draught	51 m to fintips
Mass	2.5 million kg
Payload Bay	10,000 cu m
Maximum Payload	1,000,000 kg
Crew (Commander, Pilot, Engineering, Flight Supervisor, up to eight Flight Attendants)	6
Passengers — Maximum passenger payload	125
Maximum Ship's Complement	131

Performance

Velocity	11,000 m/sec (Earth Escape)
Range	Orbital to Circumlunar
Landing/Takeoff	Horizontal Takeoff and Landing (HTOL)
Engines	Chemical Boost Single Stage to Orbit (SSTO)
Engine Configuration	Aerospike Plug-nozzle, with 24 coordinated small engines for greater efficiency and reliability

Multiple Cargo ports (8 per side) for ready cargo access

U THANT STELLAR PROBE   2017

The U Thant was part of the Stellar Series, the first interstellar probe series that traveled into the void beyond Pluto to gather the data necessary for designing interstellar spaceships. It utilized an advance in computer technology permitting program-independent thought. The U Thant discovered the presence of significant amounts of antimatter in the interstellar void.

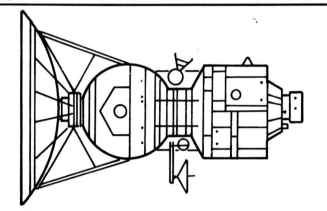

Specifications

Length	85 m
Diameter	44.5 m (Rear reflector)
Mass	8 million kg
Fuel to mass ratio	500:1
Forward Erosion Shield	12 m diameter
Fuel Sphere Volume	6000 cu m

Performance

Range	5.9 light-years (Barnard's Star)
Cruising Velocity	.104 c
Voyage Duration	2500 days
Engines	Advanced fission with ion drive
Distinctive, instrumentation	Magnetometer, Ion Detector, Multi-Spectral Imaging, Full-frequency sampling color cameras, Mass Spectronomer
Communication	Tightbeam Laser Radiotelemetry
Secondary Signaling	As a failsafe mechanism in case data transmission was unsuccessful, the U Thant was programmed to self-destruct within its star system destination in the event it detects planetary bodies; the radiation generated could be detected by Moonbase sensors

SOL SYSTEM EXPLORATIONS

Mars

Mars was the first planet in Earth's home solar system to be extensively explored and populated. A cold world with very little atmosphere, Mars is marked with channels of long-dead rivers, extinct volcanoes, crater basins and polar caps of frozen carbon dioxide and water that expand and recede on a seasonal basis. Today Mars is well settled and semi-autonomous.

Solsystem contains nine planets: three habitable; six uninhabitable

	Dist. from star ($\times10^8$km)	Diameter (km)	Revolution (Solar days & years)	Average surface temp (°c)
VENUS	1.08	12,115	225 d	27°
EARTH	1.49	12,752	365 d	15°
MARS	2.28	6,759	1.88 yrs	−7.2°

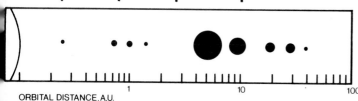

ORBITAL DISTANCE, A.U.

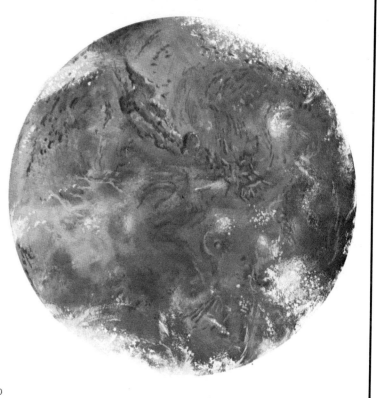

Settling the Sol System.

The first quarter of the 21st century saw an explosion of manned interplanetary exploration. Fueled by advances in fission propulsion, Mars, Jupiter, the Asteroid Belt and Saturn were visited, with bases and settlements often the result of these missions.

The unmanned Stellar Series probes were the Earth's first interstellar travelers, sending back data from a distance of five lightyears before becoming silent.

Though man was rapidly exploring the Sol System, it would still be many years before he would venture from its safe confinds and seek other worlds to explore.

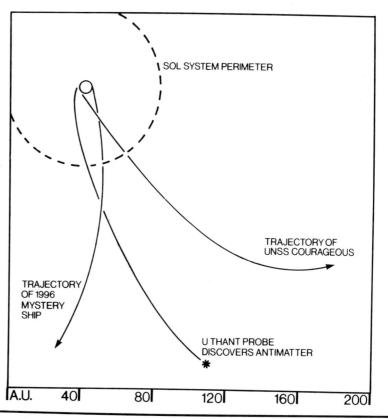

SOL SYSTEM PERIMETER

TRAJECTORY OF UNSS COURAGEOUS

TRAJECTORY OF 1996 MYSTERY SHIP

U THANT PROBE DISCOVERS ANTIMATTER

| A.U. | 40 | 80 | 120 | 160 | 200 |

THE UNITED SPACE INITIATIVE
United Nations, Plant Earth

2003

Over 200 years old, this document was a landmark in man's spaceflight progress and historic precursor to the United Federation of Planets. From this point on, the combined resources of all spacefaring nations were finally focused on the exploration of the Solar System, and eventually beyond.

Archive Log:

We the peoples of the United Nations, pursuant to our charter obligations to employ international means for the advancement of all peoples, do hereby declare:

THE UNITED SPACE INITIATIVE

This document calls for cooperation in space as follows:

Article 1—Research

All space research activities shall be coordinated to allow the maximum exchange of ideas and information. This shall include all research:
   a. in orbit about the Earth, its moon, or other celestial bodies
   b. at any research bases established on the moon, or other celestial bodies
   c. from interplanetary and interstellar probes
   d. from all other interstellar research, if and when such activity becomes technologically feasible.

Article 2—Joint Settlement

1. This Initiative reaffirms the 1967 Outer Space Treaty, declaring that space belongs to no nation but shall be utilized freely and to the benefit of all peoples.
2. All joint settlements, either in orbit, on the moon or on other planets or locations throughout the Solar System, shall be declared international zones and fall under the jurisdiction of the United Nations.
3. Local autonomy of settlements peopled by one nation or group shall not be covered by Article 2.2. However, all exchanges among autonomous settlements shall fall under the jurisdiction of the United Nations.

Article 3—Exploration and Security

1. Recognizing the future advisability of interplanetary and interstellar exploration and security, this Initiative calls for the establishment of a Solar Fleet, at such time as it becomes technologically feasible to explore the Solar System and beyond, to maintain the rule of law throughout the planets and to protect against unknown hostilities.
2. This Solar Fleet shall include, but not be limited to:
   a. a fleet of ships of a calculated range of classes
   b. a Solar Fleet Command
   c. Solar Bases for the deployment and servicing of the Fleet
   d. a monitoring system to assure solar integrity
   e. an academy to be established in the future to train officers in the specialized fields of space exploration and security.

IN FAITH WHEREOF the representatives of the governments of the United Nations have unanimously signed the present UNITED SPACE INITIATIVE.

DONE at the City of New York, the fifteenth day of October, two thousand and three.

THE FIRST SPACECHILD

2005

FARSIDE MOONBASE
HANS HOVENDAAL, M.D., CHIEF MEDICAL OFFICER

Medical Log:

It is my very great pleasure to announce that human history was made today with the birth of the first baby born in space.

Radio Telescope Technician 1st Class Rita Ashworth gave birth this morning to a 3.2 kg. boy. Mrs. Ashworth employed natural childbirth, and both mother and baby are doing extremely well. Dr. Weldon Ashworth, of the Astro-Telemetry Section, said their son will be named Jules, after the famous science-fiction writer, Jules Verne, who first envisioned man coming here.

The birth of the first human in space has been realistically considered for years, dating back to the 1970's. In fact, we at the Farside Moonbase have had the capability for doing the job for over a year, but had no expectant mothers. It is to their credit the Ashworths decided six months ago to remain here to have the child. I know it was a trying experience for them, for even the farside of the moon is no longer a safe haven from the constant inquiries of the world's press.

As assisting physician, I can report the birth was an exceptionally easy one, though I took the precaution of completing the delivery in the operating room in case complications resulted from unknown extraterrestrial causes. The operating room was kept slightly decompressed, and the lower pressure eased the mother's contractions considerably. In general, the moon's lower gravity seemed to help the whole birth process.

But the more difficult question both doctors and potential patients have asked still remains: What effect will being born and raised away from Earth have on children? The Ashworths, of course, know there are risks, which they weighed very carefully before deciding on this course of action. They should be commended for their courage. I personally will be rigorously monitoring young Jules' progress for any unusual growth signs or irregularities, though I remain confident he'll have a normal infancy.

Again, my congratulations to the Ashworths, and to this the first space baby. A new generation of man has begun.

FIRST CITY IN SPACE
250 people move into Tsiolkovskygrad.
More are expected.

2007

BORIS KARPEV, CITY SUPERVISOR

Supervisor's Log:

Ladies and gentlemen, I want to welcome you to the Earth's first spacefaring community, Tsiolkovskygrad. This magnificent structure is the result of an unprecedented amount of cooperation by the peoples of Earth, and so I would especially like to thank the Secretary General of the United Nations for traveling up here for these opening ceremonies.

Tsiolkovskygrad is both the culmination of one dream, and the beginning of another. Just a decade ago, to think we would be here at this time would have seemed foolish. But, in turning away from war and actively pursuing peace, the nations of Earth have made the impossible possible. Look around you and view the results of friendship and cooperation; more beautiful and wondrous than any that strife has created. When you tour the city, you will see the labors of two dozen countries of the Earth; all of whom played a vital part in its completion. And it is the consummate irony of life that the Earth's first truly world city . . . is in space.

But the 250 residents of Tsiolkovskygrad are just the first of many. The city will eventually house a thousand, and when we can accommodate no more, the people of the Earth will inhabit the next community in space. For we are also at the beginning of another dream. A dream that has this L-5 libration point between Earth and moon filled with humanity, hundreds of cities housing hundreds of thousands working for the betterment of the human race. It is a dream worth striving for, because it is a dream that we, all of us who call that beautiful blue ball out that window home, can make happen.

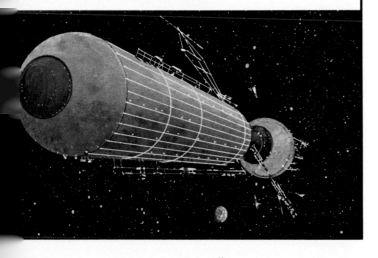

MARSBASE OPENS NEW ERA OF SPACE EXPLORATION

2012

MARSBASE 1
MARK GLYNN, DIRECTOR

Director's Log:

What with erecting the protective geodesic dome that houses Marsbase 1, unloading a year's worth of supplies for a crew of fifteen, getting the automatic refueling plant operational, and calibrating all the delicate scientific sensors, there hasn't been time enough to eat or sleep, much less commence this Log. This, therefore, is the first entry, and following Standard Operating Procedure I am entering into the Log the specific objectives for this first interplanetary base. They are:

1. Explore the geology and environment of Mars in depth
2. Take astronomical measurements to correlate with those from the Earth and moon
3. Make exploratory excursions to the Martian moons, Phobos and Deimos, to establish the feasibility of mining them for condritic minerals and other useful materials
4. Examine the long-term effects of living on another planet
5. Conduct an intensive search for any signs of Martian life, past or present.

About Objective #4, I can state the short-term effects of Mars are very bearable, even pleasant. Because of the thin atmosphere, there is a beautiful clarity and sharpness to the rocky landscape, and the low pressure and one-third-earth gravity make all physical exertion ridiculously easy. And unlike the frigid moon, daytime temperatures get as high as 20° C., almost like a spring day back on Earth.

As scientists, we can't let personal desires or aspirations interfere with our work. But there is a great unspoken hope among our research team that life in some form will be found on Mars. Writing this at my desk, where I'm being warmed by the noonday sun streaming through the porthole, it's hard for me not to believe that Martian life could exist.

THE FINAL FRONTIER OPENS
Enactment of the Space Homesteading Act

2014

This act made space attractive to individuals by creating the powerful incentive of a free space homestead for enterprising pioneers. However, while the exploration of space opened up a realm of near limitless resources for mankind, unlike the frontier of the old American West, more than sheer willingness and romantic dreams were required. Space presented a much more hazardous environment then ever before faced by man and demanded better educated, better skilled and technologically oriented individuals with a high degree of motivation.

But above the practical considerations, the Act recognized that space was truly public domain belonging to all people. Anyone wishing to stake a claim and willing to fulfill the five-year residency requirement was then entitled to a piece of space.

The Act proved to be so popular that in the decade following its enactment, the population in space multiplied by 4.5 times . . . to be followed in the next decade by a five-fold jump. For the complete history of this "People's Act," see *The Space Immigrants—The Story of the Homestead Act*, by John Bukor, published in 2214.)

Archive Log:

To encourage the colonization of space, while assuring its equitable growth and distribution among peoples, the General Assembly hereby passes the:

SPACE HOMESTEADING ACT OF 2014

Article 1—Definitions

1. A Space Homestead shall be defined as any Solar System body whose volume and/or area is up to, but not exceeding, 100 km. in diameter and approved for homesteading purposes by the U.N. Homestead Commission.

2. Right to such space shall be contingent upon:
   a. the fulfillment of five earth years residency within such volume; and
   b. the construction of at least one permanent personal dwelling environment.

Article II—Rights and Limitations

1. A Space Homestead entitles its owner to exclusive right over all traffic through, and material contained within, its volume and/or area. This specifically includes those parts of the Asteroid Belt approved for homesteading.

2. All homesteaders are entitled to unimpeded access to the Sun.

3. This Homestead Act strictly limits the amount of space a homesteader may claim to the volume and/or areas specified in this Act.

Article III—Homesteading Incentives

1. Transportation to any sector approved for homesteading purposes shall be provided by the United Nations Solar Fleet for the person and immediate family.

2. A low-interest loan, at rates determined by the Homestead Commission, shall be made available to the Homesteader, if so desired.

ANTIMATTER FOUND BEYOND ORBIT OF PLUTO
First generation interstellar probe makes incredible discovery

2017

UNP U THANT
PROBE, STELLAR SERIES

The earliest series of interstellar probes was called, appropriately enough, the Stellar Series. This project, designed by the brilliant space scientist, Jackson Roykirk, was the first to employ the controversial computer capability for elementary independent thought, a capacity then feared by many in a machine.

A total of ten of these well designed probes were launched during the years 2015–2022. One, the *Nomad*, was damaged in a meteor storm and contact subsequently lost with it in 2026. Amazingly, this probe was recently discovered in Sector 21C altered in a way that required it to self-destruct. Another, the *U Thant*, inadvertently stumbled upon the hitherto unsuspected existence of large amounts of antimatter between stars, and this discovery, recorded in the following Telemetry Log, had repercussions which decades later altered the entire scope of spaceflight.

Weekly Telemetry Readout Log:

Distance from Pluto:	120.4 A.U.
Speed:	0.104c
Elapsed Time since Pluto Flyby:	14 days
Dist from Barnard's Star:	5.162 x 10^{13} km.
Time till Barnard's Star:	2,449 days
Power System:	25.7% efficiency
Navigation System:	99.36% accuracy
Instrumentation:	All monitors functioning
Communication System:	Comp-sync laser at 98.1% opt
Propulsion System:	Accepted performance levels

Interstellar Dust Readout:

	90.7%	Fe	.07
e	8.42	Ni	.05
$_2$O	.46	Ca	.007
H	.29	Others	.003

Damage Report:

Interstellar gas collector ruptured by explosion—Cause Analysis: matter /antimatter annihilation.

Priority Input—Discovery:

Matter/antimatter annihilation indicates detectable quantities of antimatter in interstellar void.

Repeat: ANTIMATTER FOUND IN INTERSTELLAR VOID.

End Transmission

EARTH-SATURN MISSION MAKES REMARKABLE FIND

2020

UNSS LEWIS AND CLARK, AVENTEUR CLASS
SHAUN JEOFFREY CHRISTOPHER, COLONEL

Colonel's Log:

A geological survey party has just returned from the Fourth Radian Moon Ring area breathless with extraordinary news. We are not the first visitors to these moons of Saturn.

On an orbiting asteroid approximately twenty kilometers in diameter, the survey party came across mine shafts. Yes, deep mine shafts drilled entirely through the rock. And the holes were perfect cylinders, probably cut with some laser-like apparatus alien to Earth technology. It seemed whoever mined this rock removed its contents like you would core an apple.

But that's not all! On a second moon, dotted with outcroppings of metallic salts, there were signs everywhere of surface activity. I have some holographs the mystified crew took, and I can clearly make out some type of tread marks and what looks like some old-fashioned strip mining scars.

As yet, we have no estimation of the date this mining activity took place. Nor have we a clue as to who, or what, was exploiting the moons of Saturn. But this much we do know. Unless there is still some undiscovered advanced industrial civilization hiding from our probes on the outer planets, we have been visited by an extrasolar race. A race of beings who not only carve up planetary bodies at will, but who can travel between the stars at will. Which means that somewhere out there is a civilization a hundred fold, a thousand fold, greater than we are. And the age old question has today been answered: indeed, man is not alone.

EVIDENCE OF LIFE FOUND ON MARS

2021

MARSBASE 1
DR. JOHN OPPENHEIMER, SCIENCE OFFICER

Science Log:

After nine years of unremitting research, the first hard evidence of extraterrestrial life has finally been verified here at the expanded Marsbase Research Station.

Ironically, it was a natural disaster that yielded the breakthrough so long sought in vain. The recently abated sandstorm that choked the planet for three months in a deadly cloud of lacerating dust contained an unexpected silver lining. Samples siphoned from the dust contained fragments which we are now sure are fossil remains. Under the microscope, skeletal structures can be clearly viewed, and computer reconstruction indicates two small, silicon-based, insect-like creatures about 3 cm. in length and 1 cm. in width. Initial silicon isotope dating places the age of these fossils at several million years.

These preliminary results have widespread scientific and biological implications. First of all, while there is no life on Mars today that we've been able to find, it is now certain lifeforms once did exist here. Secondly, these extinct creatures seem to have had a type of organic structure totally alien to the carbon-based life found on Earth. Biologically, this means that life as we know it on our home planet represents only one possible path of evolution and more importantly, others—perhaps many others—can exist in the universe.

In accordance with Article 1 of the United Space Initiative, I am transmitting to Earth all data and preliminary results and will be sending a representative sample of fossils on the next cruiser. I have requested any and all correspondence from the members of the Institute, which I will use as an addendum to this Log.

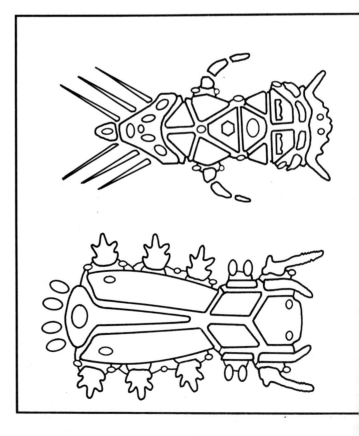

WORST TRAGEDY IN 65 YEARS OF SPACEFLIGHT
Spaceship with 62 aboard cannot return home.

2022

UNSS COURAGEOUS, WHEELER CLASS
FITZSIMMONS WALLABEE, CAPTAIN
Captain's Log:

I have before me the Engineering Damage Report, and it is, for all intents and purposes, the *Courageous'* death certificate. Yesterday, we discovered a shielding flaw in the engine room during a weekly maintenance check, and before we could return to L-5 docking for repair, a massive solar flare penetrated into the reaction chamber, with deadly consequences. Because acceleration continues at fatal full throttle, I am at this time dispatching my final log before we lose radio contact with home. Any further communication will be by Record Markers we will leave in our wake.

I've informed the crew of the grimness of our plight, and they've all taken the news well—at least as well as could be expected. Helmsman Boyle joked that we've broken the Solar speed record. And Science Officer Portillo has very thoroughly explained to us the beautiful effect near light speed has on the distant star field.

But there you go. Even under sentence of death, this marvelous crew maintains a sense of humor and scientific rigor. I would like to take this opportunity to recommend them all for the Solar Medal of Honor.

Navigation has calculated that upon leaving the Solar System, the ship won't pass near any star whatsoever on our helpless path through the Milky Way. The *Courageous* has become a modern-day *Flying Dutchman,* doomed to sail powerless to its end at the edge of the galaxy.

In a final personal note, I want to say farewell to my wife, Margaret, and our children, Robert and George. I love you all and will take your memory to my final destination.

This is the UNSS *Courageous* over and out.

HADDAD KOIRE, ENGINEERING OFFICER
Engineering Log:

Today's massive solar flare penetrated the shielding flaw in the engine room, inflicting the following damage:

—The fiber-optic computer tubes linking Engineering with Inertial Guidance and Navigation fused, resulting in complete loss of ship control.

—The feed valve to the fission magnetochamber melted, as did the Emergency Shut-down circuit, causing runaway fission reaction.

Reparative Strategy—Electromagnetic clamps fitted around the field valve have slowed input enough to prevent fission engines from turning critical and initiating a nuclear explosion. Acceleration continues at a steady rate.

Prognosis—Hopeless. Fuel supply will be exhausted within the hour, well before emergency procedures can have any effect. Acceleration will cease at a final velocity .86c (2.5 x 10^7 m/sec)

JUPITER'S RED SPOT REVEALS ITS SECRETS

2025

GANYMEDE TEMPORARY RESEARCH OUTPOST
DR. LLOYD ELKINS, SCIENCE SUPERVISOR
Science Log:

At last we're solving the riddle of the Red Spot of Jupiter. For 400 years, man has speculated over this huge enigma, three times as vast as the Earth itself. But now the data's begun to stream back from the twelve probes we've sent into the giant surface blemish, and the hard facts received are settling this astronomical mystery for good.

The first data is confirming a long-held conjecture: the Spot is the Jovian equivalent of a permanent hurricane. Within the Red Spot, the atmosphere is constantly being whipped into winds of hundreds of kilometers per hour, which rotate around local vortexes—the eye of the storm—and these vortexes themselves revolve around one another according to the magnetic field fluctuations of the inner core.

Of course atmosphere means something quite different on Jupiter, a planet composed almost entirely of hydrogen and helium. The deeper our probes penetrate into the interior of this gaseous world, the stranger the readings we get back. A thousand kilometers in, the hydrogen atmosphere liquifies due to the enormous gravitational pressures, and over 65,000 km. further, the liquid hydrogen becomes liquid metallic hydrogen, a state never before encountered in either nature or laboratory.

This last I'm really excited about, since I've spent my professional career speculating on how the laws of chemistry and physics, as we know them from terrestrial conditions, are radically altered by extreme conditions, like the gravity of Jupiter or the heat of the sun. Liquid metallic hydrogen is the best conductor of magnetism and electricity that could possibly exist, so that small deformations in the iron-silicate core of Jupiter are conducted and magnified by the time they reach the "surface." From the data we're receiving, the Red Spot appears to be a magnetically generated and sustained phenomenon, able to continue for centuries because it is a product of inner core processes and not merely an atmospheric entity. But while the mystery of the Red Spot has been finally solved, for me it in no way diminishes the awesome beauty of this greatest of planetary markings.

OVERVIEW

During this era, mankind consolidated its position in the Solar System, took its first halting interstellar steps, and right before mid-century, made face-to-face contact with intelligent aliens. This last was an epochal turning point in the history of the Earth, ending forever our world's solitude and beginning our participation in the galactic community, a community forged in part out of man's own efforts toward friendship and cooperation.

This meeting with aliens, however, was preceded by a significant portent. Radio astronomers at Farside Moonbase discovered intelligent signals emanating from a star toward the galactic center. While they could not decipher the code they knew from the star's distance what it must be—or must have been; the star's signals were 15,000 years old by the time they reached the moon—an incredibly advanced civilization to be able to broadcast with such staggering power. When man's first interstellar ships ventured to the stars, they took with them the humility borne from the evidence of overwhelming alien superiority.

Perhaps the most dramatic event in the Solar System during this period was the terraforming of the planet Venus, which had previously been considered totally unsuitable for human habitation. Its thick carbon dioxide atmosphere (100 times as dense as Earth's nitrogen/oxygen air) had created a ''greenhouse'' effect, trapping the sun's heat radiation to produce surface temperatures of a cauterizing 500°c. To reverse this greenhouse effect, the atmosphere was seeded with billions of blue-green algae, which eat carbon dioxide and give off oxygen as a waste product.* In a remarkably short time, the algae had lowered temperatures to an acceptable 30°C. and created a rich oxygen atmosphere and protective ozone layer. Also, hundreds of massive ice asteroids were freighted from the asteroid belt and sent crashing into Venus at a rate calculated to increase the planet's angular momentum. Venus not only got water enough to create vast oceans, its rate of rotation was speeded up enough to generate a radiation-Van Allen belt around the world. Botanical terraforming made the surface habitable, settlements soon followed, and today Venus has a population a tenth the Earth's own.

Mankind also continued to populate the rest of the Solar System, settling especially in the Asteroid Belt, which became a center for space mining. With a population swelled by enterprising space homesteaders, this region soon began exporting such needed raw materials as nickel and iron, allowing the Earth to revert to the pollution-free beauty of its pre-industrial past. Asteropolis, the capital city of the Asteroid Belt, is to this day the largest and most important space city in the outer planets.

Commercial spaceflights were set up to join together the ever-expanding human civilization, which had reached all the way to Pluto; a research station was established on this furthest out planet to take advantage of its great distance from the sun for precise electromagnetic readings. Because of the time it took to traverse the staggering planetary spans, the solar spaceliners were equipped with all the amenities of long-term travel:

---

*Of course, exhaustive tests were perfomed to find out if any lifeforms existed on Venus, since the remotest possibility of global genocide of organisms different from man was too horrible to permit any chance of.

racious dining, null-gravity gymnasium, a
tage and video theater, rear stellar obser-
atory. Our present starliners owe much to
he conveniences first designed for the solar
paceliners.

lso the familiar Pioneer Solar Communica-
ons System, one of the most important
echnological links to mankinds' expanded
pace development, became operational.
heir rugged viewscreens, to this stardate,
re still in use in some old-fashioned solar-
ased homes. To feed this growing popula-
on, huge windmill-shaped space farms
ere sown, each transparent blade con-
ained 500 square kilometers of controlled-
rowth micro-organisms.

he United Nations Solar Fleet (UNSF) was
ommissioned during this quarter century
o maintain the rule of law throughout the
olar System, and much of the United Fed-
ation of Planet's Star Fleet structure and
perational principles are directly taken
om the old UNSF. The Solar Fleet patrolled
om Mars to Pluto and played a vital role in
e development and testing of future inerstellar ships.

or the quest to the stars was not ignored
uring this solar consolidation. A new gen-
ation of interstellar probes superseded
e old "Stellar Series," and the reception of
is much more precise and comprehensive
ata proved essential in the construction of
ips capable of interstellar travel. In addi-
on, just as the U THANT stumbled across
e existence of antimatter with dramatic
nsequences for the future spaceflight,
e of these new probes discovered the
les in the space-time fabric that are now
lized for warp communication.

the time, however, these discoveries did

mankind little practical good. While the
theoretical applications of matter/antimat-
ter propulsion, subspace radio and the like
were discussed, dissected, proposed and re-
futed, neither the mathematics nor the
technology then existed to take advantage
of these now-familiar realities.

The first successful interstellar vessels, the
United Nations Starships ADAMEVE and
ICARUS, employed advanced fusion propulsion, which enabled them to attain relativistic speeds during their round-trip journeys
to the nearest stars thought to have any
possibility of life. The UNSS ADAMEVE's journey to Barnard's Star was extremely valuable
for the scientific insights into another star.
But the ICARUS' voyage to Alpha Centauri
changed the history of man forever.

Intelligent life was found on Alpha Centauri,
though scientists had been skeptical of finding any there. This celestial neighbor of
Earth became one of the founding members of the UFP. Theirs was a civilization
practically as advanced as our own, in accordance with Hodgkin's Law of Parallel
Planet Development. And in one extraordinary individual, it was clearly the superior—
namely Zefrem Cochrane, a genius on the
same par with Einstein or Daystrom.

Thus, in one momentus voyage, the course
of mankind was radically altered. The people
of Earth met and established friendly relations with an alien society (on the ICARUS'
return the U.N. immediately dispatched a
mission to exchange the diplomatic for-
malities of official recognition), and became
aware of the revolutionary principle of warp
drive, finally enabling the speed of light to
be surpassed and heralding for man the
true beginning of his interstellar age.

A CONCISE LOOK AT SHIPS AND EVENTS
SPACEFLIGHT CHRONOLOGY

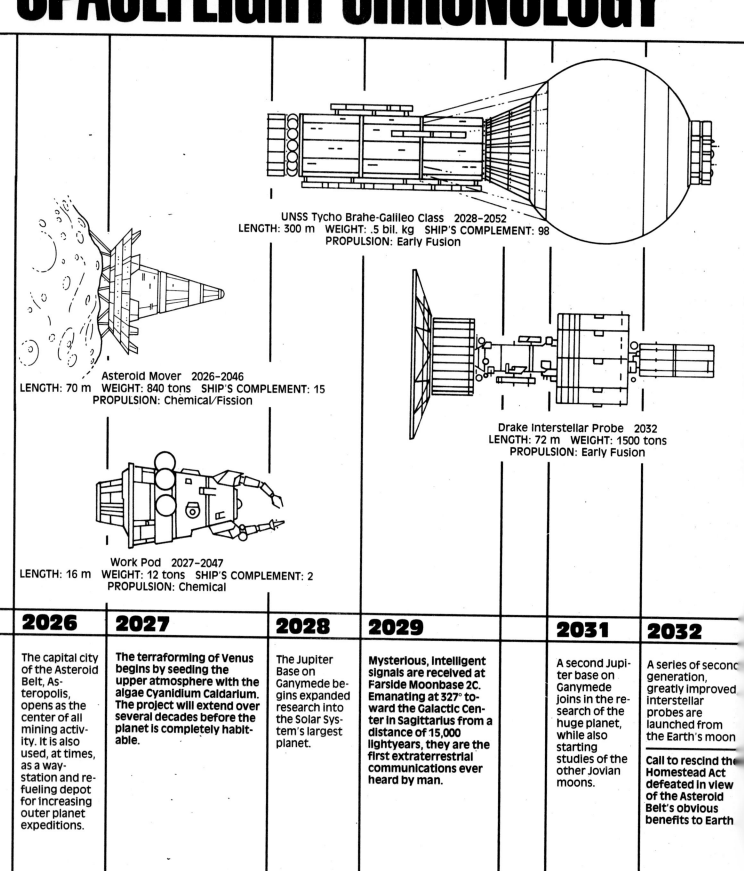

UNSS Tycho Brahe-Galileo Class   2028-2052
LENGTH: 300 m   WEIGHT: .5 bil. kg   SHIP'S COMPLEMENT: 98
PROPULSION: Early Fusion

Asteroid Mover   2026-2046
LENGTH: 70 m   WEIGHT: 840 tons   SHIP'S COMPLEMENT: 15
PROPULSION: Chemical/Fission

Drake Interstellar Probe   2032
LENGTH: 72 m   WEIGHT: 1500 tons
PROPULSION: Early Fusion

Work Pod   2027-2047
LENGTH: 16 m   WEIGHT: 12 tons   SHIP'S COMPLEMENT: 2
PROPULSION: Chemical

2026	2027	2028	2029	2031	2032
The capital city of the Asteroid Belt, Asteropolis, opens as the center of all mining activity. It is also used, at times, as a way-station and re-fueling depot for increasing outer planet expeditions.	The terraforming of Venus begins by seeding the upper atmosphere with the algae Cyanidium Caldarium. The project will extend over several decades before the planet is completely habitable.	The Jupiter Base on Ganymede begins expanded research into the Solar System's largest planet.	Mysterious, intelligent signals are received at Farside Moonbase 2C. Emanating at 327° toward the Galactic Center in Sagittarius from a distance of 15,000 lightyears, they are the first extraterrestrial communications ever heard by man.	A second Jupiter base on Ganymede joins in the research of the huge planet, while also starting studies of the other Jovian moons.	A series of second generation, greatly improved interstellar probes are launched from the Earth's moon. Call to rescind the Homestead Act defeated in view of the Asteroid Belt's obvious benefits to Earth

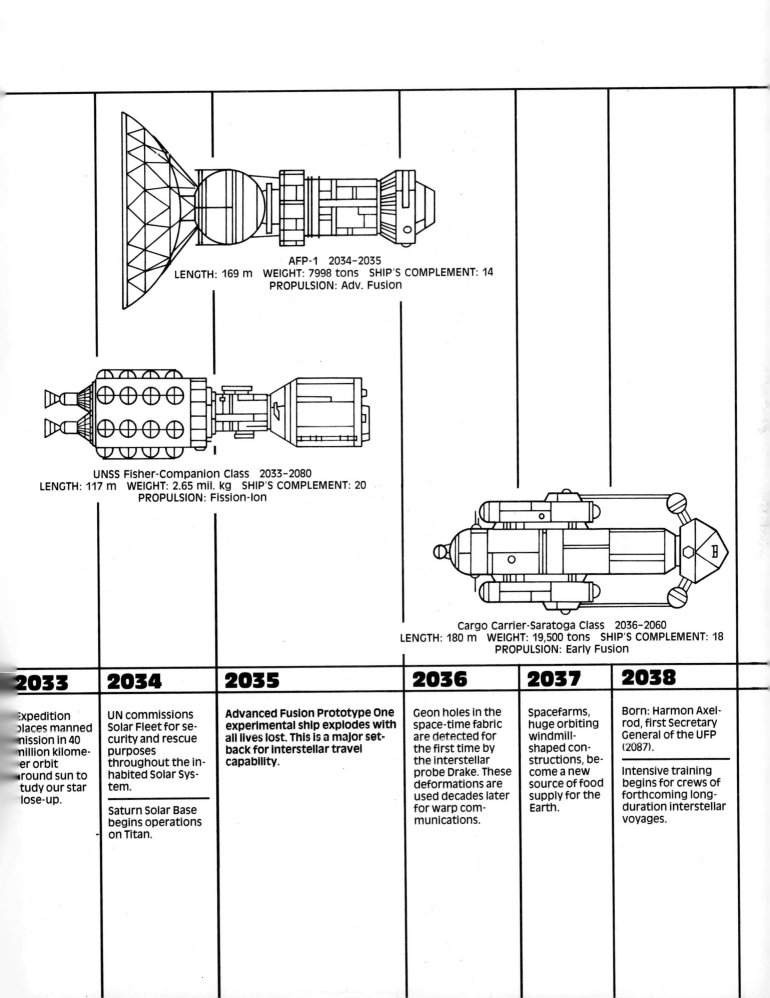

AFP-1 2034–2035
LENGTH: 169 m   WEIGHT: 7998 tons   SHIP'S COMPLEMENT: 14
PROPULSION: Adv. Fusion

UNSS Fisher-Companion Class   2033–2080
LENGTH: 117 m   WEIGHT: 2.65 mil. kg   SHIP'S COMPLEMENT: 20
PROPULSION: Fission-Ion

Cargo Carrier-Saratoga Class   2036–2060
LENGTH: 180 m   WEIGHT: 19,500 tons   SHIP'S COMPLEMENT: 18
PROPULSION: Early Fusion

2033

Expedition places manned mission in 40 million kilometer orbit around sun to study our star close-up.

2034

UN commissions Solar Fleet for security and rescue purposes throughout the inhabited Solar System.

Saturn Solar Base begins operations on Titan.

2035

Advanced Fusion Prototype One experimental ship explodes with all lives lost. This is a major setback for interstellar travel capability.

2036

Geon holes in the space-time fabric are detected for the first time by the interstellar probe Drake. These deformations are used decades later for warp communications.

2037

Spacefarms, huge orbiting windmill-shaped constructions, become a new source of food supply for the Earth.

2038

Born: Harmon Axelrod, first Secretary General of the UFP (2087).

Intensive training begins for crews of forthcoming long-duration interstellar voyages.

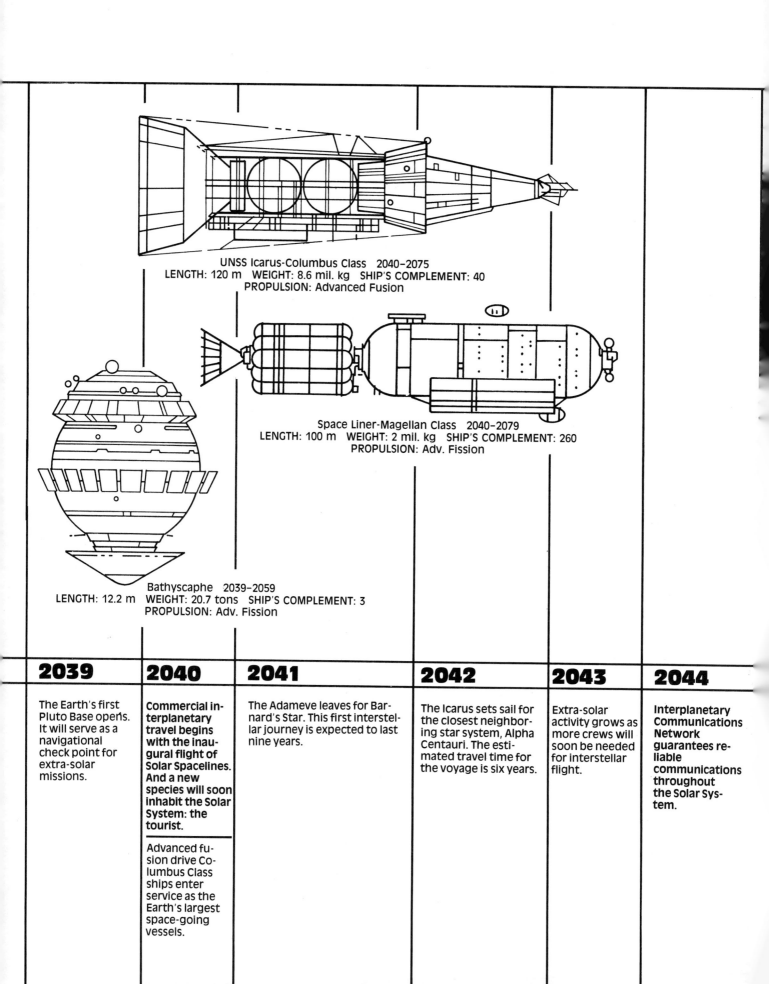

UNSS Icarus-Columbus Class   2040–2075
LENGTH: 120 m   WEIGHT: 8.6 mil. kg   SHIP'S COMPLEMENT: 40
PROPULSION: Advanced Fusion

Space Liner-Magellan Class   2040–2079
LENGTH: 100 m   WEIGHT: 2 mil. kg   SHIP'S COMPLEMENT: 260
PROPULSION: Adv. Fission

Bathyscaphe   2039–2059
LENGTH: 12.2 m   WEIGHT: 20.7 tons   SHIP'S COMPLEMENT: 3
PROPULSION: Adv. Fission

2039	**2040**	**2041**	**2042**	**2043**	**2044**
The Earth's first Pluto Base opens. It will serve as a navigational check point for extra-solar missions.	**Commercial interplanetary travel begins with the inaugural flight of Solar Spacelines. And a new species will soon inhabit the Solar System: the tourist.**	The Adameve leaves for Barnard's Star. This first interstellar journey is expected to last nine years.	The Icarus sets sail for the closest neighboring star system, Alpha Centauri. The estimated travel time for the voyage is six years.	Extra-solar activity grows as more crews will soon be needed for interstellar flight.	**Interplanetary Communications Network guarantees reliable communications throughout the Solar System.**
	Advanced fusion drive Columbus Class ships enter service as the Earth's largest space-going vessels.				

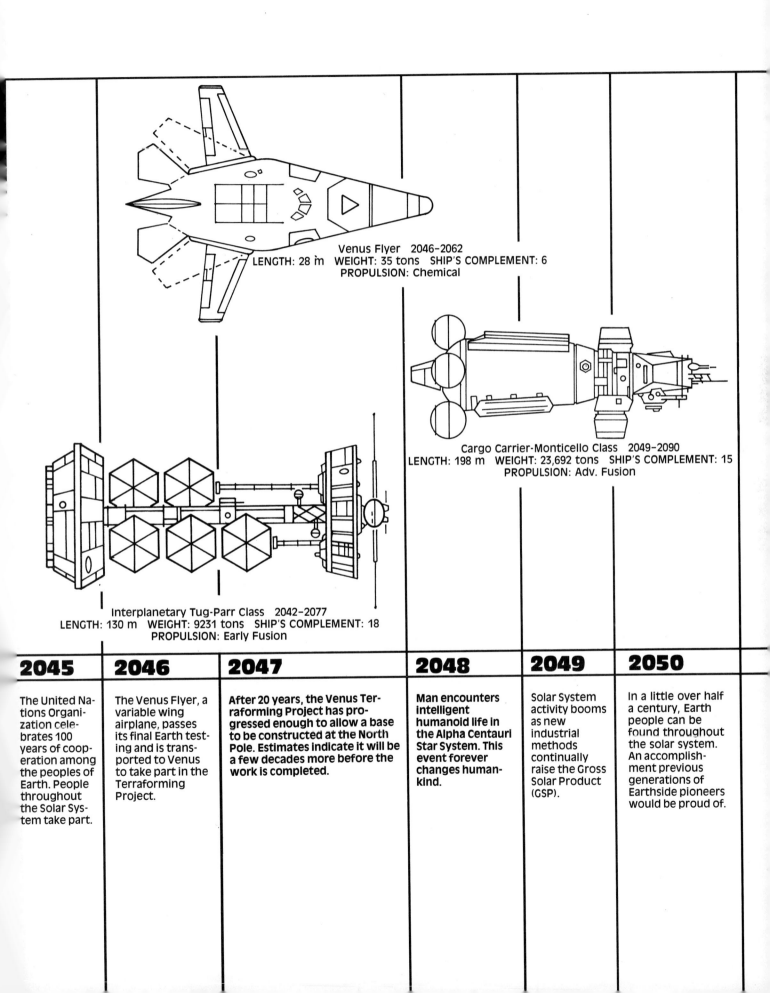

Venus Flyer   2046–2062
LENGTH: 28 m   WEIGHT: 35 tons   SHIP'S COMPLEMENT: 6
PROPULSION: Chemical

Cargo Carrier-Monticello Class   2049–2090
LENGTH: 198 m   WEIGHT: 23,692 tons   SHIP'S COMPLEMENT: 15
PROPULSION: Adv. Fusion

Interplanetary Tug-Parr Class   2042–2077
LENGTH: 130 m   WEIGHT: 9231 tons   SHIP'S COMPLEMENT: 18
PROPULSION: Early Fusion

2045	**2046**	**2047**	**2048**	**2049**	**2050**
The United Nations Organization celebrates 100 years of cooperation among the peoples of Earth. People throughout the Solar System take part.	The Venus Flyer, a variable wing airplane, passes its final Earth testing and is transported to Venus to take part in the Terraforming Project.	After 20 years, the Venus Terraforming Project has progressed enough to allow a base to be constructed at the North Pole. Estimates indicate it will be a few decades more before the work is completed.	Man encounters intelligent humanoid life in the Alpha Centauri Star System. This event forever changes humankind.	Solar System activity booms as new industrial methods continually raise the Gross Solar Product (GSP).	In a little over half a century, Earth people can be found throughout the solar system. An accomplishment previous generations of Earthside pioneers would be proud of.

UNSS TYCHO BRAHE
GALILEO CLASS

2028-2052

One of the most durable workhorses in spaceflight history, the *Tycho Brahe* and fellow Galileo class ships were extremely durable and long-lasting vessels. These early fusion ships could attain modest relativistic speeds (.2c, later .35c) and traveled to the outer planets and beyond into interstellar space. In the 2030's the Galileo was the primary ship class to the Asteroid Belt, and in the 2040's the most popular carrier to the outer planets.

Specifications

Length	300 m
Beam	120.7 m
Draught	120.7 m
Mass	empty - .5 billion kg
	loaded - 4.84 billion kg
Fuel Sphere	main - 920,000 cu m
	(3 billion kg capacity)
	engine reservoirs - 370 cu m
	(1.2 million kg capacity)
Crew compartment (6 Decks)	length - 40.8 m
	diameter - 35.5 m
Cargo volume	40,000 cu m
Forward Command Sensor Disc	35.5 m diameter

Ship's Complement

Officers (Captain, Lieutenant, Science, Engineering, Navigation, Medical)	6
Crew	92
Standard Ship's Complement	98

Performance

Range - Standard	800 mil. km (Earth - Asteroid Belt)
	5.75 bil. km (Earth - Pluto)
Maximum	10^{13} km (little over 1 light-year)
Cruising Velocity	200 million km/hr
Maximum Velocity	375 million km/hr
Typical Voyage Duration	17.4 hr (Asteroid Belt)
	45 hr (Pluto Research Station)

Maximum Voyage Duration	2.3 years (2.25 yrs Earth time)
Acceleration	0 - 1 million km/hr - 3.55 hr
	1 - 100 million km/hr - 2.85 hr
	2 - 3.5 million km/hr - 3 - 10 hr
Thrust	10 million kg per fusion eng

Systems Overview

Navigation	Interplanetary Triangulation/ Elementary Celestial Navigation
Communications	Encoded Particle Beam Telemetry
Computer	Intermediate Independent Thought Memory Scan
Life Support: Gravity	.4 g
Atmosphere	23% O_2; 10% humidity
Sustenance Duration	12 years at standard ship's complement of 6

Engineering and Science

- 24 Space Op Fusion Engines
- 10 Laser / Electron Fusion Initiators per engine
- Fuel: frozen deuterium (hydrogen 2)
- 3 detachable Fusion Engines for landing craft or emergency evacuation
- Exterior Crystal Communications Transceiver

Improvements and Innovations

- Multi-configured fusion engines quantum improvement in space-flight propulsion
- Forward Command / Instrument Disc plated with erodable material for duration shielding
- Fuel sphere covered with near-perfect reflector sheathing for radiant insulation
- First ship with elementary interstellar celestial navigation

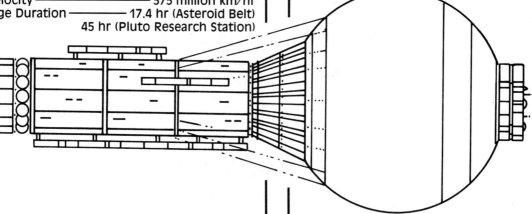

SUB LIGHT EXPLORER

UNSS ICARUS
COLUMBUS CLASS   2040-2075

The *Icarus* was the first ship to Alpha Centauri, where it made its historic contact with the Alpha Centauri civilization. Though its advanced fusion engines could produce speeds up to .75 c., new ships incorporating Zefrem Cochran's warp principles soon superseded the Columbia Class for interstellar flight. The original *Icarus* is preserved in the Moon's Spaceflight Museum.

Specifications

Length	120 m
Beam	37.2 m
Draught	37.2 m
Mass	8.6 million kg

Ship's Complement

Officers (Captain, Lieutenant, Engineering, Navigation)	4
Crew	36
Standard Ship's Complement	40

Performance

Range: Standard	5.75 bil. km (Earth-Pluto)
Maximum	8.5 light-years
Cruising Velocity	.75c (800 million km/hr)
Maximum Velocity	.85c (907 million km/hr)
Typical Voyage Duration	10 hrs. (Earth-Pluto)
	11.5 years (Earth-Alpha Centauri-Earth)
Thrust	1 billion kg

Systems Overview

Navigation	Elementary Interstellar Celestial Guidance
Communication	Laser/Particle Beam Subcarrier Radiotelemetry
Computer	Intermediate Independent Thought Memory Scan
Weapons	4 Forward Lasers 25 Fusion Torpedoes
Life Support: Gravity	.4 - .75 g (intern. cont.)
Atmosphere	22% O_2; 14% humidity
Sustenance Duration	1 - 13 yrs at standard ship's comp.

Engineering and Science

Geodyne Fusion Engine pack

Fuel	antimatter-spiked deuterium (50:1 deuterium to antimatter)

Innovations and Improvements

- Most advanced fusion ship of the twenty-first century.
- Antimatter-spiked fusion much more efficient than deuterium alone.
- First spaceship class with on-board shuttlecraft for extra-vehicular excursion.

UNSS FISHER COMPANION CLASS — 2033-2080

The Fisher was one of the most utilized escort ships during the period of intensive development and testing that resulted in interstellar spaceflight capability. From advanced fusion performance testing to warp drive prototype escort, the Fisher provided reliable backup for generations of new spaceships. Upon decommission from regular service, the Fisher was renovated and served as the Official Interplanetary Carrier for the Secretary General of the United Nations.

Specifications

Length	156 m
Beam	37.9 m diameter
Draught	37.9 m diameter
Mass	6.9 million kg
Engine Section	length: 78 m
	diameter: 37.9 m
Life Support Section	length: 40 m
	diameter: 29 m
Forward Sensor	18 m diameter

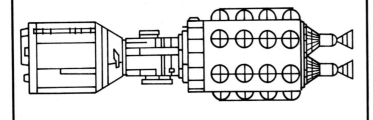

Ship's Complement

Officers — (Captain, Science, Engineering, Communications)	4
Crew	16
Standard Ship's Complement	20

Performance

Range	Up to 6 billion km
Cruising Velocity	6000 m/sec
Maximum velocity	9500 m/sec
Engine	2 Advanced fission thrusters
Fuel Capacity	1.5 million kg

Forward sensors had highly precise local sensitivity
Full-band communications receptivity

SPACELINER MAGELLAN CLASS — 2040-2079

The Prince of Wales plied the passenger lanes of the solar system for over three decades. When it first started service as a luxury spaceliner, the travel time among the planets was measured in weeks; so the Prince of Wales was designed with all the amenities of comfortable long-duration travel. Its level of excellence set a standard which even the galactic starliners of today are hard pressed to equal.

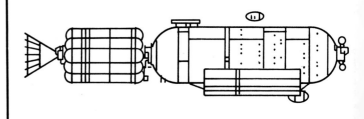

Specifications

Length	100 m
Beam	18.2 m
Draught	30.9 m
Mass	2 million kg
Engine Section	38.2 m x 18 m diameter
Passenger Section	58.2 m x 16 m diameter
Fuel Capacity	1.1 million kg
Passengers	260
Passenger/crew ratio	8.6:1

Performance

Range	800 million km (Earth-Asteroid Belt)
Cruising Velocity	50,000 m/sec
Engines	Multi-configure advanced fission
Typical Voyage length	3 weeks
Passenger Accommodations	3 dining rooms
	2 nightclubs
	1 theater/auditorium
	Low-grav gymnasium
	Rear stellar observatory

STELLAR EXPLORATIONS

Alpha Centauri

Alpha Centauri is part of a trinary star system with two planets, one inhabited, and is the closest solar system to Earth's home Sol System. A founding member of the United Federation of Planets the Alpha Centaurians have such similar physical characteristics to humans that a common ancestry has been suggested, but never established. Over the years Centaurians and Earthmen have enjoyed a strong mutual respect and admiration for each other.

A. Centauri contains two planets: one habitable (H); one uninhabitable

	Dist. from star (×10⁸km)	Diameter (km)	Revolution (Solar days & years)	Average surface temp (°c)
I(H)	1.395	13,065	342 d	24°
II	12.320	78,550	14.8 yrs	−215°

ORBITAL DISTANCE, A.U.

Galactic bound.

The advent of fusion propulsion relegated everything that came before it to the museum. This means of travel, along with great strides in navigation, communications, computer technology, and space metals, allowed for manned intersteller voyages.

Beginning with 1-3 year extra-solar tours that acclimated crews to long duration flight, time and distance away from Earth steadily grew until the advanced fusion Columbus Class ships journeyed to Barnard's Star and Alpha Centauri.

It was this latter voyage that cut the fusion age short, for a new, far greater means of travel was at hand.

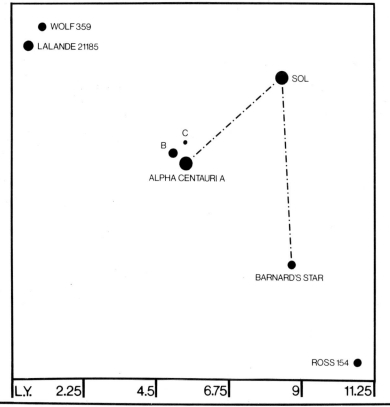

EXPLORATION ROUTES –·–·–·–·–

L.Y.	2.25	4.5	6.75	9	11.25

CLOUD SEEDING OF VENUS MEETS INITIAL SUCCESS

2027

UNSS TILLER, DY-500 CLASS
DR. WILLIAM SLATER, SCIENCE OFFICER

Science Log:

One of our truly outstanding interplanetary scientific projects has become a reality. The attempt to make our sister planet, Venus, habitable for humans is reaping its first results: the rains have started. It's been one year and seventeen days since twenty programmed probes seeded the upper Venerian atmosphere with billions of the blue-green algae Cyanidium Caldarium. At the same time, our associates have been periodically bombarding the planet with hugh ice asteroids from the Asteroid Belt. These will provide additional water for the arid world and, because of their calculated angle of impact, have already doubled the rate of rotation, which will generate a protective Van Allen belt for the planet.

For the past year, our orbiting survey team has been carefully monitoring the terraforming—the algaes' truly astronomical reproduction rate that has thinned the carbon dioxide clouds and created an oxygen atmosphere, and the slow growth in water vapor from the almost instantly vaporized asteroids (the surface temperature is 500° C.). Finally, the vapor pressure has become too great to remain gaseous. And so the rains have begun.

The planet is covered with clouds now, but these are billowing steam clouds produced when the rains approached the literally red-hot planet surface. Over the next several years, this cycle of rain and evaporation will repeat itself, each time lowering the temperature until finally, the rains will be able to remain to nourish the soil, and the inferno that was Venus will be replaced by sparkling oceans and rich oxygen atmosphere. Or so it is hoped.

I must confess my skepticism to the success of this whole project. Some of my colleagues are completely confident this radical terraforming will come off without a hitch, but I see a number of serious problems. Without an ozone layer, the artificially induced Van Allen belt might not provide enough radiation shielding. On top of that, the planet surface has high concentrations of corrosive hydrochloric and sulfuric acids. What good will sparkling acid oceans be to anyone? We might be able to make Venus look like Eden, but I doubt very much whether anyone will ever be able to live comfortably here.

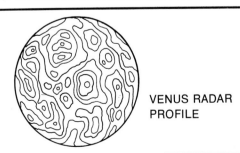

VENUS RADAR PROFILE

EXTRATERRESTRIAL SIGNALS RECEIVED AT MOONBASE
After 60 years, Project SETI has first success

2029

FARSIDE MOONBASE 2C
DR. SALVATORE MARCIANO, COMMUNICATIONS COORDINATOR

For well over a century, these signals remained undeciphered until the invention of duotronic computers in the late twenty-second century. It turned out to be a quaternary code describing the star's lifeforms, history, culture and spiritual values. Sadly, it also predicted the race's demise, which was over five thousand years ago. Their genetic vitality had been slowly fading over the millennia, and these very advanced lifeforms could predict with tragic certainty the time when they would no longer be able to maintain sufficient vigor to remain in existence. A full decoding of this Sagittarian signal can be found at Memory Alpha.

Communications Log:

I am overjoyed to report today that the huge electromagnetic ears of Project SETI have finally discovered a galactic voice. It is intelligent, it is powerful and it is *very* very far away.

Like many breakthroughs throughout history, this came as an accidental result of another experiment. Here at Farside Moonbase 2C, we've been continuing the search for galactic life begun on Earth in the twentieth century. As the scientific community is well aware, several directions have been followed: listening on various radio spectra, examining possible visual signs, searching for unusual groupings of elements. It was this last approach that provided the vital clue. The artificial element Technetium 99 is found in very few stars, our sun being unaccountably one of them. The Chief of Radio Telescope Operations, Dr. Ashworth, has been mapping these so-called S-stars for some time, and he found a peculiar triangle of them at 327° toward the galactic center in Sagitarrius.

He programmed the massive Farside radio telescope on the grouping and, to his astonishment, picked up a periodic signal emanating from its center. The signal is at the twenty-one centimeter frequency of the hydroxyl group (OH), an essential component for organic life. And the message, which repeats itself every 5.28 Earth days, is a definitely intelligent, modulated transmission. So intelligent, in fact, that Moonbase computers have been unable thus far to decode it.

The implications are staggering. This radio source appears to be roughly 15,000 light-years away from us, visible only as a hazy white dot on the infrared photos. But that image represents a civilization that was vastly more powerful 10,000 years before the dawn of our civilization than we are now. And they are calling out to the galaxy. This is a very distant, highly intelligent civilization purposely announcing its presence. And I must wonder "Why?"

ASTEROID MINING A GREAT SUCCESS
Call to rescind Homestead Act severely criticized

2032

ASTEROPOLIS, ASTEROID BELT CAPITAL SATELLITE
SVETLANA KRENSKY, GOVERNOR

Governor's Log:

I thank the General Assembly for allowing me to submit this Log into the proceedings of the Committee to Reexamine the Space Homesteading Act.

I am well aware certain critics wish to rescind this historic Act. They claim preferential treatment for space settlers, windfall profits for greedy speculators, and an unfair balance of payments between the Earth and the Asteroid Belt.

Well, there is some truth to these criticisms. Many settlers have taken advantage of the opportunities of space development to become very wealthy, and I'm sure some of them were less than completely scrupulous. This is human nature, and that stays the same whether in the Asteroid Belt or back on Earth. But most settlers have worked unbelievably hard to get where they are today. They've suffered the deprivations and deadly dangers of space, and given their youth and vitality to the making of a successful homestead. They are a special breed, these homesteaders, and I don't think many of us would trade places with them for all the riches in the Solar System.

But there are more overriding reasons for continuing the Space Homesteading Act, reasons that are extremely important to all of Earth. Let us not forget that before Asteroid mining, practically all raw materials for industrial processes had to come from the Earth itself, with the consequent pollution and ravaging of the landscape. Air quality and the fundamental quality of life for all mankind was adversely affected by the necessity of almost destroying our world to feed our industry.

The Asteroid Belt has done away with that terrible tradeoff. No longer is the Earth a receptacle for industrial pollutants. Ore mined here in the Asteroid Belt is freighted back to orbiting platforms for refining and for the manufacturing of space-related materials. The Earth as a result has been able to redirect its resources towards cleaning up the global ecology, and the planet is slowly returning to its pre-industrial purity. Without the intrepid space homesteaders supplying the Earth with needed resources, the deterioration of air, water and living quality would have inexorably destroyed the world.

I cannot believe anyone would wish us to return to that sorry state of affairs. No, space homesteading is working. Man is inhabiting his home Solar System and helping Earth realize its full potential as the home of humanity. Thank you.

EXPERIMENTAL FUSION SHIP EXPLODES
Major setback for interstellar travel
2035

UNSS FISHER, COMPANION CLASS
RICHARD HANNA, CAPTAIN

What follows is the exact transcript of the tragedy that preceded the era of advanced fusion drive. The participants in this communication were Robert Carradine, test piloting the Advanced Fusion Prototype One experimental ship and Richard Hanna, Captain of the trailing Escort Support Vehicle. Nuclear fusion proved, at times, to be difficult to tame, and, as revealed in the official inquiry of this unfortunate accident, the new vehicle was not yet ready for rigorous testing.

Captain's Channel Log:

Hanna: . . . on my mark we'll be minus ten . . . mark, ten seconds to power-up.

AFP1: Okay . . . ten seconds. Our program 9-21 is in. We've got the velocity light at nine . . . reaction prefire and energy stream detonator power levels are stable at six seconds, five, four . . . fuel pellets are switching to larger size . . . two, one

Hanna: We see your power-up.

AFP1: —and the throttle is up! The positive-g light is on . . . we're burning! Nozzle temp is going up . . . leveling off at ten thousand six. Dick, it's a very smooth firing.

Hanna: We copy; GNC and Flight Dynamics report you moving out past Marker 1, and your velocity is climbing to .389c . . . looking good.

AFP1: . . . Dick, we're getting a Master Caution and Warning alarm on the . . . wait a second. The engine is misfiring. The beams are first missing the fuel pellets and then hitting them, and it's shaking up the Engineering section. We're dropping the throttle down to the previous setting.

Hanna: Shut down the injector and turn the ship around. We want to bring you back to the inner Markers. Prepare to copy guidance instructions when you've settled the engine down.

AFP1: I don't know if we can get a total shutdown. If we stop the sequence right now, it may not be restartable within the time we have.

Hanna: All right . . . we'll get a low-g chase configured to start after you . . . and begin working on a fix for your engine from this end. How serious do you estimate your situation is right now?

AFP1: We're experiencing severe shaking when the engine fires. Something is clogging the delivery tube and it's not going to settle down.

Hanna: The Test Director wants everybody to get into the crew module and break off from the ship. Right now!

AFP1: . . . trying to dislodge the fuel in the injector . . . we'll be able to turn—what? What size is it? Twenty-five? No . . . too big . . . engine . . .

Hanna: Bob! Cut the module away! Cut the . . . Oh my God! Oh my God! One flash and five years of research and ten of friendship are vaporized. Where do we go from here?

"HOLES" IN THE UNIVERSE DETECTED
Interstellar probe suggests universe is stranger than we know.
2036

UNP DRAKE, WELLS SERIES PROBE

This second generation probe was one of fifteen launched from the Earth's moon in the early 2030's. The series had a four-fold increase in effective range and a ten-fold improvement in data gathering and analyzing capability over the earlier "Stellar Series." They also employed a significant increase in the use of artificial intelligence in their computer circuitry, enabling them to make much more complex decisions on their own, sending back whatever pictures and data they deemed important.

What the *Drake* discovered were the then unknown deformations in the space-time fabric that are fairly common in the interstellar void. These "Geon Holes" in space were harnessed forty years later for the quantum jump to warp communications.

Telemetry Readout:

—ATTENTION—
•Anomaly indicated in density pattern of interstellar dust in surrounding region.
. . . ANALYZING
•Drift examination shows attraction of hydrogen, helium and other elements of focal point approximately .117 A.U. distant.
•Attraction extends outward from point in gravity-wave patterns.
•Sensors can find no mass or energy source at center point of attraction.
—Implementing course correction for closer analysis. Approach modified to maintain .05 A.U. distance from anomaly.
—ATTENTION—
•Anomaly indicated at focal point of attraction.
. . . ANALYZING
•Interstellar dust disappearing from universe at focal point.
•Matter apparently vanished into focal point.
CONCLUSION:
Cause unknown.
Data contrary to Prime Programming Loop "Laws of Physics."
All Problem-solving circuits output impossible series converging to $\frac{1}{0}$, an undefined and impermissible endpoint.
Random-access memory integration unable to locate acceptable explanation.
Repeat Data Summary: Interstellar dust disappearing from universe. Cause unknown.

SOLAR SPACELINES INAUGURATES COMMERCIAL SERVICE
Weekly flights to Mars and Jupiter begin.

2040

UNSS PRINCE OF WALES, MAGELLAN CLASS
LARS OLMSTEAD, CAPTAIN

Captain's Log:

Good afternoon ladies and gentlemen. As Captain of the *Prince of Wales* spaceliner, I want to welcome you aboard her maiden voyage. Our inaugural flight plan, as you can see on the screen below me, will take us first to Marsbase One, a journey of some six days, then on to the capital city of the Asteroid Belt, Asteropolis, thirty days farther, and then for our remaining passengers, to our final destination in Jupiter orbit, the Ganymede Outpost.

Quite naturally, all the members of the crew are delighted about the opening of commercial cruises throughout the Solar System. I myself am a twenty-two-year veteran of the Earth/moon route and have, I don't mind saying, dreamed of the day when service between the planets would start. Not only for the adventure of it, but to be able to pilot a ship such as this. It's even hard for me to believe this is an interplanetary spaceship and not some grand hotel. We have two opulent dining rooms, stage and screen theater, null-gravity gymnasium, stellar observatory, even a wine cellar. And more. After we establish standard trajectory, the Cruise Director, Mr. Anthony, will be by to give you a complete rundown of the facilities on board. In the meantime, I ask that you remain in your seat harnesses until we've completed initial thrust sequence, about thirty minutes, and for your safety, I ask that you return to this Main Maneuvering Module whenever a major course correction or docking is scheduled.

We will be leaving Piccadilly Platform shortly on the first leg of our journey. I look forward to speaking with all of you during the course of this flight, and seating for dinner at the huge Captain's Table has been arranged on a rotating basis to assure this.

I hope you enjoy your flightcruise. Next stop is Mars.

INTERPLANETARY COMMUNICATIONS NETWORK SET UP
Pioneer System guarantees Earth to Mars transmission in minutes; Earth to Jupiter within an hour.

2044

**L-4 COMMUNICATIONS PLATFORM
MOHAMMED KAHLIL, SECRETARY GENERAL OF THE UNITED NATIONS**

More than anything else, reliable communications throughout the ever growing solar community was the long sought after wish of the early explorers and settlers. While initial costs were high as in any start-up situation, the Network has been considered by some historians as one of the most important technological advances that took place in the Sol-System. Although communications were far short of today's warp speeds, the guarantee that your call to Jupiter, or some other solar destination, will arrive and not be lost somewhere in space was nothing short of a twenty-first century miracle.

Archive Log:

Greetings citizens of the Solar System. I welcome you all to this inaugural transmission of the Pioneer Solar Communications Network.

I welcome the Earth and the moon, Solar Codes 10 and 20, respectively, who receive this videocast almost instantaneously.

I welcome Venus, Solar Code 30, who sees and hears me after a minute or two time delay.

I welcome the Marsbases, Solar Code 40, who experience a four and one-half minute delay.

Likewise, I welcome all citizens of the outer planets, Solar Code 50:

the Asteroid Belt settlers and Jovian outposts after over a half-hour delay;

the Saturn Solar Base which hears these remarks seventy minutes after I make them;

and finally, my delayed welcome to the Pluto Base, our furthest human habitation, over five and one-half hours away.

At last all mankind is connected together throughout the Solar System. The Pioneer's transmitting platforms and relay satellites, now in operation, bring our farthest-flung friends as close as our home viewscreens.

Let us pause over this feat a moment. Little over 150 years ago, Alexander Graham Bell held the first telephone conversation between two rooms in his laboratory. Today, we've not only evolved from that first crackling command to stereo/video simulcasts, we've stretched beyond that laboratory's modest confines to the very edges of our home solar system. And we're far from finished. Who knows where man's voice will reach in another 150 years?

TERRAFORMING ON VENUS BEGINS
After 20 years, man sets foot on surface.

2047

**VENUS NORTH POLE BASE
DR. WILLIAM SLATER**

Personal Log:

Well, I wouldn't have believed it. Twenty years it's been since I was last around Venus, watching the slow cycle of rains that was going to transform this world. A waste of time, I secretly thought then. Sheer folly.

So right now I'm standing on the surface of this sheer folly and I can hardly believe my eyes. The sunlight is sparkling off the new polar icecaps, and the air is cool and clear and tingling with the fresh-rain sting of ozone. One of the technical officers has attached a mini-greenhouse to the outside of our protective geodesic base covering, and inside it I can see blooming daffodils and roses. It's beautiful here.

Of course, a few flowers is not what is going to make Venus habitable. For the planetary terraforming project, huge vegetation-cultivating seafarms have been built in the newly formed oceans, complete with filters to neutralize the still high acid content of the water. And the terraforming has begun. I flew down to the equator yesterday, where the project is starting from, to spread eventually to the frost line near the poles. On the flight back, I looked at the terraformed region, lit by the warm light of the sun setting in the east, and the thin strip of green seemed like a promise of tomorrow coming true today. Venus is becoming livable.

I don't know where an old skeptic like me fits in all this. Of course, I'm something of a celebrity right now; the terraformers crowd me with questions about how it used to be, before the rains. But part of me remains a doubting fool. Can mankind start over on a new world and not spoil it with the old world attitudes?

Well, I've doubted for twenty years and it's gotten me nothing. So I'm going to spend the rest of my days working on the dream, working at making Venus the Eden it'll become. No fool like an old fool, I guess. It's good to be home.

FIRST ENCOUNTER WITH HUMANOID LIFE

6 year journey to Alpha Centauri forever changes humankind.

2048

UNSS ICARUS, COLUMBUS CLASS
ROGER TAUBER, CAPTAIN

Captain's Log:

With great pride, I am entering into the Log an Official Date of Notification. After traveling for five years, ten months and two days, the *Icarus* has just made the first contact with extraterrestrial, intelligent life: the Alpha Centaurians.

We had not expected any sort of evolved life here, since the trinary Centauri Star System produces strong, fluctuating radiation and complicated gravitational fields that can be fatal to biological development. So it was to our great surprise that once we were within 7 A.U. of Alpha Centauri, life is indeed what we found.

Inside that critical radius, we began to be bombarded by a vast array of signals emanating from a planet, signals whose complexity pointed unmistakably to an advanced civilization. I ordered a general alert, with battlestations ready, and we cautiously approached the planet at flank speed.

At 1.5 A.U. from the planet, scanners picked up four alien vessels rapidly converging on the *Icarus*. I decided against evasive or defensive action and ordered the fusion engines to dead stop, hoping to demonstrate our lack of hostile intentions.

The gambit paid off. After surrounding our ship, the alien vessels hailed us on all standard frequencies in an unknown language, then one dispatched a small craft which traveled half the distance to our ship. Understanding the gesture, I boarded our shuttlecraft and went to meet, well, I had no idea who or what I was to meet.

Who I met when I boarded their shuttlecraft was the Admiral (or their equivalent) of the interplanetary Alpha Centauri fleet. And he looked a great deal like my Uncle Alex. The Alpha Centaurians resemble homo sapiens to such a degree that it's hard not to conjecture about some common ancestry for the two races. The only physiological differences I can observe are a slightly higher forehead and their pinkies appear to function as a second opposable thumb.

Through signs and star charts, I got the Admiral to understand our origin and peaceful intentions. The Admiral has been open and friendly, allowing me and my officers free reign of his flagship. My science officer in particular has taken advantage of this openness to have extended mathematical conversations with an Alpha Centaurian scientist.

I fully recommend the commencement of diplomatic relations with these, our closest neighbors. They appear friendly, most cooperative, and an exchange of ideas and cultures may have consequences we can't even guess.

FRANK JOCASTA
SCIENCE OFFICER

Science Officer's Log:

I've just spent the two most exciting days of my scientific life talking with the Alpha Centaurian physicist Zefrem Cochrane. Of course, since neither speaks the other's tongue, we've relied almost exclusively on the language of mathematics. A lexicon of match symbols was easily established. Zefrem Cochrane drew a circle, drew its radius, pointed to the circle, then the radius, and drew a symbol which I knew immediately was their notation for pi. From such elementary steps, the whole system of mathematical thought was quickly translated, and soon we were gossiping away in scientific scribbles.

What has made these days so electrifying is a concept in theoretical physics that Zefrem Cochrane has developed, an idea I've taken to calling the warp principle. Using a math I can still only barely comprehend, he's shown that space can be visualized as moving along the curved wave of time. Straight down the curve is our normal time. But if one can cut along the warped wave of the time curve, the space-time equations of the unified field theory are radically modified.

As far as I can tell, if a ship were constructed along certain warp-dynamic lines and could generate a warp drive field around it, the vessel would integrate the normal space-time curve to produce the warp effect, and travel faster than light. Presently, there is no power known to man nor Alpha Centaurian sufficient to reach the warp threshold. However, rough computations by myself and Zefrem Cochrane suggest that matter/antimatter annihilation might provide enough power, except that, of course, there is no way known to control and focus such a reaction. But if the seemingly insurmountable technical problems can be overcome, warp drive may well become a feasible propulsion.

And if this is so, man will be able to transcend the till now limiting speed of light. Travel at warp speeds will open the entire galaxy to us. The possibilities of such a future prospect for mankind are literally unimaginable.

A. CENTAURI SHUTTLECRAFT

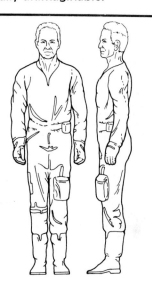

MALE A. CENTURIAN

OVERVIEW

Warp drive produced a quantum jump in the exploration of space for man, multiplying the stars accessible to him many hundreds of times over what was possible with even the most sophisticated sublight spaceships.

Unmanned stellar probes of a generation before had discovered the surprising presence of large amounts of antimatter floating in the interstellar void, and decades of follow-up work finally resulted in floating space refineries that collected and stored (in antimagnetic nacelles) sufficient antimatter to fuel starships. Then, streamlined along the geodynamic contours dictated by warp theory, warp drive starships were constructed employing the propulsion of matter/antimatter annihilation, the only uninormal reaction known to generate enough power for the warp effect.

In 2059, the first warp drive starship, the UNSS BONAVENTURE, was launched and made a twelve light-year journey to Tau Ceti. Soon, a fleet of warp drive vessels was spreading out in all directions, pointed, as might be expected, toward identified possible sources of life.

During this period, man's home Solar System was visited by two alien spacefarers, whose encounters with Earth forever changed the course of space history. In 2065, a damaged Vulcan vessel revealed its presence to a Solar Fleet ship, the UNSS AMITY, which fearlessly came to the aid of the stricken ship and so opened what ever after have remained cordial relations with our fellow UFP member Vulcan.

The meeting with Vulcan represented another great step in the evolution of man's galactic conscience. Unlike the Alpha Centaurians, who were similar enough to humans to suggest a possible common ancestral link, the Vulcan race was truly alien, physiologically and, most especially, psychologically. Though the Vulcan lack of emotion made adjustment harder than expected, the discipline of relating to an alien race made Earth's first encounter with Tellar less volatile.

For true to the feisty spirit of the race, in 2073 a Tellarite ship crossed the Pluto perimeter and immediately claimed the entire Solar System as an addition to the Tellarite Territories. With a graciousness bulwarked by firepower, the UNSS BONHOMME RICHARD's captain defused the potentially violent confrontation, and soon Tellar had been added to the list of important Earth allies.

From the growing interaction of alien worlds, a fertile exchange of knowledge and culture began. Transfer points of commercial space lanes were agreed upon, and the synergistic advantages of space relations began to be seen everywhere.

For instance, the Andorian genius Kazanga (see Volume VI-Andor) postulated the theoretical basis for warp communication. Examining one of the solutions to the Unified Field equations, shown him when Andor was encountered in 2069, he suggested the holes in space discovered b

he Drake probe decades before were sufficient to allow field-warp electromagnetic
communication to penetrate hyperspace
and emerge at distant points along the warp
curve. These communications could, of
course, attain much higher warp speeds
than a massive starship, but, limited by the
inverse-cube law of warp theory, were not
instantaneous. (See Chapter 10 for speculations about instantaneous communications.)

An extremely important historical document
was written in 2062, the Fundamental Declaration of the Martian Colonies. The settlements throughout the Solar System had
grown to such an extent that they began to
feel unevenly represented in United Nations
decisions. Much like the American Declaration of Independence almost three hundred
years before, the Fundamental Declaration
insisted on each region's right to make the
critical legislation governing their internal
life, acknowledging, however, the United
Nations' jurisdiction over matters on the
solar level. This major precedent was incorporated into the structure of the United
Federation of Planets, which makes galactic
decisions but leaves home government to
the member planets themselves.

There were some people though, for whom
all governments were equally to be
shunned. During this period, several mul-
tigenerational colony ships were launched
to seek out new worlds to settle undisturbed by any outside interference. Using by

then outmoded fusion propulsion, these
pilgrims knew they were destined almost as-
suredly never to return. And none did. The
lifeless wreckage of eight of these valiant,
doomed ships has been salvaged. One (Terra
10) survived, marooned on a barely habitable, volcanic world. One has never been
found.

On Pluto, a combined Earth-Alpha Centauri
research team finally solved the century-old
debate between correct models of the universe. Measurements relating the Big
Bang—the cataclysmic commencement of
our universe—to the furthest radio galaxies
conclusively demonstrated the superiority
of pulsating universe cosmogony to the
hyperbolic model. Instead of the universe
expanding indefinitely to maximum en-
tropy, in other words, dying, our pulsating
universe will reach a maximum breadth of
expansion, then begin to contract, eventually forming a primal nucleus from which
another Big Bang will explode to start
another cosmic cycle. The universe pulses as
surely as does a human or a Tellarite heart.

In retrospect, the incorporation of the
United Federation of Planets in the next era
seems almost an inevitable result of the
meeting and mixing of alien cultures that
took place in this quarter century. The
cooperation among isolated planets clearly
augured the institution of some political
structure to recognize and coordinate the
new galactic realities. A galactic community
was being formed, and the Earth was to be
an integral part of it.

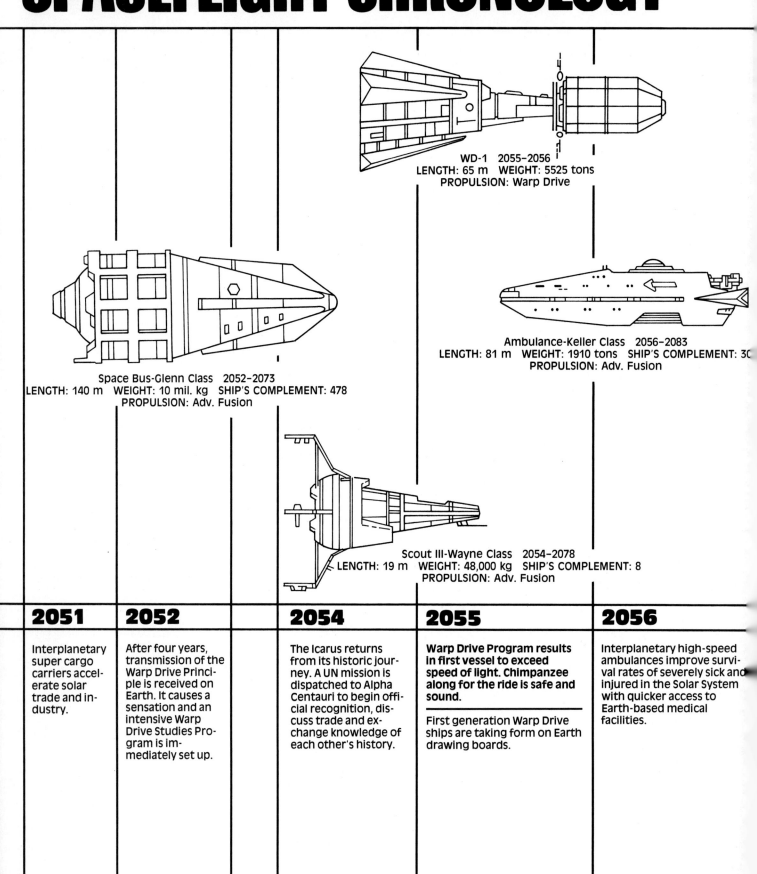

WD-1 2055–2056
LENGTH: 65 m   WEIGHT: 5525 tons
PROPULSION: Warp Drive

Space Bus-Glenn Class   2052–2073
LENGTH: 140 m   WEIGHT: 10 mil. kg   SHIP'S COMPLEMENT: 478
PROPULSION: Adv. Fusion

Ambulance-Keller Class   2056–2083
LENGTH: 81 m   WEIGHT: 1910 tons   SHIP'S COMPLEMENT: 30
PROPULSION: Adv. Fusion

Scout III-Wayne Class   2054–2078
LENGTH: 19 m   WEIGHT: 48,000 kg   SHIP'S COMPLEMENT: 8
PROPULSION: Adv. Fusion

2051	2052		2054	2055	2056
Interplanetary super cargo carriers accelerate solar trade and industry.	After four years, transmission of the Warp Drive Principle is received on Earth. It causes a sensation and an intensive Warp Drive Studies Program is immediately set up.		The Icarus returns from its historic journey. A UN mission is dispatched to Alpha Centauri to begin official recognition, discuss trade and exchange knowledge of each other's history.	**Warp Drive Program results in first vessel to exceed speed of light. Chimpanzee along for the ride is safe and sound.** First generation Warp Drive ships are taking form on Earth drawing boards.	Interplanetary high-speed ambulances improve survival rates of severely sick and injured in the Solar System with quicker access to Earth-based medical facilities.

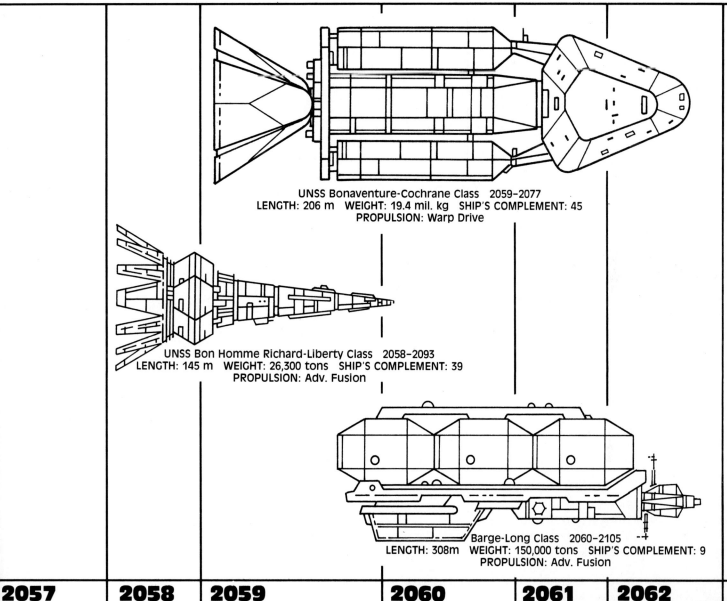

UNSS Bonaventure-Cochrane Class 2059–2077
LENGTH: 206 m   WEIGHT: 19.4 mil. kg   SHIP'S COMPLEMENT: 45
PROPULSION: Warp Drive

UNSS Bon Homme Richard-Liberty Class 2058–2093
LENGTH: 145 m   WEIGHT: 26,300 tons   SHIP'S COMPLEMENT: 39
PROPULSION: Adv. Fusion

Barge-Long Class 2060–2105
LENGTH: 308m   WEIGHT: 150,000 tons   SHIP'S COMPLEMENT: 9
PROPULSION: Adv. Fusion

2057

100 years in space poll lists encountering life on Alpha Centauri, first men on the moon, and the Venus Terraforming Project as the three most significant events in history.

Projections on the next 100 years in space refute the possibility of discovering non-humanoid intelligent life.

2058

Earth's first Warp Drive ship, the Bonaventure, undergoes testing. It proves to be the remarkable craft its designers had hoped it would be.

2059

The Bonaventure begins Earth's Warp Drive era with a voyage to the star system, Tau Ceti, 12 light-years from Earth.

UN mission that left Earth in 2054 arrives at Alpha Centauri and official recognition begins.

Advanced Pluto Research Station opens.

2060

The Warp Drive ship, UNSS Powell, journeys to Alpha Centauri and is hailed as a remarkable achievement.

Industrial Space Ark concept proposed as a potential boon to space economy.

2061

The return of the Powell brings Zefrem Cochrane to Earth. He is accorded all the pomp and pageantry any native earth hero would receive.

Solar Spacelines has special tourist flights to view Halley's Comet close-up.

2062

The Fundamental Declaration of the Martian Colonies grants every inhabited region in the Solar System local autonomy over their own affairs.

Trade with our celestial neighbor begins in earnest with these first generation Warp Drive ships.

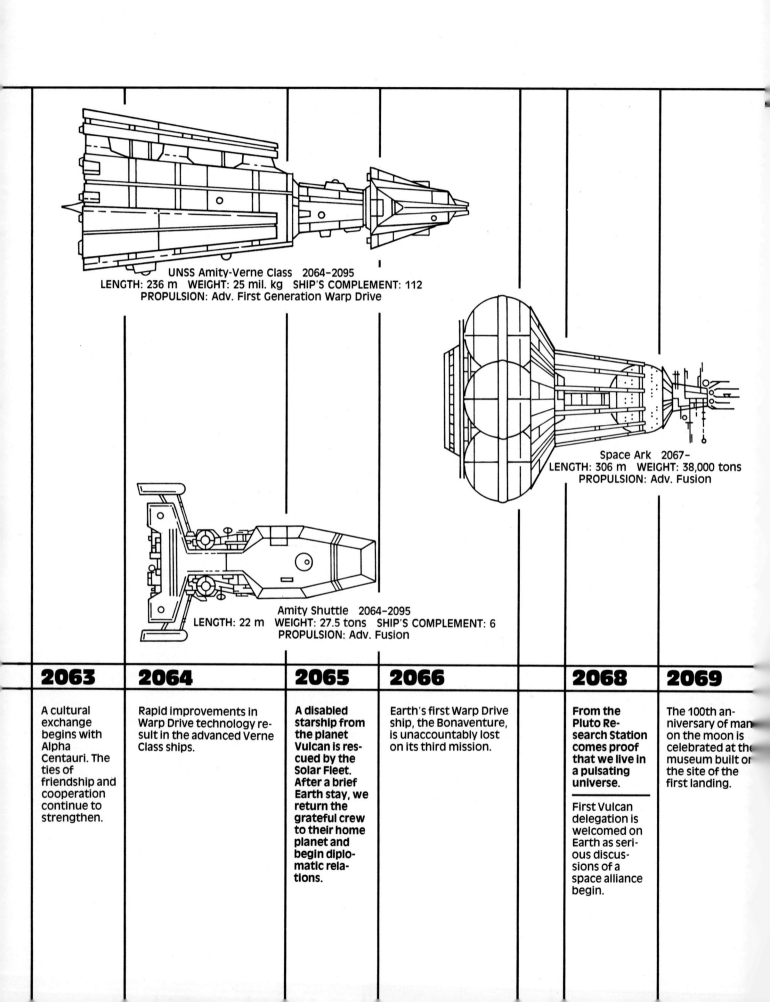

UNSS Amity-Verne Class   2064–2095
LENGTH: 236 m   WEIGHT: 25 mil. kg   SHIP'S COMPLEMENT: 112
PROPULSION: Adv. First Generation Warp Drive

Space Ark   2067–
LENGTH: 306 m   WEIGHT: 38,000 tons
PROPULSION: Adv. Fusion

Amity Shuttle   2064–2095
LENGTH: 22 m   WEIGHT: 27.5 tons   SHIP'S COMPLEMENT: 6
PROPULSION: Adv. Fusion

2063	**2064**	**2065**	**2066**		**2068**	**2069**
A cultural exchange begins with Alpha Centauri. The ties of friendship and cooperation continue to strengthen.	Rapid improvements in Warp Drive technology result in the advanced Verne Class ships.	**A disabled starship from the planet Vulcan is rescued by the Solar Fleet. After a brief Earth stay, we return the grateful crew to their home planet and begin diplomatic relations.**	Earth's first Warp Drive ship, the Bonaventure, is unaccountably lost on its third mission.		**From the Pluto Research Station comes proof that we live in a pulsating universe.** First Vulcan delegation is welcomed on Earth as serious discussions of a space alliance begin.	The 100th anniversary of man on the moon is celebrated at the museum built on the site of the first landing.

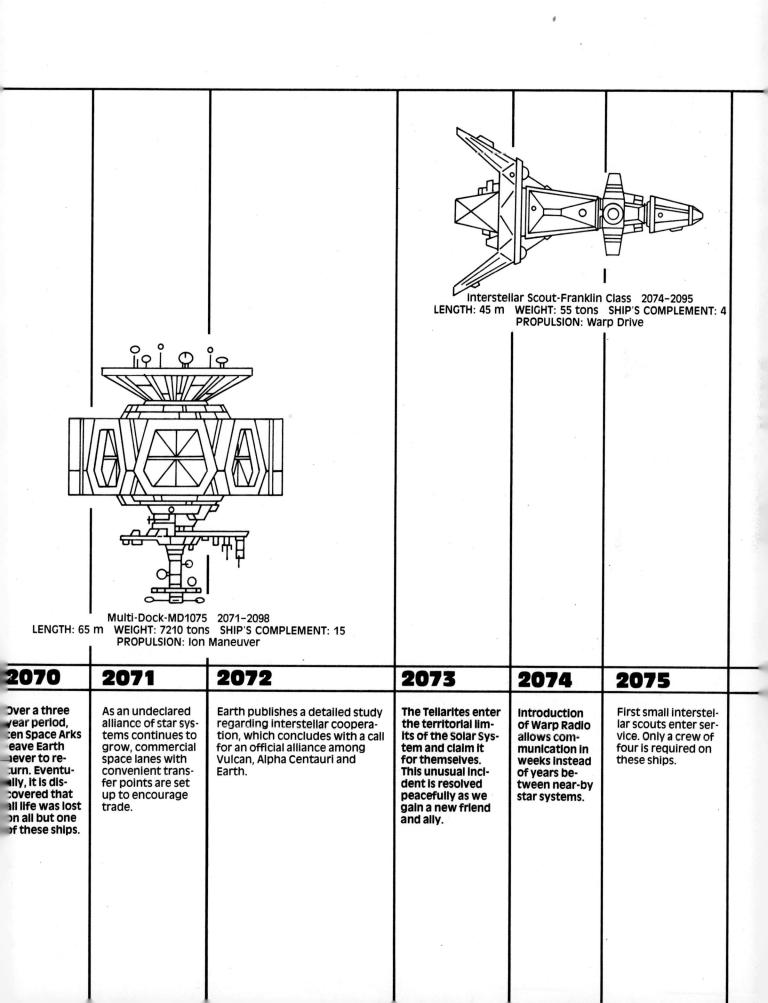

Interstellar Scout-Franklin Class   2074–2095
LENGTH: 45 m   WEIGHT: 55 tons   SHIP'S COMPLEMENT: 4
PROPULSION: Warp Drive

Multi-Dock-MD1075   2071–2098
LENGTH: 65 m   WEIGHT: 7210 tons   SHIP'S COMPLEMENT: 15
PROPULSION: Ion Maneuver

2070	**2071**	**2072**	**2073**	**2074**	**2075**
Over a three year period, ten Space Arks leave Earth never to return. Eventually, it is discovered that all life was lost on all but one of these ships.	As an undeclared alliance of star systems continues to grow, commercial space lanes with convenient transfer points are set up to encourage trade.	Earth publishes a detailed study regarding interstellar cooperation, which concludes with a call for an official alliance among Vulcan, Alpha Centauri and Earth.	The Tellarites enter the territorial limits of the Solar System and claim it for themselves. This unusual incident is resolved peacefully as we gain a new friend and ally.	Introduction of Warp Radio allows communication in weeks instead of years between near-by star systems.	First small interstellar scouts enter service. Only a crew of four is required on these ships.

UNSS BONAVENTURE
COCHRANE CLASS

2059-2077

The *Bonaventure* was the first ship to have warp drive. After more than a decade of design, construction and validation testing, the *Bonaventure* and its fellow Cochrane class ships inaugurated a new era in spaceflight exploration. Inaccessible interstellar spans became reasonable distances, as demonstrated by this ship's journey in 2061 to Tau Ceti, nearly 12 light-years away. On its third voyage, to Sirius, the *Bonaventure* was unaccountably lost.

Specifications

Length	206 m
Beam	63.4 m to radiator wings
Draught	66.7 m
Mass	19.4 million kg
Engine Section: Diameter	20 m
Length	85.2 m
Life Support Section	33.3 m x 57.3 m x 63.48 m
Heat Radiator Wings	Length: 42.8 m
Diameter	66.7 m

Ship's Complement

Officers (Captain, Lieutenant, Science, Engineering, Navigation)	5
Crew	40
Standard Ship's Complement	45

Performance

Range: Standard	25 light-years
Maximum	40 light-years

Cruising Velocity	Warp 2 (8c)
Maximum Velocity	Warp 2.5 (15.6c)
Typical Voyage Duration	3.8 years (Sun - Tau Ceti)
Maximum Voyage Duration	6 years

Systems Overview

Navigation	Warp Celestial Guidance
Communication	Laser Radiotelemetry
Computer	Intermediate Independent Thought Memory Scan
Weapons	2 forward lasers
Life support: Gravity	.4 - 1.0 g
Atmosphere	20% O_2; 11% humidity
Sustenance Duration	4.5 yrs at Standard Ship's Complement

Engineering and Science

- 1 Stellarjet Warp Drive Engine
- 3 Geodyne Fusion Power Packs
- Fuel — 75:1 matter to antimatter mix
- Exhaust plating of dispersion-strengthened hafnium carbide. Radiator wings needed for heat dispersion

Improvements and Innovations

- First ship with warp drive
- First ship to travel with warp celestial navigation
- Fusion engines used to generate warp field effect
- Detachable Life Support Segment in case of warp engine emergency
- First ship to utilize extraterrestrial components (warp celestial guidance system)

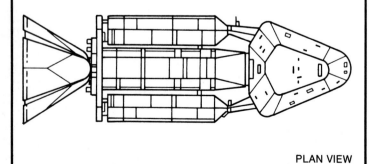

PLAN VIEW

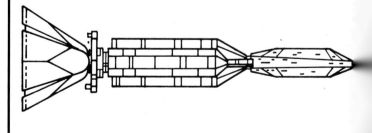

ELEVATION VIEW

WARP 2.7 CRUISER

UNSS AMITY
VERNE CLASS
2064-2095

A dramatic upgrading of warp drive design, the Verne class vessels were the most popular of the early warp spaceships. Used for both interplanetary and interstellar missions, the *Amity* not only made the first historic contact with Vulcan, but was also the ship that carried the stranded Vulcan survivors back to their home world.

Specifications

Length	236 m
Beam	80.4 m
Draught	50 m
Mass	25 million kg

Ship's Complement

Officers (Captain, Lieutenant, Science, Engineering, Navigation, Medical, 3 Ensigns)	9
Crew	103
Standard Ship's Complement	112

Performance

Range: Standard	35 light-years
Maximum	50 light-years
Cruising Velocity	Warp 2.5 (15.6c)
Maximum Velocity	Warp 2.7 (19.7c)
Typical Voyage Duration	1.5 years (Sun - Epsilon Eridani)
	2.5 years (Sun - Altair)

Systems Overview

Navigation	Warp Celestial Guidance
Communication	Particle Subcarrier Radiotelemetry
Computer	Independent Thought Memory Scan
Weapons	8 Forward Lasers 50 Fusion torpedoes
Life support: Gravity	.5 g - 1.0 g
Atmosphere	24% O_2; 11% Humidity
Sustenance Duration	5.3 years at Standard Ship's Complement

Engineering and Science

- Separated Dual-drive Warp Engines
- Fuel: 35:1 matter to antimatter
- Exhaust Heat Radiator Fins

Improvements and Innovations

- Separate warp engines provide much more efficient warp drive

SPACEBUS GLENN CLASS 2052-2073

These Space Buses served as the principal surface-to-orbit carriers during the second half of the 21st century. Over 200 were built to accommodate the increasingly heavy traffic among the Earth, orbiting satellite-cities, Mars, Venus and the Asteroid Belt. Perhaps the most distinctive feature of the Space Buses were their adaptability. With convertible interiors, they could be used for both industrial transport and passenger service.

Specifications

Length	140 m
Diameter	56.5 m
Mass	10 million kg
Passenger Area	length: 38.4 m
	diameter: 45 m

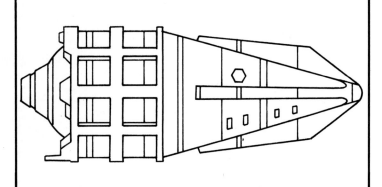

Ship's Complement

Officers (Captain, Pilot, Navigation, Engineering, Flight Supervisor)	5
Crew	23
Standard Ship's Complement	28
Passengers	Up to 450

Performance

Range	800 million km (Earth - Asteroid Belt)
Cruising Velocity	175 million km/hr
Typical Voyage Duration	20 hours (Earth - Asteroid Belt)
Engines	SpaceOp Advanced Fusion Engine
Fuel	Frozen deuterium

Forward docking ribs fit standard docking ports on all satellite cities, planetary bases and asteroid belt settlements

---

SPACE ARK 2067-

The Space Ark was originally conceived as a huge interplanetary industrial spaceworks, but its design flexibility was too narrow to keep pace with the rapidly evolving technology of the 21st century. Instead, it was cheaply purchased by a consortium of like-minded people, who refitted it as a multi-generational colony ship.

Specifications

Length	306 m
Diameter	140 m
Mass	34.6 million kg
Living Sphere	Diameter: 57.5 m
	Volume: 100,000 cu m
	Decks: 10
Fuel Spheres (4)	diameter: 64 m
	Total Fuel Volume 550,000 cu m

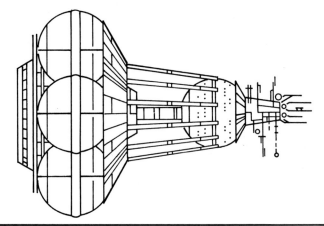

Performance

Range	Unknown*

*(As far as is known, only one of these multi-generational ships survived; and that one stranded its passengers on a totally hostile planet)

Cruising Speed	.5
Voyage Duration	Multi-generational
Engines	Multi-configured advanced fusion
Life Support	The ships were refitted to be totally self-sufficient for decades. They had their own food-grow tanks, manufacturing facilities, resource collectors, schools, stores, recreational facilities and chapel

STELLAR EXPLORATIONS

Vulcan

Vulcan is a founding member of the United Federation of Planets. Appearing deep red from space, the planet is a harsh and, in some places, extremely hostile world with half its land mass made uninhabitable by volcanoes and dust storms. Vulcan is the third planet in the Epsilon Eridani binary star system and is slightly larger in mass than the Earth and closer to it's Sun. The atmosphere is thin by Earth standards and surface temperatures vary from 10° to 60°c in the temperate regions to temperatures in the desert regions as high as 120°c.

Epsilon Eridani contains seven planets: one habitable (H); one potential (P); five uninhabitable

	Dist. from star (×10⁸km)	Diameter (km)	Revolution (Solar days & years)	Average surface temp (°c)
II(P)	.72	8,872	212 d	550°
(Vulcan) III(H)	1.40	12,952	389 d	50°

ORBITAL DISTANCE, A.U.

Earth joins the interstellar community.

With warp drive capability, Earth became a member of the interstellar community. This remarkable means of propulsion allowed man to begin diplomatic relations and trade with several star systems, which inevitably lead to greater dependence on one another.

As this undeclared alliance of worlds grew, voyages of up to twenty lightyears became commonplace for Earth starships, as their velocity and range were continually uprated.

In this era, man was traveling between stars the way his previous generation traveled between planets. A jump never seen before, or since.

MAJOR COMMERCIAL ROUTES ———————

EXPLORATION ROUTES –·–·–·–·–·–

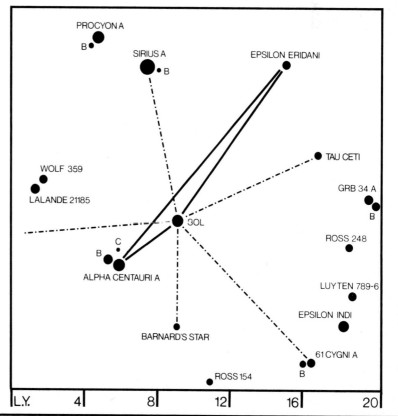

EXPERIMENTAL VESSEL EXCEEDS SPEED OF LIGHT

Unmanned Warp Drive vehicle allays fears concerning travel at invisible speeds.

2055

UNSS FISHER, COMPANION CLASS
RICHARD HANNA, CAPTAIN

Captain's Log:

We've just recovered the warp drive prototype WD-1 at the outer limits of the Pluto Test Area after its first experimental run, and it sure looks like we have an "All-Go" here. We had the model on visual and laser tracking as it accelerated up to warp threshold, then it disappeared from all sensors. Just a half minute later, when the warp engine disengaged after only ten seconds of firing, the prototype dramatically reappeared *ten* million kilometers away, a warp of approximately 1.5. Amazing!

We've brought the prototype on board and its in-ship sensors indicate the successful conversion of matter/antimatter annihilation into warp propulsion. The efficiency still isn't anything to log home about, and we're going to have to clean that warp engine up before it'll have any practical use for interstellar travel. Also, the matter/antimatter integrator burned out, for reasons the engineering boys are still working on. But I'm happy to report warp drive works. Warp drive really works! And one more thing. The solid crystal recording of warp threshold from the on-board camera is everything I hoped it would be. What a star show!

MANUEL GASSET, M.D.

MEDICAL LOG:

Rosy the chimpanzee, who rode on the warp drive test run, is safely back in her cage, alive and very well indeed. I've done a preliminary checkup on all her vital signs, and except for her pulse rate, which is somewhat slowly returning to normal, all readings are satisfactory. This appears to answer those critics who swore life could not survive the warp effect. Organic life cannot transcend the normal laws of physics, they denounced. Well, they should tell it to Rosy, who's presently screeching for her lunch in a decidedly undead clamor. It's a good thing some of us have vision and confidence and are willing to try . . . or else I don't know where we would be!

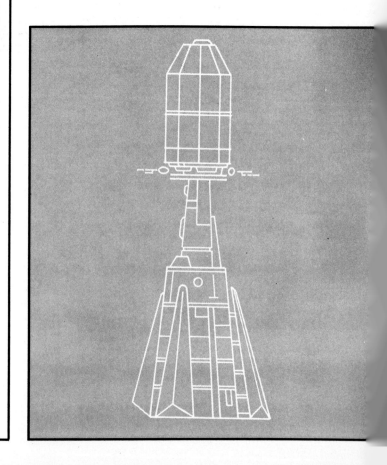

100 YEARS IN SPACE
Space Centennial celebrated throughout Solar System.

2057

PLANET EARTH
UNITED NEWS SERVICE

Archive Log:

The U.N. Public Affairs Poll recently completed a survey of all Earth and Earth-originated people asking them to name, in their own opinion, the ten outstanding landmarks of the first century of spaceflight. The response was by far the largest in the history of poll-taking, possibly due to the public's new-found interest in space exploration because of the promise of warp drive and the advent of interstellar flight.

The list was computer-compiled from wrist, public and some microcomputer inputs, planetary batch transmission and interstellar laser relays. The following represents the consensus response of 5,875,212,149 Terrans which is 61.2 percent of the total population.

1. Encountering advanced life on Alpha Centauri
2. *Apollo 11*—first men on the moon
3. Venus Project—the terraforming of the planet Venus to accommodate human habitation
4. The "Sagittarian Signals"—first sign of superior extraterrestrial life
5. Astropolis Belt—the asteroid cities and mining complexes
6. *Sputnik*—first artificial satellite
7. *Vostok 1*—first man in space
8. First interstellar flight by UNSS *Adameve*
9. Discovery of the warp principle
10. The Space Shuttle—first reusable spacecraft, responsible for opening up space

WARP DRIVE ERA BEGINS
UNSS Bonaventure greatly expands explored galaxy.

2059

UNSS BONAVENTURE, COCHRANE CLASS
HADRIAN HUCKLEBY, CAPTAIN

This Log was recorded in 2061.

Captain's Log:

After traveling less than two years in the interstellar void, it is hard for me to believe we are about to enter the gravitational influence of Tau Ceti, a star that is approximately twelve light-years from home. In my previous experience, in fact, in any starship captain's previous experience, a two-year flight meant no more than one and a half light-years out. So it becomes very obvious that man is about to explore the nearby galaxy the way he once explored the Solar System. And I'm glad I'm part of that.

The ship itself has functioned near flawlessly on the first leg of this record-breaking voyage, and the only one to register any complaints has been my Helmsman, who half-jokingly still doesn't trust the computer reconstruction that replaces the visual field screen.

Now that we've come out of warp drive for our approach to Tau Ceti, I've turned the onboard telescope back towards home. From almost twelve light-years away, our mighty sun is just another insignificant sparkle in the star field and I'm left with the thought that the early explorers had when they first looked back at the Earth from space: Man never was the center of the universe . . . and never will be.

IAN MACGREGOR, CHIEF ENGINEER
Engineer's Log:

Weekly Warp Drive Systems Check

—Matter/Antimatter Integrator
- (✓) Reaction Chamber cleaned and inspected for surface imperfections
- (✓) Emergency Bypass Valve checked and operative
- (✓) Integrator timing computer-recalibrated to 1.5×10^{-8} tolerance

—Antimatter Storage Field
- (✓) Field inspected for invariant containment 69.433% capacity in antimatter storage field

—Warp Control Panel
- (✓) All switches checked and operative
- (✓) Meter levels calibrated to 7.5×10^{-6} degree accu:

—Warp Drive
- (✓) Warp 1.0: performed to specifications
- (✓) Warp 1.5: performed to specifications
- (✓) Warp 2.0: performed to specifications
- (✓) Warp 2.5—Emergency: slight breakdown of power

FUNDAMENTAL DECLARATION OF THE MARTIAN COLONIES PASSED

2062

MARTIAN COLONIES
JOHN HAMMERLICH, GOVERNOR

As mankind evolved from a geo-centered to a solar-wide civilization, its political structure underwent a similar decentralization. A separate political forum was needed to address each planet's unique needs, and in 2062, representatives of every inhabited region in space met on Mars and formally recognized this need in the "Fundamental Declaration." The Earth still remained man's ultimate governing body, but local autonomy was granted the planets over their own internal affairs. The Fundamental Declaration was subsequently extended into interstellar space and has become a major galactic precedent.

Archive Log:

THE FUNDAMENTAL DECLARATION OF THE MARTIAN COLONIES

When in the course of human events, it becomes necessary for Planets to dissolve the Political Bands which have connected Them with their Home Planet Earth, and to assume with the Earth a separate and autonomous status, a decent Respect to the Opinions of Mankind requires that They should declare the causes which impel Them to the Separation.

We contend that the great distances and differing Planetary realities among Planets and the Earth have given rise to numerous inequities and misunderstandings.

We further contend that the representation afforded Planets in any Earth-centered Political Forum cannot provide a sufficient voice for our Needs and Aspirations.

We, therefore, the Representatives of all Inhabited Regions of the Solar System, met here at the Martian Colonies, do, in the Name, and by the Authority of the good People of these Regions, solemnly Publish and Declare, that these Regions are, and of Right ought to be, FREE AND AUTONOMOUS.

This Declaration implies no malice nor animosity toward the Planet Earth. It recognizes the Authority of the Earth over intraplanetary affairs and pledges Full Participation in the Maintainence and Security of the Solar System.

However, the FREEDOM AND AUTONOMY of these Regions must be considered an inviolable principle, which hereafter, must be honored by all peaceful Governments and will be Defended by these Regions with the full weight of their Honor, their Fortunes, and their Lives.

SIGNED at these MARTIAN COLONIES, 2062
JOHN HAMMERLICH, GOVERNOR OF
THE MARTIAN COLONIES

EARTH RESCUES ALIENS FROM VULCAN IN DISABLED SHIP

2065

UNSS AMITY, VERNE CLASS
PETER O'BRIAN, CAPTAIN

Captain's Log:

ATTENTION - PRIORITY - TRANSMISSION TO:
UNSF COMMAND

I have extraordinary news to report. We have peaceful contact with an advanced alien civilization. They call themselves Vulcans.

While on routine sector patrol the *Amity* tracted an unknown emerging from the radar blackout behind Neptune. The moving body immediately began broadcasting—in precise but strangely inflected English—the following Ship In Distress Signal:

"Hailing all ships. Emergency. We are a nonviolent alien vessel experiencing rapid loss of life support systems. Unless evacuated within 59.837 minutes, standard earth time, all crew shall die. Life saving assistance is urgently requested."

Since any communication with Solar Fleet Command would have taken longer than the stated time remaining, I alone had to decide our course of action, and I chose to answer the distress call as I would for any ship in space. Consequently, the *Amity* executed *EOP*-113, Deep Space Rescue, and recovered forty-two alien survivors, including four wounded.

Once safely aboard, the Vulcan skipper, Captain Sparon, formally greeted me on behalf of his world and thanked me for saving his crew from the life support failure, which he attributed to a "most illogical coincidence involving a random combination of break down parameters." That's how Vulcans express themselves. He also consented to answer some preliminary inquiries to accompany this historic transmission.

Vulcan, the alien's home world, is the third planet in the Epsilon Eridani Star System, a close binary system 10.7 light years from our sun. It's a planet slightly larger than Earth and closer to its star. Appearing deep red from space, Vulcan has a thin atmosphere, though high in oxygen and water vapor, with surface temperatures varying from 10°-60°C: I'm also including my medical officers log for data concerning the Vulcan species.

According to Captain Sparon, Vulcans are a very private species, with an advanced technological civilization thoroughly grounded in logic and nonviolence. He made me aware they've been to our solar system several times before, going back a century and more.

When I asked Captain Sparon why he trusted us to ask for help, he replied, "We've studied your world quite extensively, so we knew that with the advent of your interstellar space flight program, it was inevitable our planets would someday meet. And while your species exhibits a passionate emotionalism that makes accurate predictions impossible, we counted on your curiously consistent altruism to overcome what would have been a completely rational reluctance to assist us. Some planets wouldn't, you know."

This last remark intrigues me, since it implies other intelligent worlds the Vulcans know of. For right now though, this first truly alien race can occupy our full energys, so let me forwarn our diplomats of a Vulcan trait that makes communication surprisingly difficult. Vulcans have no emotions.

MIGUEL ORTEZ, M.D.

Medical Log:

There are presently four wounded Vulcans in Sick Bay. I've been pressed for their proper diagnosis, treatment and prognosis; readings of Vulcan vital signs indicate a physiognomy totally unlike man's! I plastiset a compound fractured leg of one crew member, but the other three have suffered internal injuries, and I can do little for them but keep Sick Bay at a sweltering 35°C, which Vulcans find comfortable, and let them rest undisturbed. I strongly recommend their return to Vulcan at the earliest possible opportunity. From discussion with the broken legged Vulcan, I have assembled the following preliminary species report: Physiological—Vulcans are tall and lithe, with light green skin and dark hair, though one crew member has white hair and dark olive complexion. The most striking outward characteristics are their upswept eyebrows and pointed ears. They appear to have a lower blood pressure and higher heart beat and respiration rate than humans, though objective readings are difficult because Vulcans seem to have great voluntary control over their physiological processes.

To adapt to their sun's rays, Vulcans have evolved a copper-based bloodstream with a higher boiling point than our iron-based blood, and additionally, have a second, nictitating eyelid to shield their sight from accidental blindness. Reproduction is a taboo subject for discussion with outsiders, but I gather it follows some sort of cyclical process. The rest of the Vulcan physiology likewise remains an enigma at this time. Though several Vulcans have volunteered to be examined for this preliminary study, my medical instruments can make no sense of their interior anatomy. And there is at this time no explanation for the pointed ears.

Neurological—The Vulcan race's mental ability has developed in a similar fashion to man's, however, Vulcans appear to have no emotional functions in their mental makeup. It's hard to believe this is an innate lack, and I would tend to think their cold logic is more a result of rigorous training and societal pressure than genetic neurology.

In addition, Vulcans appear to have an extra-conscious, psionic power, which manifests itself in certain forms of telepathy. The Vulcans refer to it as the Vulcan mind touch, or sometimes, mind meld, which is another degree of the same psionic aptitude, and it allows Vulcans to establish mental contact with each other and with other lifeforms.

In summary, Vulcans have certain similarities to humans, but their physiological and neurological structure is in many ways totally foreign to all known Earth medicine. Unlike the Alpha Centaurians, Vulcans are a completely alien race.

POSITIVE PROOF FOUND FOR PULSATING UNIVERSE

2068

PLUTO RESEARCH STATION
HERBERT SAMUELSON, SENIOR ASTRONOMER

Science Log:

As we watched the new year ring in on Earth on the monitors, we were in the midst of the biggest party ever seen on Pluto. The reason for our bash wasn't for the year 2068, but rather because we have, once and for all, answered the century-old question of whether the universe is pulsating or hyperbolic. I can now say *it is definitely pulsating.*

Ever since the steady-state theory fell into theoretical disfavor, the debate has been between the hyperbolic universe model (where the stars will continue to expand indefinitely) and the pulsating universe one (where after a certain time, the expansion will reverse itself and the universe will fall back into a "cosmic egg," from which a new Big Bang will create another universe cycle). Because of previous deficiencies in measuring accuracy, it's been hard to choose between the two. But on Pluto the data is better and the choice is now clear.

Conclusive support comes from two sources. First, the most distant galaxies in the universe—and consequently the oldest—are receding at a velocity that is in variance with the rate predicted by Hubble's Law. This means that the present rate of expansion has slowed down since the dawn of the universe, a fact incompatible with an ever expanding cosmology. Also, measurements of the angular distance between components of distant binary radio galaxies decreases to a limit and then begins increasing further out, additional confirmation that our universe is not expanding irreversibly outward.

Of course, these results tickle my Alpha Centaurian assistant Zeena, who has informed me that the concept of the universe growing and dying and growing again is one of the basic tenets of the Centaurian worldview. I've consistently championed the hyperbolic, ever-expanding model, and the two of us have had a friendly wager riding on the outcome of this theoretical debate. But I can't refute the data we now have. The universe pulses as surely as my heart. I paid up this New Year's Eve.

SPACE ARK SEEKS NEW WORLD
Disenchantment with Solar Community causes families to leave forever.

2070

TERRA 10, MULTI-GENERATIONAL COLONY SHIP
MIRIAM AKKOORD, DECK 3 SUPERVISOR

Personal Log:

I have just been informed we've passed the orbit of Pluto, which means we are officially out of the territorial limits of the Solar System and on our way to our new home. Wherever that is.

While we're still in contact with Earth, I have been asked by the Colony Council to submit this Personal Log into the Earth Log Archives in case we don't have another opportunity to have our voice heard by mankind. For we're going to be gone a long, long time. Longer than I or my children, or their children will live . . . perhaps forever. And I know how hard it has been for family, friends, and people in general to understand our motives and aspirations. So let me, once again, try to explain.

Quite simply, we seek a new world for ourselves and our descendents. People have said there's room enough and more for everyone in the Solar Community. Or that with the beginning of interstellar flight new worlds will open up. But there is a price to be paid in both these views, and that price is outside interference. We've all seen it happen too often in the Asteroid Belt and elsewhere, either by governments or assertive neighbors to doubt it wouldn't surely befall us, too.

Instead, we of *Terra 10* have this dream. We will sail to the stars, we will find a new world out there somewhere, and we'll settle it and build our homes and raise our families to be who and what we choose to be. We'll do it all ourselves, by ourselves, for ourselves.

Of course, we're all scared of the unknown void we have chosen to sail into. What dangers and perils await us out there may easily overwhelm our humble resources. But some day, perhaps, we'll find a little planet somewhere. And we'll call it home and live happily ever after.

It's a simple dream. A dream we have found many share. But the people aboard this ship are those hardy, idealistic souls who are willing to risk everything for that dream . . . even their lives. Which, in spite of it all, leaves me with a sense of confidence about our journey. Because I already know I have found my home.

CELESTIAL NEIGHBORS CLAIM OUR SOLAR SYSTEM
Earth and Tellar begin alliance after unusual incident

2073

UNSS BONHOMME RICHARD, LIBERTY CLASS
ABEL NIWEN, ADMIRAL

While this first meeting between Tellar and the Earth had its awkward moments, as described by the following Log, these two worlds went on to become allies and trading partners. After over a decade of growing interaction and disputation, Earth and Tellar joined together with other charter members to form the United Federation of Planets.

Admiral's Log:

The crisis is over and the first interstellar hostilities have been resolved without a single laser being discharged. I've relaxed Fleet Battlestations and halted the Sixth Fleet reinforcement advance at Neptune. The war's over before it began, and it appears, though I'm damned if I understand it, that we've just gained a new interstellar ally, the Tellarites.

I'm proud to report our Solar Defense Perimeter functioned superbly in this, its first test ever. Pluto Base stellar radar picked up the rapid approach of an alien vessel, and by the time it arrived, ten cruisers had been deployed to meet the ship, a modest-looking craft with foreign markings.

Then things turned peculiar. In crude, gutteral English, a gruff voice broadcast to us the surprising news that we had just been claimed as an addition to the Tellarite Territories, and that if we did not immediately surrender, we would be summarily destroyed.

Here was a lone, somewhat backward-looking ship threatening ten heavily armed cruisers with extinction. Did they have a secret super-weapon on board? I doubted it. So in my best diplomatic voice, I called their bluff. I welcomed them to our Solar System, said we were always delighted to meet new intelligent lifeforms, and told them if they made a single hostile movement, we would destroy their ship.

A very long silence followed, broken finally by the still gruff voice accepting our offer of friendship and exclaiming that as allies we would be an invincible duo.

So there it is. We have met the Tellarites and apparently are now their allies. I wonder if they're always so combative. It's the strangest war I've ever fought.

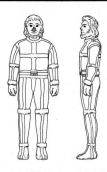

GREAT ADVANCE IN COMMUNICATIONS
Warp radio allows transmissions at 64C.

2074

FARPLUTO TRANSMITTING PLATFORM
BELA ABRUZZI, UNITED NATIONS REPRESENTATIVE

I would like to inaugurate this first Interstellar Communications Network by welcoming our fellow participants, Vulcan and Alpha Centauri. At last, we'll end the fifteen year technological lag between travel and communication. Until now, we've been able to physically contact our neighboring planets sooner than we could converse with them. No longer. With the network of transmitting platforms built near the geodynamometric holes closest to each star system, we will be able to contact our neighbors in weeks instead of years. I speak for all Earth when I express my optimism that this new network will bring our planets ever closer. We are now no longer simply Vulcans or Earthmen, but are citizens of the galaxy.

OUTER ERIDANI TRANSMITTING PLATFORM
T'PAU, VULCAN ACADEMY OF SCIENCES REPRESENTATIVE

As Vulcan representative to the inauguration of the Interstellar Communications Network, I would like to amplify the remarks made by the distinguished Earth representative concerning the advantages of this system. The present warp drive capability averages warp 2.203 for interstellar journeys. This means a typical Earth-Vulcan journey takes 410.597 solar days. With this communications warp producing warp 4 at the present time, a call can be made in 68.313 solar days. A similar time-savings can be realized among Earth or Vulcan and Alpha Centauri, and with Tellar, when that system's transmitting platform is finished construction. The exchange of scientific informations should produce a strong impetus to technological progress in all areas, and it is only logical that diplomatic correspondence will stimulate mutual cooperation. This is a most sensible network.

CENTAURI TRANSMITTING PLATFORM
ZORMER GANDERANE, ALPHA CENTAURI REPRESENTATIVE

I would like to depart a little from my colleagues' focus on the present advantages of this great warp communications network and look instead into the future. The exploration of new worlds and discovery of other races is almost certain to increase. Already the Tellarites have described a trading planet where dozens of aliens sell their system's goods and services. And much as I applaud this network, I believe the time will come when other communications systems will be necessary.

Particularly for those exploring starships not near any hole in space with a transmitting platform broadcasting into it. Starships will someday have to be equipped with warp broadcasting capabilities of their own.

Using the expertise acquired from the construction of this network, warp communication, I believe, will be common in the not-too-distant future. Today we salute this landmark, tomorrow we move beyond it.

OVERVIEW

The galaxy continued to open to man's exploration as this era opened. A quantum leap in the number of known inhabited planets occurred when the Tellarites introduced Earth traders to the Rigel Trading Planet. The second of the twelve worlds that comprise the Rigel Star System, the Rigel Trading Planet has long been known as a galactic trading center, where space traders from all sectors could meet and exchange the unique goods of each region. Earth rapidly established a reputation for the high quality of its spaceworthy metal alloys and its advanced electronic technologies. Today there is a permanent Earth legation to coordinate the myriad transactions that take place on Rigel.

Increasing interaction among alien cultures was likewise reflected in the first Earth-alien crews. Even before the UFP, Earth pioneered the commission of alien crew members to complement the strengths of its human crew. For all their belligerence, Tellarites proved adept engineers, and Andorians showed an uncanny knack for interstellar communication and navigation. This spaceflight cooperation brought planets ever closer, until political alliance seemed the only logical next step.

For the momentum to formalize the growing interdependence among planets had been growing for decades, as friendly worlds leaned even more heavily on one another for vital goods and services. Inevitably, the most important political event in the Interstellar Age came to pass. In 2087, the United Federation of Planets was formally incorporated at the Interplanetary Conference at Babel. Founding members were the Earth, Vulcan, Alpha Centauri, Tellar, Andor and Rigel, and later many other members were admitted at periodic intervals by consent of member planets. And the UFP's continuing vitality and growth stands as an eloquent testament to the wisdom of forming this acclaimed alliance.

So much of what we take for granted was decided upon and inaugurated by those visionary founding fathers. Our monetary system of Federation Credits was established then, as were the Standard Interstellar Symbols every child learns with his ABC's. The space/time matrix of stardates was instituted as the Federation's official chronology, so that descrepancies caused by the special relativity theory (2087 on Earth would be 2092 on Alpha Centauri, etc.) could be reconciled among planets. In addition, a space census was ordered—Earth registered 10 billion planetary residents, 8 million solar citizens, and 354,000 interstellar pioneers—and has been repeated every decade since.

Responding to the obvious need for interstellar security, the UFP Star Fleet was mustered at this first Babel Conference, and the brilliant strategic placement of Starbase was outlined by Star Fleet Command. These Starbases serve as the Federation's outposts throughout its defined territories. They are responsible for sector security and stellar emergencies, and they also serve as complete maintenance and refitting depot for starships. Starbases also coordinate galactic communication, initiate new research activity, and provide welcome shore leave for spaceweary starship crews.

The exploration of unknown sectors of space was also recognized at this time as a primary goal of the new UFP and given a very high priority. Though one of the first starships launched for that purpose, the USS ARCHON, was unaccountably lost in the vicinty of the Beta III star system, other ships, like the USS HORIZON, which explored toward the edge of the galaxy, vigorously pursued this goal.

Space medicine made great leaps forward during this harmonious mingling of alien cultures, and the field of comparative anatomy took on a whole new meaning. Valuable insights were gained into such problems as long-term sensory deprivation, radio immunization and space stress (the Vulcan "vacation"—a self-induced state of restful suspended animation—was studied for use in combating this problem of space stress, unsuccessfully, however: Vulcans are the only ones capable of taking this type of vacation). Equipment such as the medical scanner and bone-setting laser was designed. In addition, a clearing-house of planetary medical societies was begun to guard against unknown epidemics like the "Pluto Plague," which mysteriously decimated all life at the Pluto Research Base (it was later found to be a mutant strain of Omega Virus clinging to a souvenir sold to a researcher by an unscrupulous Orion trader).

There were, however, some unfortunate growing pains that accompanied the founding of the UFP. The new Star Fleet was quickly integrated with crews and captains from member planets, too quickly as it turned out. A space war game disaster in 2089 tragically highlighted the lack of standardized training for Star Fleet officers. To remedy this chaotic chain of command, Star Fleet Academy was chartered to provide centralized training for Fleet officers, and from then on, all starship captains have been graduates of the Academy.

In 2100, the Earth Centenary Conference was assembled to assess the previous century of spaceflight and to offer predictions for the coming hundred years. Authorities traced the evolution of propulsion, communications, electronics, and the development of political and economic alliances among the UFP members and other worlds. Other speakers looked to the future with forecasts ranging from the prophetic to the pathetic. Transporters were predicted, as was the impossibility of speeds faster than warp four. All in all, the character of mankind—its foolishness as well as its vision—was aptly illustrated at this Centenary Conference, the second of which was held in 2200.

As the Earth-dated twenty-first century drew to a close, the UFP had consolidated its position as a galactic presence. And none too soon. For there was another galactic presence beginning to make its existence felt, through acts of savagery at the borders of the Federation. The Romulan Empire, once thought to be little more than a Vulcan children's fable, was thirsting for conquest.

A CONCISE LOOK AT SHIPS AND EVENTS
SPACEFLIGHT CHRONOLOGY

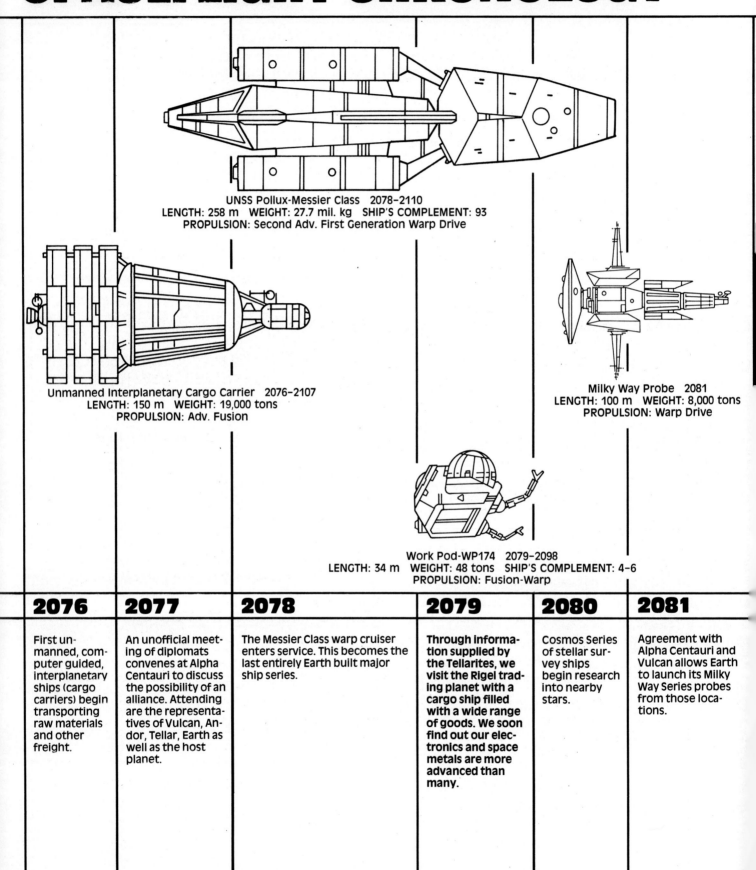

UNSS Pollux-Messier Class   2078–2110
LENGTH: 258 m   WEIGHT: 27.7 mil. kg   SHIP'S COMPLEMENT: 93
PROPULSION: Second Adv. First Generation Warp Drive

Unmanned Interplanetary Cargo Carrier   2076–2107
LENGTH: 150 m   WEIGHT: 19,000 tons
PROPULSION: Adv. Fusion

Milky Way Probe   2081
LENGTH: 100 m   WEIGHT: 8,000 tons
PROPULSION: Warp Drive

Work Pod-WP174   2079–2098
LENGTH: 34 m   WEIGHT: 48 tons   SHIP'S COMPLEMENT: 4–6
PROPULSION: Fusion-Warp

2076	**2077**	**2078**	**2079**	**2080**	**2081**
First un-manned, com-puter guided, interplanetary ships (cargo carriers) begin transporting raw materials and other freight.	An unofficial meeting of diplomats convenes at Alpha Centauri to discuss the possibility of an alliance. Attending are the representatives of Vulcan, An-dor, Tellar, Earth as well as the host planet.	The Messier Class warp cruiser enters service. This becomes the last entirely Earth built major ship series.	**Through informa-tion supplied by the Tellarites, we visit the Rigel trad-ing planet with a cargo ship filled with a wide range of goods. We soon find out our elec-tronics and space metals are more advanced than many.**	Cosmos Series of stellar sur-vey ships begin research into nearby stars.	Agreement with Alpha Centauri and Vulcan allows Earth to launch its Milky Way Series probes from those loca-tions.

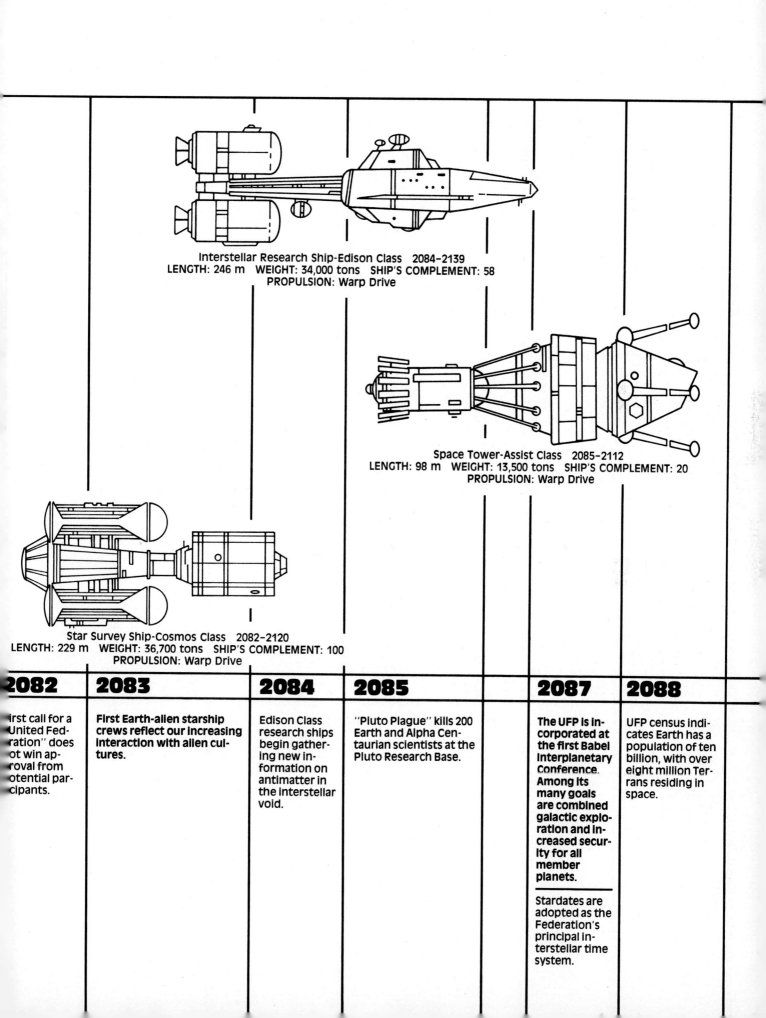

Interstellar Research Ship-Edison Class   2084–2139
LENGTH: 246 m   WEIGHT: 34,000 tons   SHIP'S COMPLEMENT: 58
PROPULSION: Warp Drive

Space Tower-Assist Class   2085–2112
LENGTH: 98 m   WEIGHT: 13,500 tons   SHIP'S COMPLEMENT: 20
PROPULSION: Warp Drive

Star Survey Ship-Cosmos Class   2082–2120
LENGTH: 229 m   WEIGHT: 36,700 tons   SHIP'S COMPLEMENT: 100
PROPULSION: Warp Drive

2082	2083	2084	2085		2087	2088
First call for a "United Federation" does not win approval from potential participants.	First Earth-alien starship crews reflect our increasing interaction with alien cultures.	Edison Class research ships begin gathering new information on antimatter in the interstellar void.	"Pluto Plague" kills 200 Earth and Alpha Centaurian scientists at the Pluto Research Base.		The UFP is incorporated at the first Babel Interplanetary Conference. Among its many goals are combined galactic exploration and increased security for all member planets. Stardates are adopted as the Federation's principal interstellar time system.	UFP census indicates Earth has a population of ten billion, with over eight million Terrans residing in space.

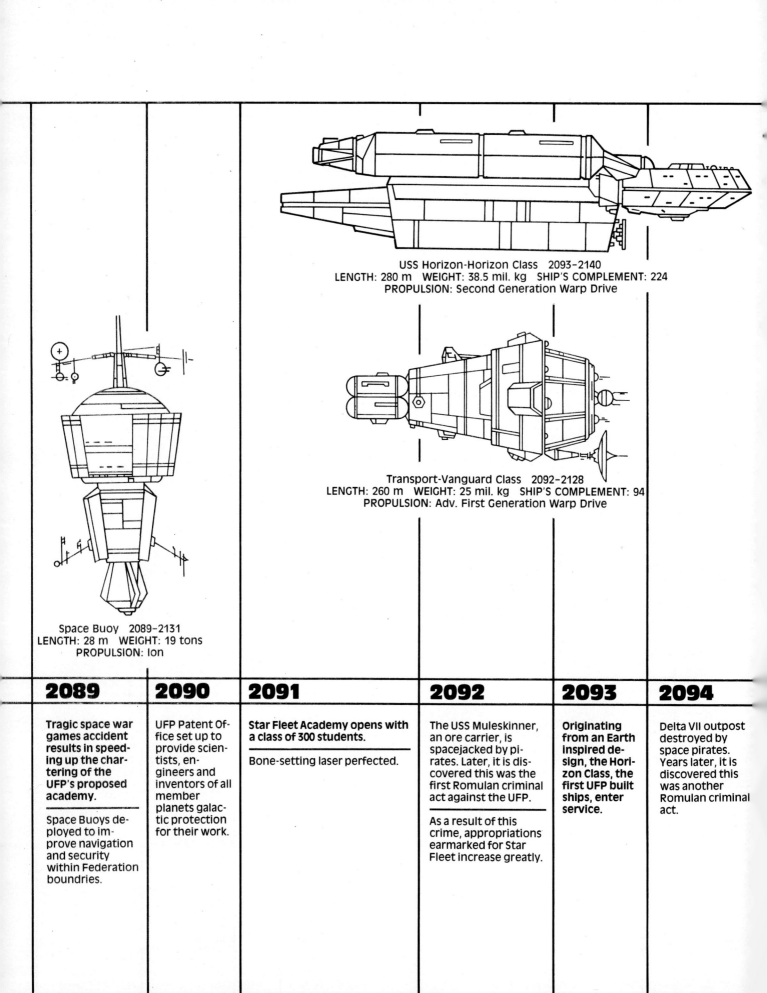

USS Horizon-Horizon Class 2093–2140
LENGTH: 280 m WEIGHT: 38.5 mil. kg SHIP'S COMPLEMENT: 224
PROPULSION: Second Generation Warp Drive

Transport-Vanguard Class 2092–2128
LENGTH: 260 m WEIGHT: 25 mil. kg SHIP'S COMPLEMENT: 94
PROPULSION: Adv. First Generation Warp Drive

Space Buoy 2089–2131
LENGTH: 28 m WEIGHT: 19 tons
PROPULSION: Ion

2089

Tragic space war games accident results in speeding up the chartering of the UFP's proposed academy.

Space Buoys deployed to improve navigation and security within Federation boundries.

2090

UFP Patent Office set up to provide scientists, engineers and inventors of all member planets galactic protection for their work.

2091

Star Fleet Academy opens with a class of 300 students.

Bone-setting laser perfected.

2092

The USS Muleskinner, an ore carrier, is spacejacked by pirates. Later, it is discovered this was the first Romulan criminal act against the UFP.

As a result of this crime, appropriations earmarked for Star Fleet increase greatly.

2093

Originating from an Earth inspired design, the Horizon Class, the first UFP built ships, enter service.

2094

Delta VII outpost destroyed by space pirates. Years later, it is discovered this was another Romulan criminal act.

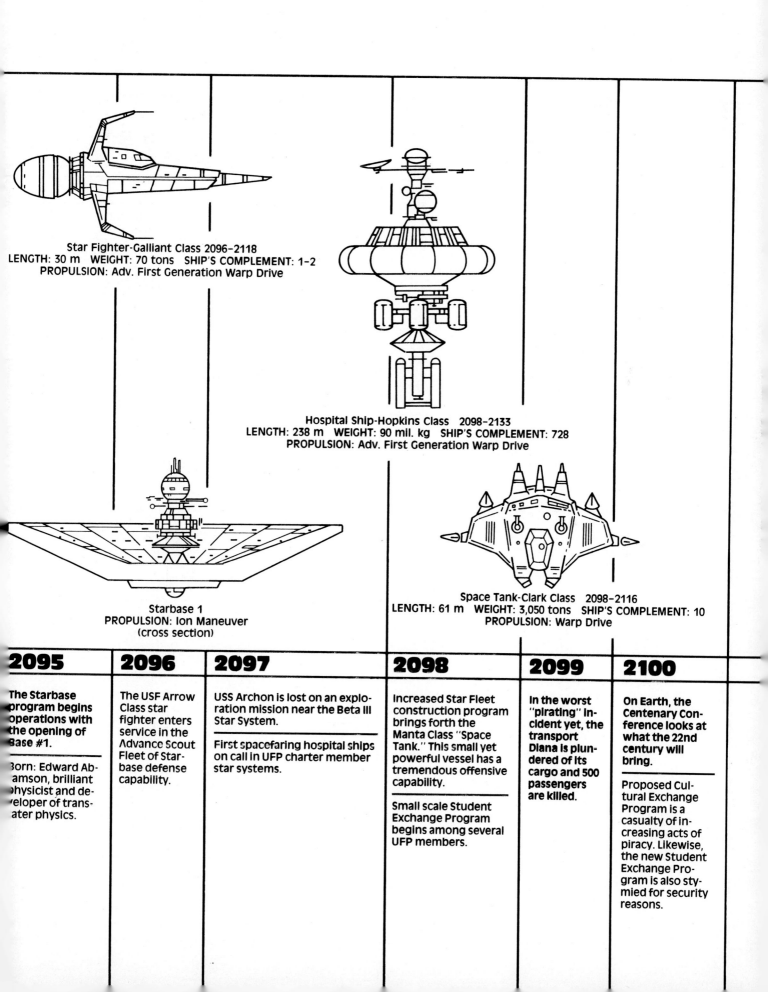

Star Fighter-Galliant Class 2096–2118
LENGTH: 30 m   WEIGHT: 70 tons   SHIP'S COMPLEMENT: 1–2
PROPULSION: Adv. First Generation Warp Drive

Hospital Ship-Hopkins Class   2098–2133
LENGTH: 238 m   WEIGHT: 90 mil. kg   SHIP'S COMPLEMENT: 728
PROPULSION: Adv. First Generation Warp Drive

Starbase 1
PROPULSION: Ion Maneuver
(cross section)

Space Tank-Clark Class   2098–2116
LENGTH: 61 m   WEIGHT: 3,050 tons   SHIP'S COMPLEMENT: 10
PROPULSION: Warp Drive

2095	2096	2097	2098	2099	2100
The Starbase program begins operations with the opening of Base #1. Born: Edward Abramson, brilliant physicist and developer of transwater physics.	The USF Arrow Class star fighter enters service in the Advance Scout Fleet of Starbase defense capability.	USS Archon is lost on an exploration mission near the Beta III Star System. First spacefaring hospital ships on call in UFP charter member star systems.	Increased Star Fleet construction program brings forth the Manta Class "Space Tank." This small yet powerful vessel has a tremendous offensive capability. Small scale Student Exchange Program begins among several UFP members.	In the worst "pirating" incident yet, the transport Diana is plundered of its cargo and 500 passengers are killed.	On Earth, the Centenary Conference looks at what the 22nd century will bring. Proposed Cultural Exchange Program is a casualty of increasing acts of piracy. Likewise, the new Student Exchange Program is also stymied for security reasons.

UNSS POLLUX MESSIER CLASS

2078-2110

The last exclusively Earth-built major series, the *Pollux* and its fellow Messier class warp ships were the first to have integrated Earth-alien crews. At the formation of the UFP, Star Fleet Command ordered additional Messier class starships for its deployment strategy until Federation-designed ships came on line. Refitted for military use, the *Pollux* saw considerable action during the Romulan War.

Specifications

Length	258 m
Beam	113.8 m
Draught	72 m
Mass	27.7 million kg
Engine Section	125 m x 113.8 m x 72 m
Living Section	110 m x 38 m x 55.8 m

Ship's Complement

Officers (Captain, Lieutenant, Science, Engineering, Navigation, Medical, 2 Ensigns)	8
Crew	85
Standard Ship's Complement	93

Performance

Range - Standard	50 light-years
Maximum	80 light-years
Cruising Velocity	Warp 2.75 (20.8 c)
Maximum Velocity	Warp 2.9 (24.4 c)
Acceleration	0 - .999c—2.34 hrs
	.999c - warp engage: 4.55 min
	Warp 1 - 2—87.9 sec
	2 - 2.75—30.4 sec
	2.75 - 2.9—70.3 sec

Systems Overview

Navigation	Computer-assisted warp field reader (with stellar distortion program)
Communication	Warp Communication
Weapons	4 forward lasers
	2 Particle beam cannons
	55 fusion torpedoes
Life Support: Gravity	.5 - 1.1 g, intern. variable
Atmosphere	19% O_2; 13% humidity
Sustenance Duration	4 years at Standard Ship's Complement

Engineering and Science

- Advanced first generation warp engines
- Fuel —————————— 20:1 matter to antimatter
- Computer capable of complex independent problem-solving and self-programming
- Forward statolith sensors

Improvements and Innovations

- First ship designed to accommodate extraterrestrial lifeforms
- Statolith sensors use incredibly sensitive organic components
- First ship equipped with warp communication capabilities
- Shielding and weaponry uprated for Romulan War

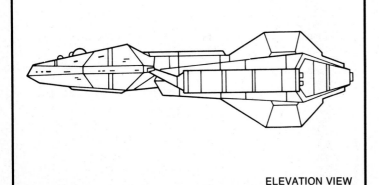

ELEVATION VIEW

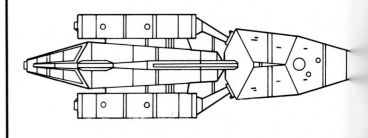

PLAN VIEW

WARP 3.25 CRUISER

USS HORIZON
HORIZON CLASS   2093-2140

The *Horizon* was one of the most important ships and classes in spaceflight history. The flagship for early UFP space exploration, the USS *Horizon* journeyed to the edge of the galaxy, encountering many new worlds in its numerous voyages. At the end of its commissioned life, it was retired to Star Fleet's Spaceflight Museum on Memory Alpha.

Specifications

Length	280 m
Beam	136.5 m
Draught	57.8 m
Mass	38.5 million kg

Officers	(Captain, Lieutenant, Science, Engineering, Medical, Navigation, Communications, 5 Ensigns)	12
Crew		212
	Standard Ship's Complement	224

Performance

Range: Standard	150 light-years
Maximum	500 light-years
Cruising Velocity	Warp 3 (27c)
Maximum Velocity	Warp 3.25 (34.3c)
Engine	2nd Generation Warp Drive
Fuel	20:1 matter to antimatter

Systems Overview

Navigation	Celestial Warp Reader
Communication	Warp Communication
Weapons	4-8 Forward lasers*
	2-6 Particle Beam Cannons*
	50-250 photon torpedoes*

*Uprated for Romulan War

Life Support: Gravity	.2 - 1.2 g
Atmosphere	20% O_2; 11% humidity
Sustenance Duration	Up to 40 years if outfitted for long-duration exploration

Engineering and Science

- Work Pods for exterior maintenance and experimentation
- Equipped with impulse drive prototype as auxiliary engine

Improvements and Innovations

- First UFP-sponsored starship class
- New metal/ceramic alloys used in superstructure construction gave greater strength at less weight

TRANSPORT VANGUARD CLASS   2092-2128

This was the largest commercial/industrial ship of the 21st century and served as the primary multipurpose starship in the early years of the UFP. Its side loading bays and adaptable cargo interior made for ready accommodation of different payloads, from small craft to raw ore to nearly 1000 passengers. Later models were uprated to keep pace with advances in warp technology.

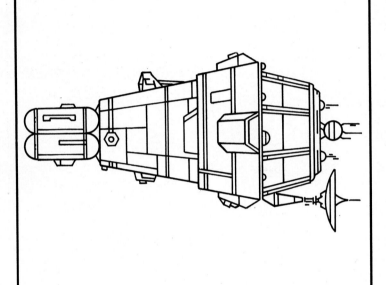

Specifications

Length	260 m
Maximum Diameter	98.7 m
Forward Cargo Volume (paneled)	150,000 cu m
Midships Cargo Volume	300,000 cu m
Mass (Empty)	25 million kg
(Maximum)	50 million kg

Ship's Complement

Officers (Captain, Lieutenant, Navigation, Engineering, Cargo Supervisor, Flight Coordinator)	6
Crew	88
Standard Ship's Complement	94

Performance

Range	100 light-years
Cruising Velocity	Empty: Warp 2.75
	Loaded: Warp 2
Engines	Advanced First Generation warp drive engines
Fuel	20:1 matter to antimatter

HOSPITAL SHIP HOPKINS CLASS   2097-213̶3̶

Along with the Horizon class, these interstellar hospital ships were among the first created by and for the newly-incorporated UFP. Each member planet contributed its particular design needs, so that the Hospital ships could address the medical problems of all the lifeforms then known. Later, these ships played an integral part in the Federation's Medical Assistance Program and were dispatched to sectors or systems experiencing severe medical emergencies.

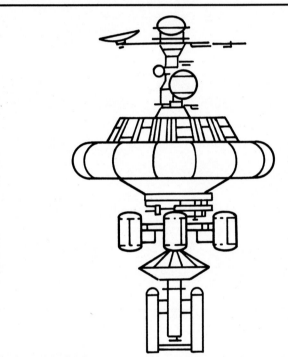

Specifications

Length	238
Diameter	150
Life Support Toroid	diameter: 150
	width: 25
Mass	90 million k
Landing Bays (4)	length: 28.2
	diameter: 16

Performance

Range	40 light-yea
Cruising Velocity	Warp 2
Maximum Velocity	Warp 2.?
Engines	Advanced First Generatio warp drive engine
Fuel	20:1 matter to antimatt
Crew	
Medical Staff	1
Patient Capability	Up to 6
Support Craft	five space ambulanc

STELLAR EXPLORATIONS

Rigel

Rigel is one of the most populated systems in the galaxy. With four of its twelve planets supporting life, this fellow founding member of the UFP is known for such diverse assets as mining ores, cabarets, bureaucrats and, of course trading. Rigel IV is the trading center for the known galaxy, and the entire planet is devoted to interstellar commerce.

Rigel contains twelve planets: four habitable; eight uninhabitable

	Dist. from star ($\times 10^8$km)	Diameter (km)	Revolution (Solar days & years)	Average surface temp (°c)
II	1.28	5,476	142 d	65°
IV	2.55	7,671	314 d	42°
V	3.03	8,542	2.47 yrs	38°
VII	20.10	32,150	24.41 yrs	5°

ORBITAL DISTANCE, A.U.

The United Federation of Planets opens the galaxy further.

The founding of the UFP created a great pool of science and technical knowledge which enabled a vastly more spaceworthy generation of starships, the Horizon Class, to be built.

This in turn, accelerated the integration of the newly formed Federation as voyages of 30-50 lightyears became more practical.
Explorations to the territorial limits of the Federation were also made possible as a result of the Horizon Class ships.

But the dark side of this expansion was the encountering of space pirates, who increasingly terrorized and destroyed Federation starships. The spacejacking of the ore freighter USS *Muleskinner* and the destruction of the transport *Diana* were among the most prominent instances because of their close proximity to major Federation trade routes.

MAJOR COMMERCIAL ROUTES ———

OTHER ROUTES – – – – – –

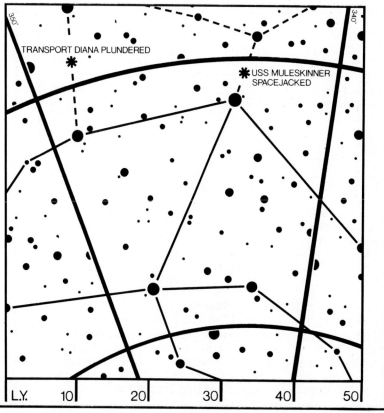

RIGEL TRADING PLANET DISCOVERED
2079

UNSS MARCO POLO, MERCHANT CLASS
LORENZO MALFATTI, CAPTAIN

Rigel is, of course, one of the founding members of the United Federation of Planets. A twelve-planet system, Rigel is known for its trade, mining and, strangely enough, bureaucrats. For more information on this system, see Volume III: Rigel.

Captain's Log:

I've just returned from my first exposure to the Rigel Trading Planet, and it's wilder than the Tellarites could ever have told us. Who would have thought this insignificant looking planet, the second smallest in the 12-world Rigel system, would be the trading capital of the galaxy.

Scowling Tellarites, scornful Andorians, hawkeyed Rigellian bargain-hunters all crowd the twisting streets of the main city of Rralrark. Plus there are literally dozens of aliens we had no idea existed, pushing their world's wares. I won't soon forget the sight of a ciliated creature, something like a fuzzy-spiked porcupine, angrily waving his front tentacles at a Rigellian jeweler, who was refusing the creature's offer for a diamond as big as my fist.

Fist-sized diamonds are not the only wonder available on Rigel. There is more than everything imaginable here, since I don't know half the items for sale. A liquor called Saurian brandy, for instance, is especially popular and fetches premium prices on Rigel. There is every type of food, clothing and recreation available, and I'm told whole cities on the planet are devoted to heavy machinery, or spaceships, or even, I've heard, a blackmarket trade in slaves.

This was just a sightseeing tour, feeling out the market. We had no idea what commodities would be tradable, so the Marco Polo's holds are stuffed with a whole motley of goods: clothes, coal, oxygen, art, argon, carbon-epoxy composites, boron-steel, etc. Of all these, the space metals should be the big sellers. I had eager Rigellians rush from their booths to examine my titanium belt buckle and offer me absurdly high sums for it. But even more sought for was my wrist computer. Aliens of every description asked me what it was, and where they could get one. Apparently, Earth's electronics and metals technology are more advanced than other worlds.

Tomorrow I'll return to Rralrark and test the demand for Earth goods. If what I think is true, we might be able to really boost the GSP (Gross Solar Product by trading at Rigel. But right now I'm going to sample some of this Saurian brandy I swapped my belt buckle for.

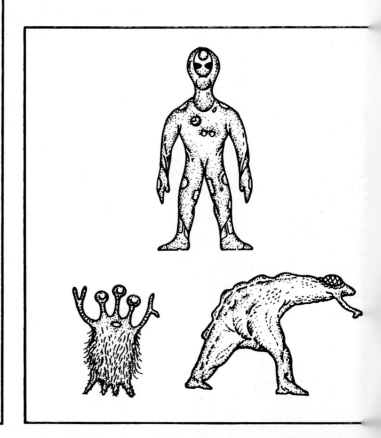

FIRST EARTH-ALIEN CREWS
Generally we work well with our neighbors from space.

2083

UNSS POLLUX, MESSIER CLASS
SHU TSE SUM, CAPTAIN

Captain's Log:

The Vulcan Communications Officer Mr. Supak has finished his first month of active duty aboard the *Pollux*, and this Log stands as his preliminary evaluation. Solar Fleet Headquarters asked me to include my subjective reactions in my review, so that is to be found here along with the standard critique.

Mr. Supak's duty performance as Communications Officer has been superb. He has not made a single operational mistake or oversight—in fact, he once corrected me on a bit of procedure—and all communications have been flawlessly transmitted and received. I could not ask for more.

Except I find myself inwardly doing just that, asking for more from the Vulcan, and I'm not even sure more of what—more involvement, or more intuitive initiative, or more something. He mans his console day after day, performing his duty, and nothing else. Ever. I would have thought that I couldn't ask for otherwise from a subordinate. But emotionless excellence is harder to coexist with than I anticipated. If only he would smile.

SUPAK, COMMUNICATIONS OFFICER

Communications Log:

Pursuant to UNSF Directive DL-1142—"All participants in the interstellar exchange of crew members are requested to log, at monthly intervals, their reactions to the aforesaid exchange." I enter this log as my evaluation of duty aboard the UNSS *Pollux*, Shu Tse Sum, Captain.

I have been able to suitably discharge my responsibilities as Communications Officer and have responded to all commands issued me by superiors. The work is interesting, and I have gained thirteen new insights into communications theory and practice.

However, I must submit my difficulty in responding to certain statements addressed me by the Earth crew. They refer to them as "shooting the breeze," or "kidding around," but I can only understand them as a most illogical arrangement of ungrammatical syntax and complete nonsense. The Engineer, for instance, states when he reluctantly initiates an action: "Might as well, too windy to haul gravel." 48.7 hours of reflection have yet to reveal to me the meaning of that statement.

In summary, my duties are engaging, but the rampant illogical emotionalism on board does strain me. I therefore must reserve judgement at this time as to the advisability of integrating Vulcan and Earth crews. There may well be no future merit in the arrangement.

INCORPORATION OF UNITED FEDERATION OF PLANETS

2087

BABEL INTERPLANETARY CONFERENCE
HARMON AXELROD, SECRETARY GENERAL

Proclamation Log:

As your newly-elected Secretary General, it is my very great pleasure to officially proclaim the incorporation of the United Federation of Planets this stardate at Babel.

I welcome, as founding member planets, the Earth, Vulcan, Tellar, Andor, Rigel and Alpha Centauri. I am sure this number will grow as new lifeforms are encountered and as we demonstrate the utility and wisdom of this Federation.

But what exactly is this utility, this wisdom? Why have we joined together here? We are very different planets, with different needs and aspirations. But there are some goals we all share in common, and perhaps the first is the mutual respect we have for each others' uniqueness. The United Federation of Planets has not been inaugurated to diminish a planet's sovereignty but to assist it in its galactic development.

Exploration is a goal we have all agreed upon. New worlds and new lifeforms will be met in the coming future, and we feel it our responsibility to be in the forefront of these meetings, to seek out new allies wherever they live in the galaxy.

Galactic health and the promotion of social progress are also high priorities of the UFP, if I may use the initials that will no doubt soon be our Federation's standard reference. To guarantee all citizens good health and social equity is a noble ideal, and the possibility of making it reality is, I feel, within this organization's power.

Lastly, the United Federation of Planets will provide for the allied security of its member planets. The dark side of exploration is the possibility, and we must face it, of encountering violent or aggressive worlds. With the commissioning of a Star Fleet and the construction of the strategic Star Base network, the Federation will go a long way to guard the integrity of its members. I have no doubt there are grave perils in the galaxy. We will be ready for them.

I would like to applaud all the delegates to this historic Babel Interplanetary Conference. Out of the diplomatic give and take has emerged a viable, even visionary, blueprint for the future. We now have a United Federation of Planets; let's make its dreams come true.

The polished document that is the Articles of Incorporation of the United Federation of Planets does not reflect the struggle and uncertainty that preceded its adoption. The delegates to the Babel Conference spent incredible amounts of time and energy drafting an outline for the future that was agreeable to all participants. This log, subsequently declassified, illustrates the delicate state of negotiations that led to final compromise and incorporation.

HUMPHREY STANNIS, AMBASSADOR
Supplemental Log:

—CONFIDENTIAL—Ambassador's Report on Progress of Negotiations at Interplanetary Conference at Babel (Declassified Stardate 3345.7)

It has been a long and not very productive Conference so far. While I remain optimistic about the successful outcome of the Conference, progress has thus far been painfully slow. Blue-skinned Andorians lisp savagely at green-skinned Vulcans, who logically debate with the illogical Tellarites, who bully the Rigellians, who are blackmailing us for ten billion credits for a pro-incorporation vote. The current status of negotiations is as follows:

ANDOR—The Andorians are pressing their claim for some of the Rigel territories, even though they have never been within ten parsecs of the territories in question. The Andorians claim sovereignty over all stars visible to the eye from Andor. This has yet to be resolved.

RIGEL—Although plainly terrified by the aggressiveness of the Andorians, Rigel continues to maintain its neutrality with respect to membership in the United Federation of Planets. Their Ambassador has indicated that as little as eight billion credits might overcome Rigel's reservations.

TELLAR—Tellarites continue their tradition of arguing for argument's sake. I scored a decisive point for federation when I suggested to the Tellarite Ambassador that a United Federation of Planets would provide a permanent forum for debate. He immediately disagreed, which I take as a positive sign.

VULCAN—Vulcan remains a staunch proponent for incorporation. Although the constant bickering among greedy or violent planets must be distasteful to the Vulcan sensibility, they consistently maintain the logical advantages of such a union are the preeminent consideration.

ALPHA CENTAURI—Along with Vulcan, Alpha Centauri is committed to a United Federation of Planets. After all their planet and ours have enjoyed a similar but unincorporated alliance for almost forty years, so they are well aware of the advantages of federation.

EARTH—I continue to recommend federation. The chance for hostility and absence of any economic or political coordination in the present chaos cannot be allowed to endure. I believe we must all stand together or separately fall at each other's throats.

PACE WAR GAMES DISASTER

2089

SS SCYTHE, VERNE CLASS
ENRI FOURRIER, CAPTAIN

he following log was recorded during a war games exercise
eld shortly after the formation of the UFP. Because of a mis-
nderstood combat-simulation procedure, the USS *Scythe*
as accidentally blind-sided by a small corvette, swinging the
rge destroyer's lasers fatally through two other Federation
estroyers, the USS *Hammer* and the USS *Enmity,* with the
ss of 232 lives. It was this horrendous spaceflight disaster
at was the prime motivating force for speeding up the char-
ering of Star Fleet Academy.

aptain's Channel Log:

aptain: Opening Captain's Channel. All crew at battle-
           stations. Condition Red. *Scythe* under simu-
           lated attack by enemy vessels. Sensor report.

cience: Enemy vessels approaching at 1.7 along inter-
           cept trajectories.

aptain: Navigation. Execute Evasive Maneuver #2 and
           bring ship to warp 2.

elm: Executing. Warp 2 achieved.

cience: Enemy maintaining synchronized intercept.

aptain: Prepare counter-weaponry. Set Angle Error
           well starboard of the ships, Mr. Henry. We
           don't need any near misses; this is only an
           exercise.

elm: Roger, Captain. Forward lasers set at wide-
           angle array 30° off starboard beam.

aptain: Fire forward lasers.

elm: Forward lasers fire . . .

aptain: What the—What the hell was that?

cience: Collision of unknown cause on rear port side.
           Ship's axis of symmetry swinging . . .

aptain: My God, the lasers! Halt fire.

elm: Controls not responding. They're jammed.

aptain: Manual override, dammit, we're going to cut
           those ships out there in two.

cience: Direct hit recorded on USS *Hammer.*

elm: Manual override not responding, Sir.

aptain: Then pull the plug on the weapons center!

cience: USS *Enmity* destroyed by forward lasers.

elm: Engineering reports weapons center energy
           input jettisoned, Captain.

aptain: Too damned late. . .Prepare to rescue . . .

cience: No lifeform readings coming from the wreck-
           age of either ship. They're all dead, Sir.

aptain: How could this happen? Two ships lost. All
           hands dead. How could this happen?

STARFLEET ACADEMY OPENS

2091

STAR FLEET ACADEMY
STAVROS NIARCHOS, ACADEMY COMMANDANT
Commandant's Log:

Ahoy, Cadets, and welcome aboard. You three hundred
fledgling officers, representing both sexes and every
planet in the UFP, also represent the future of Star Fleet.
In a very real sense, Star Fleet will become what this class
and succeeding classes of Cadets make it. This important
responsibility will require you to make a total commitment to the Academy; for anything less will not do.

Here you will learn celestial navigation, warp engineering
and communication, as well as the essentials of classical,
relative and warp, physics, chemistry and astro-biology.
You will also be given a firm grounding in Federation
history and law, since it is the maintenance of the galactic rule of law which is one of your highest duties.

But more importantly, you will be taught how to command; how to be a Star Fleet Officer. This will be the
hardest part of your rigorous training, and some,
perhaps many of you, will not make it through. But by the
time you receive your Star Fleet commission, you will be
able to command, or you will not graduate. That is a sol-
emn pledge from me.

I also want to stress the deadly seriousness of this
Academy's education. The recent war games' disaster involved seasoned and competent commanders who did
not have the same training, the same experience. You
Cadets will not have that handicap. You'll all possess the
same disciplined knowledge and skills upon graduating,
so as you rise through the ranks, so will the standardized
training rise with you.

Of course, personal initiative is the hallmark of all true
leaders, and there will be recognition enough for outstanding individuals. But that is not this Academy's primary concern. Our specific job is to provide the solid
foundation which will enable you to command. And we
will.

In closing, let me say that you Cadets are the hope of Star
Fleet, of the United Federation of Planets, of all peace-
loving planets everywhere. Good luck to you all, and
enough chatter. Let's weigh anchor and get this
Academy launched.

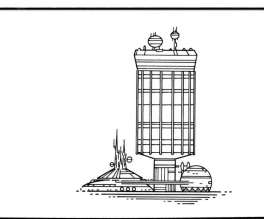

FIRST STARSHIP CLASS BUILT WITH COMBINED UFP EXPERTISE ENTERS SERVICE

2093

USS HORIZON, HORIZON CLASS
SERGE KOSYGIN, CHIEF ENGINEERING OFFICER

Engineering Log:

The *Horizon*'s Engineering Validation Phase has been concluded and I, for one, am convinced that this bear can bounce to the edge of the galaxy and back as easy as scooping honey from a hollow tree.

All performance monitors registered above computer-design specs, and the Fault Detection circuitry didn't record a single component breakdown for the whole flight-preliminary test sequence. And I pushed these new warp engines, pushed them a Pluto of a lot harder than I ever would have considered working a first generation warp engine. After running at maximum warp 3 for a hundred revolutions around the Centauri Test Orbit, I redlined the *Horizon* into warp 3.25 for five more orbits without exceeding stress parameters. These engines burn.

I especially like the *Horizon*'s new semi-independent modules. With the engines separate from the bridge, and lower hull, a much greater efficiency can be squeezed out of the warp engines, because we don't have to worry about gamma wastes contaminating the living areas. They'll be easier to maintain, too.

My validation assessment is they're unqualified Condition Green Go. Launch can proceed on schedule, and I'm confident the *Horizon* will become the flagship explorer in the Federation. If only they could improve the food as much.

STARBASE 1 BEGINS OPERATIONS
Huge station ends year long tow to Sector 3A. Personnel take up residence.

209

STARBASE 1
FELIX PJINDIK, COMMODORE

Commodore's Log:

The Starbase program is off to a fine start. I've just com pleted my first tour of all facilities and am very satisfie with my findings. Starbase 1 is a technological wonder. is a stellar-designer's dream come true. And none to soon. We've just opened for business and already th Maintenance Deck is working overtime refitting two star ships with the new warp engines. Chief Engineer Hobbe tells me his boys are getting so good at swapping en gines they can overhaul a starcruiser in a week or so. hope he's right.

On the other hand, Sick Bay has only five patients righ now: one coronary recovery, an alcohol-detoxificatio case—a drunk helmsman on R&R who's going to catch nova's worth of trouble from his captain when he' discharged—and three radiation victims spacelifted fror Meta.

The Research Deck is functioning smoothly, and the Rec reation Decks are, shall I say, models of sailorly relaxatior No violent incidents reported this stardate.

Finally, the Forward Alert Defense Deck reports all sur rounding sectors clear of unidentified intrusion. The Ac vance Scout Fleet has not made any unusual contac whatsoever.

Yes, the Starbase program is off to a fine start. And I'r worried. Very worried. It's almost as if whatever or who ever's out there is lying low for now, letting us forget th still too recent incineration of *Delta VII*, or the spacejack ing of the ore freighter *Muleskinner*. What are they wait ing for?

I know some at Star Fleet Command think I'm bein paranoid about asking for extra Scout Fleet protectior There's nothing out there but your imagination, the scoff. Well, they should save their scorn for the charre remains of the twenty-eight men, women and childre of *Delta VII*. There is something out there. And it is hos tile. I pray we are ready.

COMMERCIAL TRANSPORT DESTROYED BY SPACE PIRATES
Over 500 killed in brutal incident.

2099

USS INTREPID, MESSIER CLASS
HENRY MCKENNA, CAPTAIN
Captain's Log:

I'm reporting the retrieval of the remains of the Transport *Diana*. The crew and all 500 passengers have been murdered, and the cargo holds have been split open and completely plundered, along with all valuable personal effects. I would classify this as a Class 1 Space Piracy offense, and I'm forwarding all evidence to Star Fleet Security Council for their investigation and prosecution.

Two extremely disturbing facts stand out about this particular piracy. The first is, whatever tool was used to slice the ship's hull, it is not to be found in any alien technologies I know of. The precision of the cut seems to indicate some sort of advanced laser drill specifically designed for plunder. These are sophisticated space pirates. (Shortly thereafter, they were discovered to be the Romulans.)

The second is the sheer horror of seeing so many bodies lying about. Never have I encountered such a sight in all my service in space. I can only conclude there is a horrible menace behind this act of piracy. All inhabitants of this sector should be alerted to the presence of this unknown, violent danger. Accordingly, I am requesting increased patrols throughout the sector, until these pirates are caught or killed. Let's hope that won't be too long.

MAJOR EARTH SPACEFLIGHT CONFERENCE
Limits to growth of exploration predicted.

2100

STARBASE 5
DR. MILTON KORNHEISER, SPEAKER
Archive Log:

I would like to thank the organizers of this Earth Centenary Conference for inviting me to speak on the future of spaceflight. I have very much enjoyed the other speakers' discussions of terraforming, pre-warp history, interstellar politics and the like, and I hope I can be as informative, if not provocative, as they have been.

After twenty-five years of designing interstellar spacecraft, I feel confident in my ability to foretell what the coming century will bring. First of all, there are some theoretical limitations which coming generations of ships will not be able to exceed. Even if the matter/antimatter reaction becomes 100% efficient in terms of its exhaust products, we will not be able to achieve speeds greater than a factor of approximately warp 4. The energy just isn't there. This, in turn, places a limit on the extent of new exploration and plans such as the exploration of the galactic center are, I'm afraid, destined to remain little more than wishful thinking.

Now I don't want to sound too pessimistic. Given the number of civilizations and interesting star systems we have already encountered, warp 4 speeds will mean a very large assortment of new worlds within our feasible reach. What new Vulcans or Rigels await our discovery out there is anyone's conjecture. And advances in technology that are already on the computer simulators, will allow bigger and longer-ranging ships to be built; vessels which will shame our present state-of-the-art.

However, I've heard so much wild speculation during this Conference I feel it my responsibility to inject a note of cold realism. Speeds of warp 7 or warp 10 or even higher that have been bandied about as if they were just around the corner are theoretical impossibilities. One speaker even blithered on about the alchemy of molecular reintegration; destroying a being for the purpose of transporting his remains elsewhere, as if the splintered bundle of loose molecules could ever be restitched into a living creature. This sort of idea belongs in a magic show, not a scientific conference.

In summing up, I look forward to a century of ever-bigger ships, traveling as fast as warp 4, and bringing us to more and more new worlds. Modest goals, to be sure, but goals I am sure we will attain before the century is over.

22nd
CENTURY

OVERVIEW

The opening of the twenty-second century was darkened by the advent of the only major interstellar conflict in Federation history: the Romulan War. It had been building for years in a pattern of escalating violence. An ore freighter was spacejacked, a small settlement at Delta VII destroyed, a transport plundered and 500 defenseless passengers killed. Then, in 2103, Starbase 1 was destroyed, and Star Fleet was placed on its first Mobilization Alert. Three years later, in 2106, the patrolling USS PATTON happened across the advance flank of a Romulan Invasion Fleet. Left with no choice, Official Hostilities were declared by the UFP, and the Federation entered into its first and only interstellar war.

While such terms as the Cochrane Deceleration Maneuver and engagements like the decisive Battle of Cheron are part of common Federation folklore, a definitive account of this bleak period may be found in THE WAR TORN GALAXY: A HISTORY OF THE ROMULAN WAR, by John Gill, published in 2202.

However, certainly much of the credit for the termination of conflict went to the development by the UFP of an advanced laser weaponry system. These effective and versatile weapons provided the crucial strategic difference in the war.

By 2109, the war was over, and a peace established which has, with minor exceptions, endured to this stardate. The UFP has always refrained from claiming victory in the Romulan War, although the tempo of the strife was clearly in its favor when armistice was declared. For victory signifies little when considered against the thousands lost in the bloody struggle. There is no glory in war; there is only suffering and death and brave lives spent to sustain a free way of life for all Federation worlds.

With peace reigning once more, the exploration of space and expansion of the frontiers of knowledge which had been epitomized by the famous USS HORIZON, could again proceed. New star systems and planets were continually being discovered, such as Pyrimiis I and II, Gamma Spica, Janus VI, among others.

It became clear from the meeting of diverse cultures that some aliens possessed types of mental abilities very much out of the ordinary. These have been grouped together under the heading "psionic," meaning mental power, and range from the psychokinetic ability of the Platonians to move objects to the telepathic Vulcan mind touch. All are manifestations of similar neurochemical matrixes and can be found, at least in potential, in most advanced brain structures, humans included.

Of course, advanced mental capabilities are no guarantee of a species' survival. In 2120 the oldest known and long extinct civilization in the galaxy was found on planet 522 IV. Estimated from star maps found on the planet to be 7.5 billion years old (the Earth itself is only 4.5 billion years old and man [homosapiens] much younger still, perhaps 200,000 years old as a species), the remain indicate a race that had incredible psionic powers which, however, did not save them from whatever mysterious fate brought about their extinction. The artifacts of their amazing civilization have been marvelously preserved. Of the race itself, there is not a single trace remaining.

The Federation continued its role as both coordinator and sponsor of galactic activities. The UFP's Deneva Research Station was opened, the first of many Federation facilities that have provided the cutting edge of scientific progress for the past century. For instance, it was at Deneva that researchers, utilizing the still-new field of transtator physics, forged the breakthrough in warp communication responsible for our present stardate subspace radio.

Previous warp communication had to rely on the exploitation of local aberrations in the geodynamometric structure of space, where giant relay stations were constructed to process faster-than-light communications. Subspace radio, on the other hand, does not depend upon outside boosters, since its signal "rides" on a stream of warp accelerated, computer-encoded particles. The initial warp 15 transmission speed of subspace radio, which has of course grown greatly in the past century, knitted the galaxy together more than any breakthrough since warp drive.

Also, to bring planets closer together, the UFP sponsored the Galactic Cultural Exchange Project. Touring starships of the Federation's leading actors, artists, kineticists, musicians, smell-shapers, dancers and tactilists, spread each world's unique cultural heritage throughout the Federation, and the sense of wonder and appreciation generated by this exchange brought member planets in closer harmony with one another. For almost a hundred years, the Galactic Cultural Exchange has grown in scope and variety, until presently there are hundreds of starships cruising the Federation to bring great art to all planets, colonies, starbases and outposts.

At the end of this era, a galaxy-shaking, but still unexplained, event occurred. A starship encountered a probe that had come from outside the galaxy, most likely from the Small Magellanic Cloud. Suddenly the closeness among the planets seemed a puny thing, indeed, for here was something, or someone, reaching out 56,000 parsecs to our Milky Way Galaxy. It was a staggering and humbling feat, and to this stardate, we know no more about whatever or whoever sent the probe in our direction than the probe itself, which can be viewed at the Star Fleet Museum on Memory Alpha.

This was a tempestuous quarter-century, starting in war and ending in enigma. The United Federation of Planets survived its first military test and came out the stronger for it, when it redeployed its war-oriented energies in the fields of research, exploration and cultural exchange. It was just this ability of the UFP to recover so well from the horrors of galactic war that assured its vitality and growth during the past century.

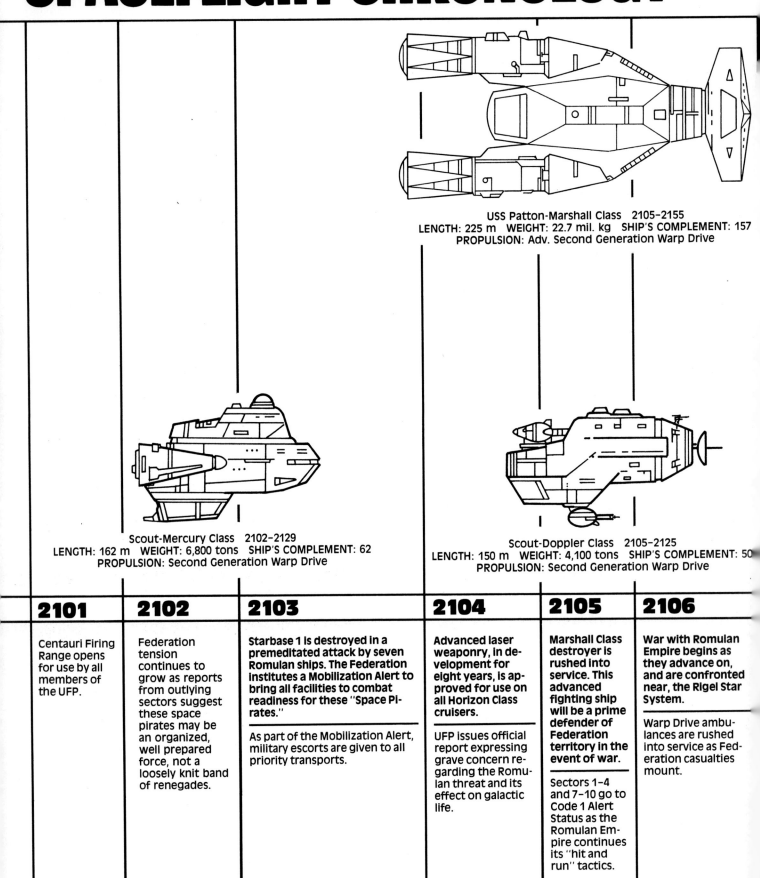

USS Patton-Marshall Class   2105-2155
LENGTH: 225 m   WEIGHT: 22.7 mil. kg   SHIP'S COMPLEMENT: 157
PROPULSION: Adv. Second Generation Warp Drive

Scout-Mercury Class   2102-2129
LENGTH: 162 m   WEIGHT: 6,800 tons   SHIP'S COMPLEMENT: 62
PROPULSION: Second Generation Warp Drive

Scout-Doppler Class   2105-2125
LENGTH: 150 m   WEIGHT: 4,100 tons   SHIP'S COMPLEMENT: 50
PROPULSION: Second Generation Warp Drive

2101	**2102**	**2103**	**2104**	**2105**	**2106**
Centauri Firing Range opens for use by all members of the UFP.	Federation tension continues to grow as reports from outlying sectors suggest these space pirates may be an organized, well prepared force, not a loosely knit band of renegades.	Starbase 1 is destroyed in a premeditated attack by seven Romulan ships. The Federation institutes a Mobilization Alert to bring all facilities to combat readiness for these "Space Pirates." As part of the Mobilization Alert, military escorts are given to all priority transports.	Advanced laser weaponry, in development for eight years, is approved for use on all Horizon Class cruisers. UFP issues official report expressing grave concern regarding the Romulan threat and its effect on galactic life.	Marshall Class destroyer is rushed into service. This advanced fighting ship will be a prime defender of Federation territory in the event of war. Sectors 1–4 and 7–10 go to Code 1 Alert Status as the Romulan Empire continues its "hit and run" tactics.	War with Romulan Empire begins as they advance on, and are confronted near, the Rigel Star System. Warp Drive ambulances are rushed into service as Federation casualties mount.

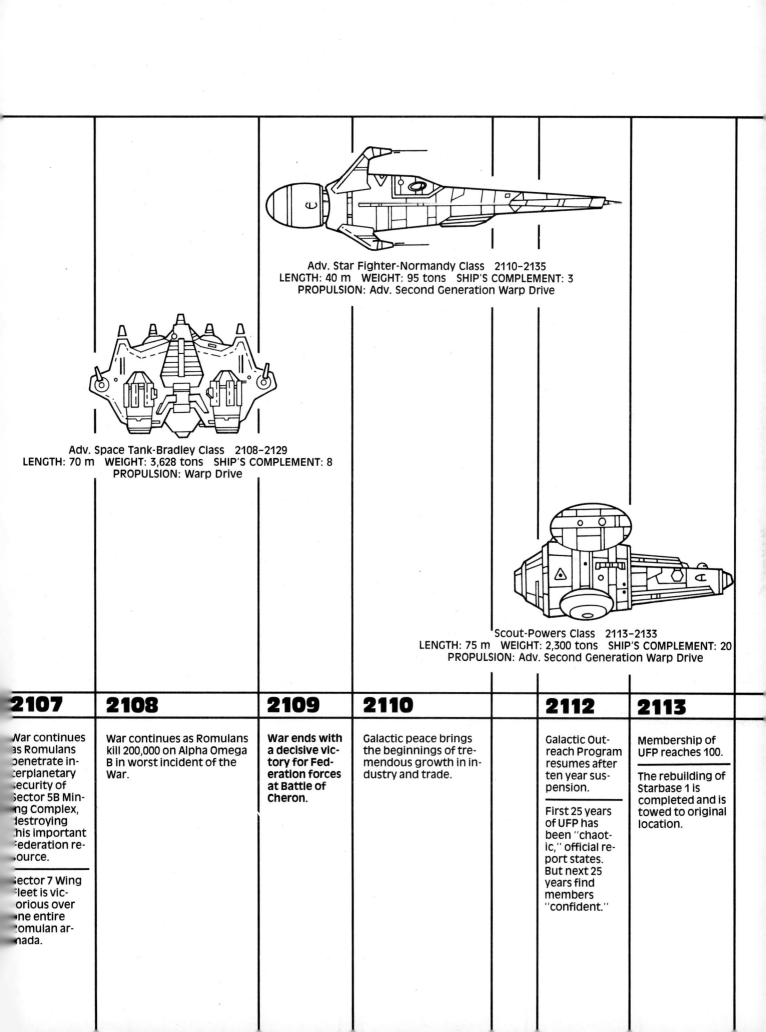

Adv. Star Fighter-Normandy Class 2110–2135
LENGTH: 40 m WEIGHT: 95 tons SHIP'S COMPLEMENT: 3
PROPULSION: Adv. Second Generation Warp Drive

Adv. Space Tank-Bradley Class 2108–2129
LENGTH: 70 m WEIGHT: 3,628 tons SHIP'S COMPLEMENT: 8
PROPULSION: Warp Drive

Scout-Powers Class 2113–2133
LENGTH: 75 m WEIGHT: 2,300 tons SHIP'S COMPLEMENT: 20
PROPULSION: Adv. Second Generation Warp Drive

2107	2108	2109	2110		2112	2113
War continues as Romulans penetrate interplanetary security of Sector 5B Mining Complex, destroying this important Federation resource. Sector 7 Wing Fleet is victorious over one entire Romulan armada.	War continues as Romulans kill 200,000 on Alpha Omega B in worst incident of the War.	War ends with a decisive victory for Federation forces at Battle of Cheron.	Galactic peace brings the beginnings of tremendous growth in industry and trade.		Galactic Outreach Program resumes after ten year suspension. First 25 years of UFP has been "chaotic," official report states. But next 25 years find members "confident."	Membership of UFP reaches 100. The rebuilding of Starbase 1 is completed and is towed to original location.

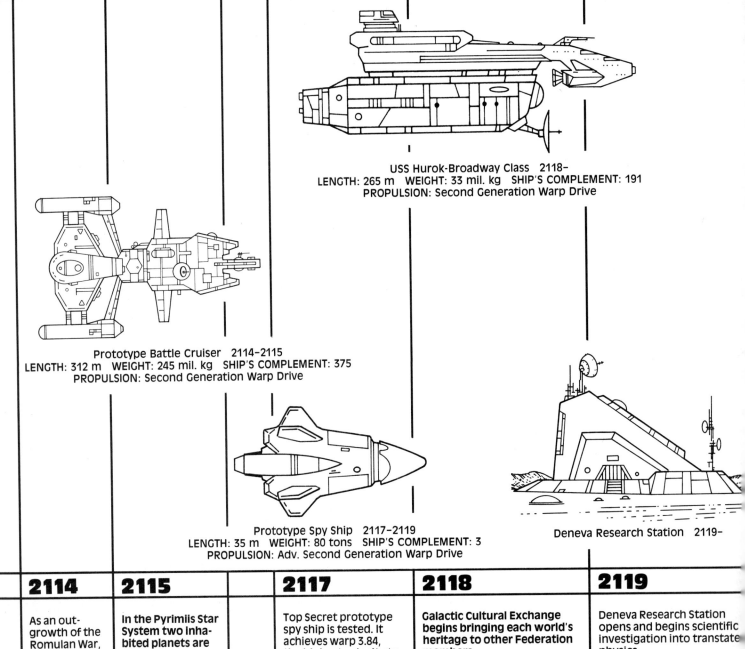

USS Hurok-Broadway Class   2118–
LENGTH: 265 m   WEIGHT: 33 mil. kg   SHIP'S COMPLEMENT: 191
PROPULSION: Second Generation Warp Drive

Prototype Battle Cruiser   2114–2115
LENGTH: 312 m   WEIGHT: 245 mil. kg   SHIP'S COMPLEMENT: 375
PROPULSION: Second Generation Warp Drive

Prototype Spy Ship   2117–2119
LENGTH: 35 m   WEIGHT: 80 tons   SHIP'S COMPLEMENT: 3
PROPULSION: Adv. Second Generation Warp Drive

Deneva Research Station   2119–

2114	**2115**		**2117**	**2118**	**2119**
As an out-growth of the Romulan War, a huge pro-totype Federa-tion battle-cruiser is completed and under-goes testing. It fails to meet requirements and is put in storage.	In the Pyrimiis Star System two inha-bited planets are found on the same orbit, on a collision course.		Top Secret prototype spy ship is tested. It achieves warp 3.84, the highest velocity to date.	Galactic Cultural Exchange begins bringing each world's heritage to other Federation members.	Deneva Research Station opens and begins scientific investigation into transtate physics.

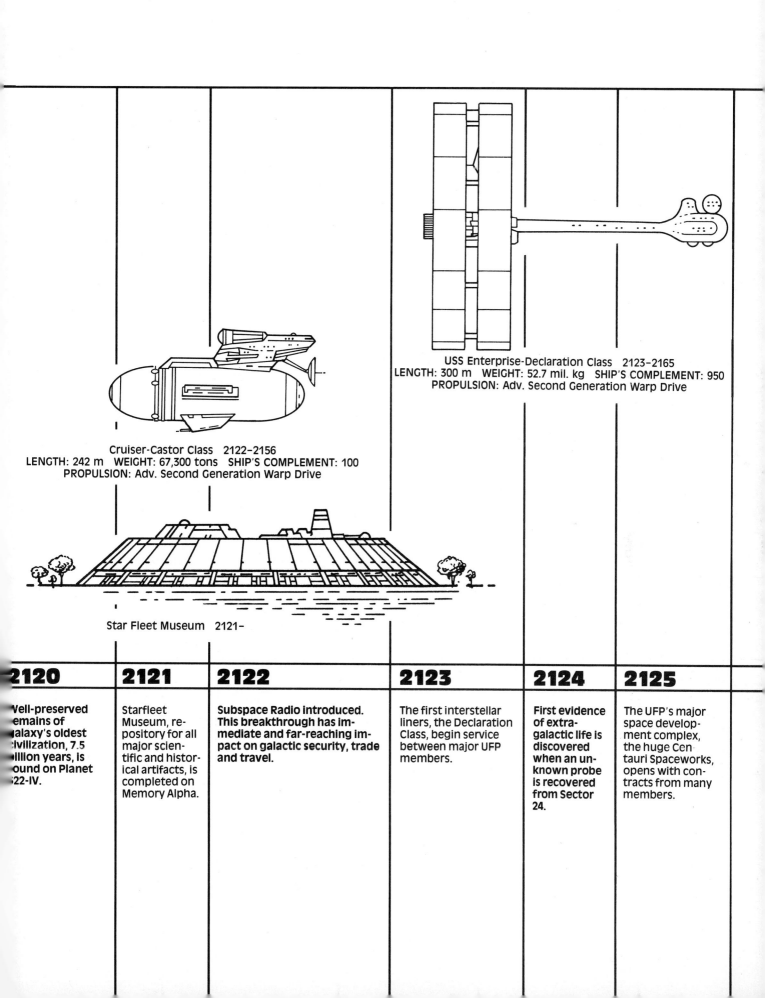

Cruiser-Castor Class   2122–2156
LENGTH: 242 m   WEIGHT: 67,300 tons   SHIP'S COMPLEMENT: 100
PROPULSION: Adv. Second Generation Warp Drive

USS Enterprise-Declaration Class   2123–2165
LENGTH: 300 m   WEIGHT: 52.7 mil. kg   SHIP'S COMPLEMENT: 950
PROPULSION: Adv. Second Generation Warp Drive

Star Fleet Museum   2121–

2120	**2121**	**2122**	**2123**	**2124**	**2125**
Well-preserved remains of Galaxy's oldest civilization, 7.5 million years, is found on Planet 22-IV.	Starfleet Museum, repository for all major scientific and historical artifacts, is completed on Memory Alpha.	**Subspace Radio introduced. This breakthrough has immediate and far-reaching impact on galactic security, trade and travel.**	The first interstellar liners, the Declaration Class, begin service between major UFP members.	**First evidence of extragalactic life is discovered when an unknown probe is recovered from Sector 24.**	The UFP's major space development complex, the huge Centauri Spaceworks, opens with contracts from many members.

SHIPS

USS PATTON
MARSHALL CLASS

2105-2155

The ambush and loss of the USS *Patton* began the Romulan War. The Marshall class was the Federation's staunchest line of defense, and these ships' superior performance and firepower provided a crucial tactical edge. In fact, the class supposed to succeed it could not better its specifications and so was never built, the reason the Marshall class had the longest commissioned lifespan in interstellar history.

Specifications

Length	225 m
Beam	117 m
Draught	45.5 m
Mass	22.7 million kg
Engine Nacelles	Length 130 m
	Diameter 31.2 m
Forward Command / Attack Section	104 m x 37.7 m x 20.8 m

Ship's Complement

Officers (Captain, Lieutenant, Science, Engineering, Navigation, Communications, Medical, Weaponry, 4 Ensigns) — 12
Crew — 145
Standard Ship's Complement — 157

Performance

Range	Standard 300 light-years
	Maximum 1000 light-years
Cruising Velocity	Warp 3.5 (42.9c)
Maximum Velocity	Warp 3.8 (54.9c)

Acceleration

0-.99c: 1.5 hr
Warp Engage: 2.31 min
warp 1 - 2: 40.7 sec
2 - 3.5: 29.6 sec
3.5 - 3.8: 37.3 sec

Systems Overview

Navigation — Celestial Warp Reader with extensive evasive action programming
Communication — Warp Communication
Weapons — 14 forward lasers
8 rear lasers
8 forward particle beam cannons
2 rear particle beam cannons
400 photon torpedoes
Life Support: Gravity — .5 - 1.1 g intern. variable
Atmosphere — 19% O_2; 13% humidity
Sustenance Duration — 6.2 years at Standard Ship's Complement

Engineering and Science

- Engines — Advanced 2nd Generation Warp Drive
- Fuel — 10:1 matter to antimatter
- Low-mass design for superior fighting performance
- Separated dual-warp generators
- Computer-programmed for multiple attack/defense scenarios

Improvements and Innovations

- Separated engine nacelles produced dramatic increase in power levels
- Detachable Command section for damage jettisoning
- Efficient hull-cooling to dissipate energy beam assault
- First ship equipped with warp-generated defensive shielding

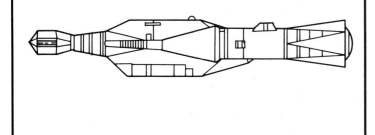

ELEVATION VIEW

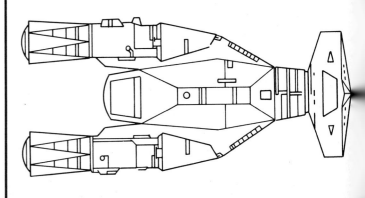

PLAN VIEW

WARP 3.2 STARLINER

USS ENTERPRISE DECLARATION CLASS 2123-2165

This original *Enterprise* was the first spaceliner built specifically for the major Federation space lanes (such as Earth - Alpha Centauri). The travel demand that blossomed in the 22nd century resulted in 957 of these Declaration class ships being commissioned. The *Enterprise*'s name lives on in the current refitted heavy cruiser (Constitution-II Class).

Specifications

Length	300 m
Diameter	210 m
Living Section Width	28.7 m
Mass	52.7 million kg

Ship's Complement

Crew and Service Personnel	100
Passenger Capacity	850
Standard Ship's Complement	950

Performance

Range: Standard	350 light-years
Maximum	1,200 light-years
Cruising Speed	Warp 3.2 (32.8c)
Voyage Duration: Standard	3 months
Maximum	2.5 years

Systems Overview

Navigation	Celestial Warp Reader
Communication	Subspace Radio
Recreation	Null-grav gymnasium
	5 dining rooms
	3 theaters
	3 nightclubs
	Forward and Rear stellar observatories
Life Support: Gravity	.2 - 1.2 g
Atmosphere	20% O_2; 11% humidity
Sustenance Duration	Up to 40 years if outfitted for long-duration exploration

Engineering and Science

- Advaced 2nd Generation Warp Drive
- Fuel: 10:1 matter to antimatter
- Separated engine and living sections for improved efficiency

Improvements and Innovations

- First class of ship equipped with subspace radio
- Most popular passenger carrier of its time

PROTOTYPE BATTLECRUISER 2114-2115

During the darkness of the Romulan War, when the prospect of prolonged hostility seemed only too real, Star Fleet Command ordered this battlecruiser prototype built and feasibility tested. However, the ship proved tremendously unwieldy and never entered active service. Its failure to perform to specification was a major reason why both the Horizon and Marshall classes enjoyed such an extended commissioned life.

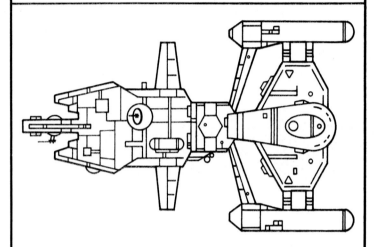

Specifications

Length	312 m
Beam	196 m
Draught	95.6 m
Mass	245 million kg

Ship's Complement

Officers (Captain, Lieutenant, Science, Engineering, Navigation, Communications, Medical, 6 Ensigns)	13
Crew	362
Standard Ship's Complement	375

Performance

Range	1700 light-years
Cruising Speed	Warp 3.5 (42.9 c)
Maximum Speed	Warp 3.9 (59.3 c)
Weaponry	2 main forward lasers
	2 secondary forward lasers
	4 flank lasers
	4 forward particle beam cannons
	4 rear particle beam cannons
	8 forward fusion torpedo tubes
	8 rear torpedo tubes

USS HUROK BROADWAY CLASS 2118-

The Hurok was the flagship for the UFP Galactic Cultural Exchange Project. A hybrid ship, it was originally a Merchant-Class cargo ship that was renovated to accommodate the specific needs of its complement of cultural ambassadors. Through the decades, the Hurok was refitted with the latest warp engines, and this incredibly sturdy classic can still be seen in operation at various ports of call.

Specifications

Length	250 m
Beam	51.5 m
Draught	61.9 m
Mass	33 million kg
Living Section (6 decks)	103.5 m x 46 m x 28.7 m
Command Tower (6 decks)	34.5 m x 25.8 m x 20 m
Engine/Fuel Section	length: 100 m diameter: 28.7 m

Ship's Complement

Officers (Captain, Navigation, Engineering)	3
Crew	30
Passenger Capacity	158
Standard Ship's Complement	191

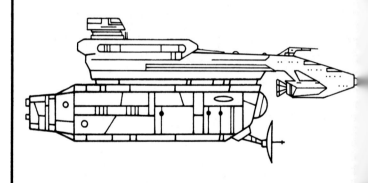

Performance

Range	100 - 1200 light-years*
Cruising Velocity	Warp 3 - 4.5*
Engines	2nd Generation - Advanced 3rd Generation*
Fuel	10:1 - 1:1 matter to antimatter
Support Craft	4 Shuttlecraft 1 zoo/cargo ship

- Ampitheater for on-board performances
- Ample practice rooms, stage and gymnasiums

*The Hurok was uprated over the decades to keep pace with changing warp technology

FIRST EVIDENCE OF EXTRA-GALACTIC CIVILIZATIONS

2124

USS GREYHOUND, CASTOR CLASS
DR. WILLIAM POMEROY, SCIENCE OFFICER
Science Log:

I sit here in my lab, staring at the probe, and can't shake the suspicion it's staring back at me. I've run tests on it till I'm blue, and haven't learned much more than what I can see with my own incredulous eyes. It is a cylinder two meters long with a width of 357 millimeters diameter. There are no exterior seams and no protruding antennae or other appendages. The metal itself is an unknown alloy of incredible density which has resisted every effort at x-raying, sonar sounding, or microsampling. Simply put, the probe is impenetrable, indestructible, and to all investigation, a dead hunk of metal. There is really only one thing known about it for sure. This inert probe before me doesn't come from this galaxy.

Its ion trail proved that conclusively. Up to thirty parsecs away, the telltale residue of interstellar ion dust leads in an unwavering line straight out of the galaxy towards the Small Magellanic Cloud. The excited state of the ions also indicates the probe was traveling at unimaginable speeds we can only take a stab at estimating in the vicinity of warp 30.

But something caused it to decelerate abruptly, and I can't help but believe that something was us. For it braked abruptly out of warp, radically realigned its trajectory towards the *Greyhound,* then stopped cold within 0,000 kilometers of our ship, for all the world like rolling over and playing dead. After observing it for a full star-date, the Captain finally ordered it brought aboard and dumped it in my lap.

And I've found out just about zero. It is an inert cylinder which shows no sign of recording or transmitting data. We've encountered our first extra-galactic object and have learned nothing from the meeting. And I still think 's staring at me.

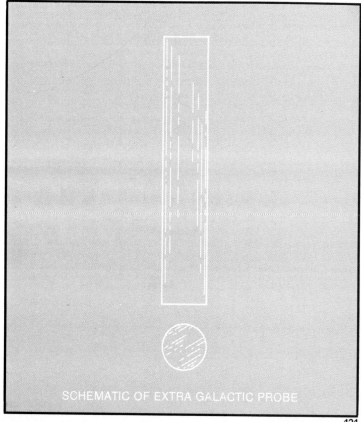

SCHEMATIC OF EXTRA GALACTIC PROBE

OVERVIEW

The painful memory of the Romulan War had thankfully diminished by the opening of this quarter century, and the UFP entered into an era of quiet growth and prosperity. Though there were the seemingly inevitable planet conflicts, plagues and space catastrophes, the welcome placidity of this period as a whole began what has become known as the Golden Age of Space. For almost a century now, there has been a steady progression of peaceful exploration of space and steady expansion of the frontiers of knowledge.

There is perhaps no better indication of this period's tranquility than the veritable explosion in space ridership, the number of people who enjoyed interstellar travel. Space tourism blossomed into a major interstellar industry, with luxurious new generations of starcruisers to pamper the traveler. Exploiting the natural wonders of the cosmos, sightseeing tours were organized to such marvels as the Jewel Stars of Corona Major. These are Cepheid Variables, stars which change brightness, whose unpredictable, flashing bursts of color have dazzled countless legions of amazed tourists.

Moreover, whole planets adapted themselves to the tourist trade, like the nightclub world of Argelius II, or the famed vacation paradise that is Beta Colony VII. No longer the exclusive domain of intrepid explorers and avaricious traders, space opened its treasures to people from every walk of life.

Including students. The educational possibilities of space were developed more and more. For instance, collegiate excursions were made to planets in early stages of development so that the paleozoology students could witness firsthand, an actual dinosaur age. The uses of space seem endless.

The variety of new worlds discovered also appears limitless. During this period, the first highly intelligent flying creatures were found on Alpha Virginis. On this geologically unstable planet, the most advanced lifeform evolved in the most stable medium, the air, and the Canaris of Alpha Virginis possessed a well-developed ethical and cultural civilization.

As often seems the case, there was a theoretical breakthrough in this era that only decades later produced what is now known as the transporter. For many years, a heated debate had raged between biologists and physicists over whether form of life could be broken down into constituent parts and reassembled without destroying the fragile spark of life in the process. Previous experiments had always supported the naysaying biologists. But the increasing sophistication of matter/antimatter reactions, new generations of computer intelligence and the successful application of transtator physics, developed by the brilliant twenty-second century physicist Abramson, finally achieved in a controlled laboratory situation, what had been thought impossible: life could, in fact, be transported. It could be energized into personal energy engrams, beamed to another location, and faithfully reassembled into a living entity. However, these first successes dealt only with single-cell protozoa. It would be another forty years before the process was perfected enough to permit the safe transporting of a human being.

Other advances were made in the field of galactic astronomy. Black holes were studied for their insights into multiple continuums—other complete universes coexisting with our own in a different space/time matrix. The antimatter universe is just such a continuum, whose occasional presence in our own has been harnessed for warp drive. In fact, large antimatter lodes have been found in certain sectors of space, for reasons still unclear, which are now the sites for the major antimatter refineries.

Another galactic mystery concerned the string of novas that plagued a particular space sector one solar year. A special task force was assigned to discover the source of these novas, and the answer they found was linked to a completely new field of science called galactic tectonics, or the study of the patterns of galactic evolution. The novas traced a galactic fault line along the whole of the Omega finger of the Milky Way's Orion arm. While there isn't yet any technological solution to this hazard, at least other star systems along the fault have been alerted to the danger, so that they can monitor their troubled stars closely. They were found to be the result of a galactic fault, a line of instability caused by unbalanced stresses from the rotating galaxy.

Unfortunately, not all astronomical research can be done within the safe confines of a research station. The research ship USS KEPLER was sent to observe closehand, the collapse of a Giant Type I star into a Black Hole, a body with so great a density that its gravitational forces don't permit any radiation to escape, including light or radio waves. The star literally disappears. This collapse was to have been the first within the reach of Federation spaceflight, and the KEPLER was there. Tragically, however, the KEPLER's computers had miscalculated the mass of the star. Instead of collapsing steadily into a black hole, the not-quite massive though star went supernova, the cataclys-

mic explosion of dying stars. The KEPLER and all crew were instantaneously incinerated. There should be no illusions: space is still a very dangerous place.

One of the innovations that has made space a little safer was the medical tricorder invented during this era. This piece of equipment allows all vital lifesigns to be measured by a portable, handheld device which can output instant diagnoses. Also employing transtator circuitry, tricorders are now standard equipment on all starships.

Galactic health has the highest priority within the UFP, and in fact, it is one of the only possibly permissible exceptions to the Prime Directive, the overriding prohibition against interference into a planet's internal affairs. Few others are tolerated, and it was in this era that the first starship captain was convicted of violating the Prime Directive. Though his "crime" was certainly understandable—he intercepted a wave of nuclear missiles that was about to start a world war on Vega Proxima that would have killed millions—it was nevertheless a reprehensible intrusion into a planet's history, with incalculable effects on that world's future. The Star Fleet Special Court Martial had no alternative; the captain was relieved of his commmand, his rank and commission.

Despite this black mark and the interplanetary war near the Romulan Neutral Zone that had Star Fleet Command on edge for a while, this era was uncommonly peaceful. Breakthroughs in science, advances in technology, and the increase in galactic travel all added up to a period of placid growth, a period that extended through the next quarter-century, and has largely delineated our present stable, technologically advanced society.

SPACEFLIGHT CHRONOLOGY

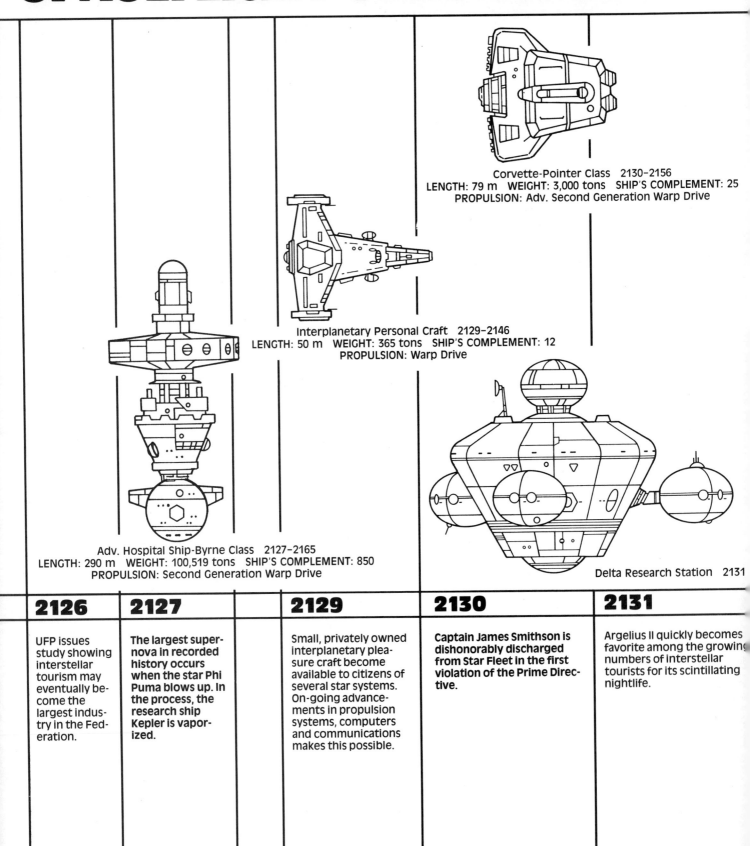

Corvette-Pointer Class   2130–2156
LENGTH: 79 m   WEIGHT: 3,000 tons   SHIP'S COMPLEMENT: 25
PROPULSION: Adv. Second Generation Warp Drive

Interplanetary Personal Craft   2129–2146
LENGTH: 50 m   WEIGHT: 365 tons   SHIP'S COMPLEMENT: 12
PROPULSION: Warp Drive

Adv. Hospital Ship-Byrne Class   2127–2165
LENGTH: 290 m   WEIGHT: 100,519 tons   SHIP'S COMPLEMENT: 850
PROPULSION: Second Generation Warp Drive

Delta Research Station   2131

2126	2127	2129	2130	2131
UFP issues study showing interstellar tourism may eventually become the largest industry in the Federation.	**The largest supernova in recorded history occurs when the star Phi Puma blows up. In the process, the research ship Kepler is vaporized.**	Small, privately owned interplanetary pleasure craft become available to citizens of several star systems. On-going advancements in propulsion systems, computers and communications makes this possible.	**Captain James Smithson is dishonorably discharged from Star Fleet in the first violation of the Prime Directive.**	Argelius II quickly becomes favorite among the growing numbers of interstellar tourists for its scintillating nightlife.

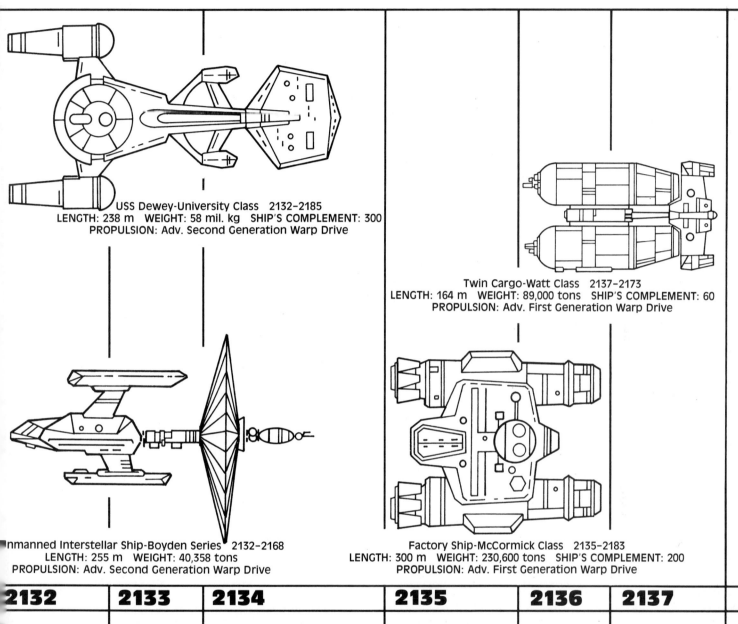

USS Dewey-University Class   2132–2185
LENGTH: 238 m   WEIGHT: 58 mil. kg   SHIP'S COMPLEMENT: 300
PROPULSION: Adv. Second Generation Warp Drive

Twin Cargo-Watt Class   2137–2173
LENGTH: 164 m   WEIGHT: 89,000 tons   SHIP'S COMPLEMENT: 60
PROPULSION: Adv. First Generation Warp Drive

Unmanned Interstellar Ship-Boyden Series   2132–2168
LENGTH: 255 m   WEIGHT: 40,358 tons
PROPULSION: Adv. Second Generation Warp Drive

Factory Ship-McCormick Class   2135–2183
LENGTH: 300 m   WEIGHT: 230,600 tons   SHIP'S COMPLEMENT: 200
PROPULSION: Adv. First Generation Warp Drive

2132	**2133**	**2134**	**2135**	**2136**	**2137**
First unmanned Interstellar cargo ships, the Boyden Class, begin plying the long-haul trade routes. Delta Research Station completed and draws scientists from all sectors of space.	Worlds in Evolution Program enables students to witness firsthand, various eras in the lifecycle of developing planets.	Like many planets in the Federation, the Milky Way Galaxy itself contains ''faults'' that cause violent disruptions. After years of study the mystery novas in Sector 27 are found to be caused by these forces.	The theory of molecular reintegration achieves a major breakthrough with the first successful transmission of organic life.	Funding for a new generation of warp ships not approved. Horizon and Marshall Classes remain first line of defense.	After 50 years, the UFP has matured into a stable, ever growing alliance of star systems.

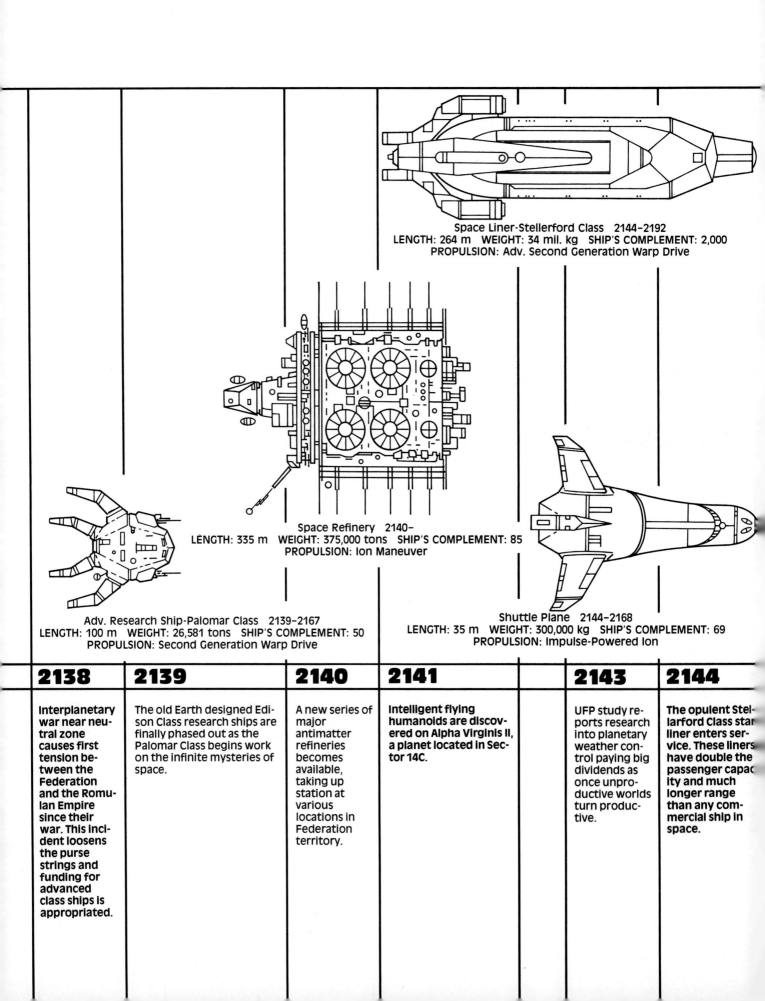

Space Liner-Stellerford Class   2144–2192
LENGTH: 264 m   WEIGHT: 34 mil. kg   SHIP'S COMPLEMENT: 2,000
PROPULSION: Adv. Second Generation Warp Drive

Space Refinery   2140–
LENGTH: 335 m   WEIGHT: 375,000 tons   SHIP'S COMPLEMENT: 85
PROPULSION: Ion Maneuver

Adv. Research Ship-Palomar Class   2139–2167
LENGTH: 100 m   WEIGHT: 26,581 tons   SHIP'S COMPLEMENT: 50
PROPULSION: Second Generation Warp Drive

Shuttle Plane   2144–2168
LENGTH: 35 m   WEIGHT: 300,000 kg   SHIP'S COMPLEMENT: 69
PROPULSION: Impulse-Powered Ion

2138	2139	2140	2141		2143	2144
Interplanetary war near neutral zone causes first tension between the Federation and the Romulan Empire since their war. This incident loosens the purse strings and funding for advanced class ships is appropriated.	The old Earth designed Edison Class research ships are finally phased out as the Palomar Class begins work on the infinite mysteries of space.	A new series of major antimatter refineries becomes available, taking up station at various locations in Federation territory.	Intelligent flying humanoids are discovered on Alpha Virginis II, a planet located in Sector 14C.		UFP study reports research into planetary weather control paying big dividends as once unproductive worlds turn productive.	The opulent Stellarford Class star liner enters service. These liners have double the passenger capacity and much longer range than any commercial ship in space.

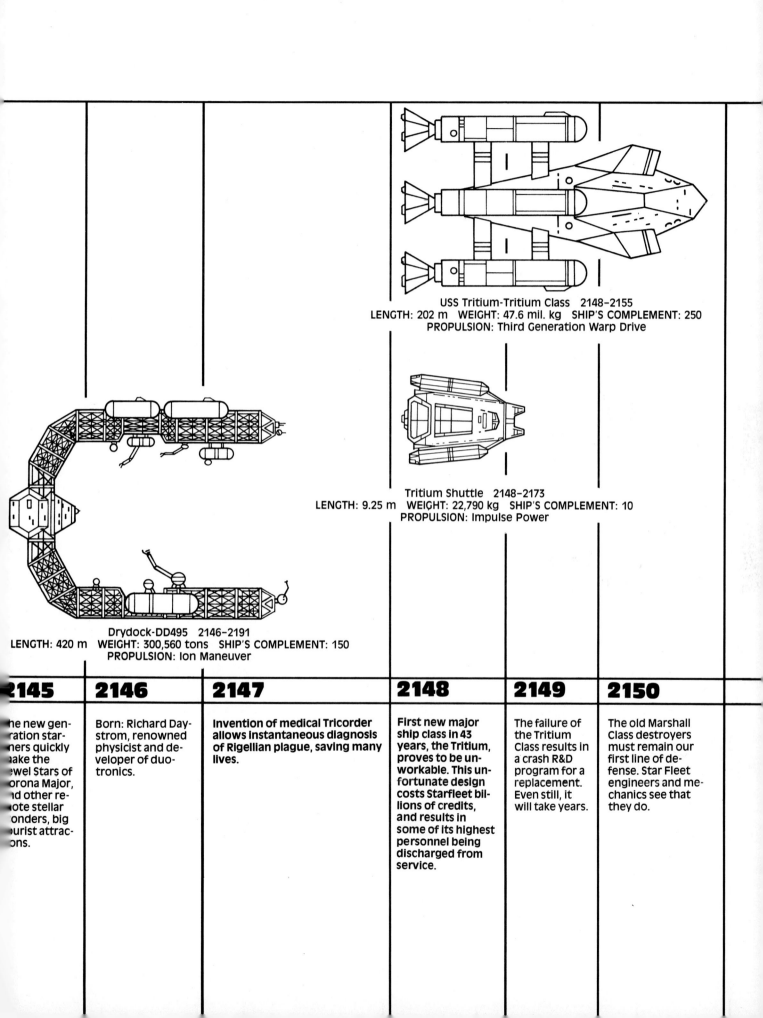

USS Tritium-Tritium Class   2148–2155
LENGTH: 202 m   WEIGHT: 47.6 mil. kg   SHIP'S COMPLEMENT: 250
PROPULSION: Third Generation Warp Drive

Tritium Shuttle   2148–2173
LENGTH: 9.25 m   WEIGHT: 22,790 kg   SHIP'S COMPLEMENT: 10
PROPULSION: Impulse Power

Drydock-DD495   2146–2191
LENGTH: 420 m   WEIGHT: 300,560 tons   SHIP'S COMPLEMENT: 150
PROPULSION: Ion Maneuver

2145	2146	2147	2148	2149	2150
he new gen-ration star-ners quickly ake the ewel Stars of orona Major, d other re-ote stellar onders, big urist attrac-ons.	Born: Richard Day-strom, renowned physicist and developer of duo-tronics.	Invention of medical Tricorder allows instantaneous diagnosis of Rigellian plague, saving many lives.	First new major ship class in 43 years, the Tritium, proves to be un-workable. This un-fortunate design costs Starfleet bil-lions of credits, and results in some of its highest personnel being discharged from service.	The failure of the Tritium Class results in a crash R&D program for a replacement. Even still, it will take years.	The old Marshall Class destroyers must remain our first line of de-fense. Star Fleet engineers and me-chanics see that they do.

USS KING CHARLES STELLARFORD CLASS

2144-2185

The most luxurious starliner ever conceived, the *King Charles* set a standard of opulence and comfort still unsurpassed. It had double the passenger capacity of previous Declaration class spaceliners, and its much greater range opened up the galaxy to all peoples. Catering especially to the burgeoning tourist industry, these Stellarford series ships made excursions to such galactic wonders as the Jewel Stars.

Specifications

Length	264 m
Beam	105.6 m
Draught	96.8 m
Mass	34 million kg
Living Dirigible	220 m x 65.1 m x 105.6 m
Engine Section	60 m x 28.2 m x 52.8 m
Forward Antenna length	56.3 m

Ship's Complement

Officers (Captain, Lieutenant, Science, Engineering, Navigation, Communications, Medical (4), Cruise Director, Recreation, 12 Deck Supervisors)	24
Crew	176
	200
Passenger Capacity	1800
Standard Ship's Complement	2000

Performance

Range	Standard: 400 light-years
	Maximum: 1500 light-years
Cruising Velocity	Warp 3.5 (42.9c)

Voyage Duration	Standard: 2 months
	Maximum: 4 years
Acceleration	0 - .99c: 2.5 hr
	Warp Engage: 2.3 min
	Warp 1 - 2: 56.4 sec
	2 - 3.5: 41.9 sec

Systems Overview

Navigation	Starbase-triangulated warp celestial guidance
Communication	Subspace radio
Life Support: Gravity	0 - 1.2 g, intern. variable
Atmosphere	18% - 25% O_2; variable according to function
Sustenance Duration	Luxury consumables: 4.5 years
Standard Consumables	Unlimited, (self-sufficient food-growth capability)

Accommodations

- First, Second and Excursion class staterooms
- 2 gymnasiums, one null-grav, one 1 g
- 10 dining rooms
- 5 theaters
- 2 auditoriums
- 12 nightclubs
- 4 stellar observatories

Engineering and science

- Engines: Advanced 2nd Generation warp drive
- Fuel: 10:1 matter to antimatter
- Separated dual-warp engines for excellent engine response
- Largest capacity starship in Federation history
- Forward antennae array with multi-redundant distress signaling capability
- Flank stabilizers for smoothest possible voyage

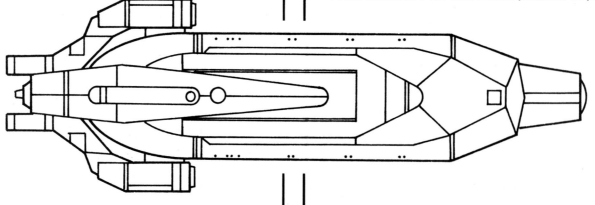

USS TRITIUM
TRITIUM CLASS

2148-2155

The USS *Tritium* has the dubious distinction of being the worst major ship ever built by the UFP. Insurmountable design flaws surfaced during its validation phase, and though six other Tritium class ships were constructed in a vain attempt to overcome glaring shortcomings, the Federation finally cut its losses and canceled the series. As a costly reminder to future generations, the *Tritium* may also be viewed at the Spaceflight Museum on Memory Alpha.

Specifications

Length	202 m
Beam	161 m
Draught	118.6 m
Mass	47.6 million kg
Nacelles (3)	length: 100 m
	diameter: 26 m
Exhaust Nozzle Diameter	42.4 m
Main living/command segment	77.7 m x 190.7 m x 70.6 m
Nacelles Cross Strut length	50 m

Ship's Complement

Officers	(Captain, Lieutenant, Science, Engineering, Medical (3), Navigation, Communication, Ensigns (6))	15
Crew		235
	Standard Ship's Complement	250

Performance

Range	(Estimate) 800 light-years
	Actual 30 light-years
Cruising Velocity	(Estimate) Warp 4 (64c)
	Actual Warp 3 (27c)
Maximum Velocity	(Estimate) Warp 4.75 (107.2c)
	Actual Warp 3 (27c)
Standard Voyage Duration	The Tritium never successfully completed a standard voyage.

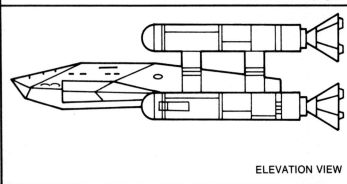

ELEVATION VIEW

Acceleration	0 - .99c (est & act) 59 min
	.99c - warp engage (est) 1.8 min
	(act) 2.4 min
	Warp 1 - 2 (est) 29.7 sec
	(act) 45.3 sec
	Warp 2 - 4 (est) 24.5 sec
	(act) Warp 4 never attained

Systems Overview

Navigation	Starbase-synchronized warp celestial guidance
Communication	Subspace Radio
Weapons	6 Laser Banks
	8 Particle Beam Cannons
	250 Photon Torpedoes
Life Support: Gravity	.2 - 1.2 g
Atmosphere	20% O_2; 11% humidity
Sustenance Duration	Up to 10.5 years if outfitted for long-duration exploration

Engineering and Science

- Engines — Second generation warp drive
- Fuel — 5:1 matter to antimatter
- Tri-Nacelles engine configuration for proposed synergistic coupling of warp field
- Wide-flanged radiator nozzles for proposed better waste heat management

Improvements and innovations

- First third generation warp drive engines
- First starship equipped with Tricorder
- Tri-Nacelle design had terrible performance record, three engines setting up disruptive warp principle harmonies
- Waste heat management impractical; extra weight of nozzles negated proposed efficiency gain

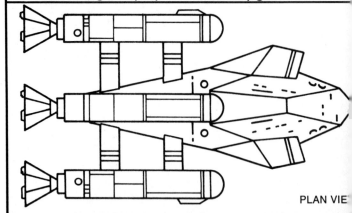

PLAN VIEW

USS DEWEY
UNIVERSITY CLASS   2132-2185

The *Dewey* was a spacefaring school, transporting students on a wide range of educational excursions, the best known being the still-popular "Worlds in Evolution" course that visited planets representing different stages of life-form development. A derivation of the Marshall class using second generation warp propulsion, the *Dewey* and its fellow school-ships opened up a galaxy of educational opportunities.

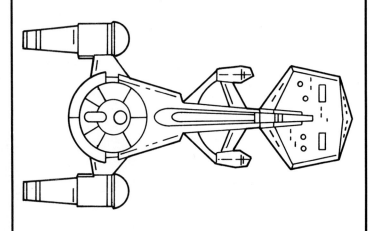

Specifications

Length	238 m
Beam	196 m
Draught	66.7 m
Mass	58 million kg
Side Auditorium pods	length: 38 m
	diameter: 15 m
Forward Classroom/	76.2 m x 57 m x 50 m
Command Section	
Crew	47
Faculty	33
Students	220
Standard Ship's Complement	300

Performance

Range	100 - 1000 light-years
Cruising Velocity	Warp 3 (27c)
Engines	2nd Generation Warp Drive
Fuel	10:1 matter to antimatter

2 Side lecture ampitheaters
35 classrooms
5 laboratories
Extensive computer library
4 Shuttlecraft for surface educational excursions

SHUTTLEPLANE
2144-2168

This very large Shuttleplane was designed for use with Stellarford Class starliners. Excellent life-support systems and multi-redundant automatic distress signaling made this a sought-after interplanetary craft in its own right. With its 65-passenger capacity, the Shuttleplane proved to be a perfect life rescue ship for interstellar travel.

Specifications

Length	35 m
Beam	25 m to wing tips
Draught	12 m
Mass	300,000 kg

Ship's Complement

Crew	4
Passenger Capacity	65
Standard Ship's Complement	69

Performance

Range	Interplanetary
Landing/Takeoff Velocity	200 knots
Atmosphere Cruising Velocity	Mach 8 (9500 km/hr)
Launch Mode	Horizontal Takeoff/ Landing (HTOL)
Engines	Impulse-powered ion propulsion

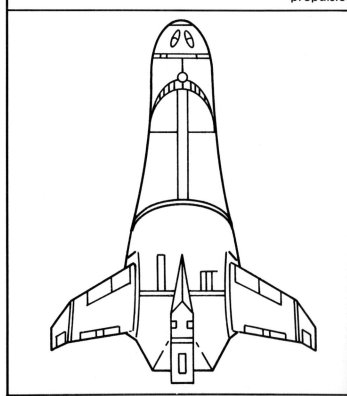

STELLAR EXPLORATIONS

Alpha Virginis II

The second planet in the Alpha Virginis star system is notable for having one of the most evolved lifeforms, flying creatures, in the galaxy. Because most of the land area on the surface is subject to seismic upheaval, the calm and relatively thick atmosphere compared to Earth's became the most stable evolutionary environment. The Canaris are also notable for having no aggressive instincts whatsoever.

Alpha Virginis contains six planets: one habitable (H); one potential (P); four uninhabitable

	Dist. from star (×10⁸km)	Diameter (km)	Revolution (Solar days & years)	Average surface temp (°c)
II(H)	1.79	11,274	1.21 yrs	18°
III(P)	2.43	9,343	1.89 yrs	11°

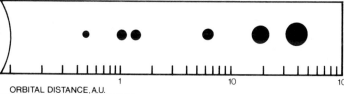

ORBITAL DISTANCE, A.U.

Tourists from all over, travel all over.

The Golden Age of Space tranquility created a tremendous demand for interstellar liners capable of taking innumerable tourists to see the many stellar wonders of the UFP. In this era, the Declaration Class became the largest class ever built, its 957 ships making attractions like *Argelius II* one of the most popular in the Federation.

In 2144, the Stellarford Class liners made it possible for travelers to really get away from it all by opening up more remote sectors of space with its increased speed, range and comforts.

STARLINER ROUTES — — — — — — —

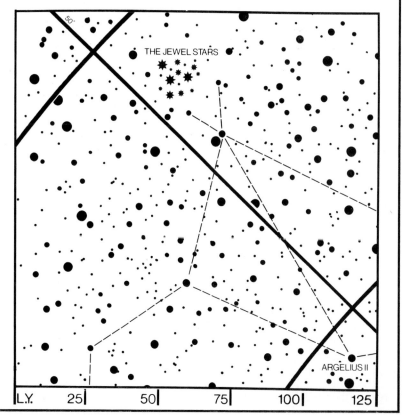

THE JEWEL STARS

ARGELIUS II

L.Y.   25   50   75   100   125

GALAXY'S GREATEST SUPERNOVA
Research ship vaporized by explosion
2127

USS KEPLER, NEWTON CLASS
WILHELM HENKE, SCIENCE OFFICER

Science Log:

The collapse of the red giant Phi Puma has been proceeding for 57.5 minutes, and our sensors are monitoring every reading possible for good reason: this is the most important astronomical event in Federation history, in human history as well. Only twenty-five stars a year in the whole galaxy go nova, and only a small fraction of those are sufficiently large to collapse into a black hole, that most fascinating of stellar phenomena. We're incredibly lucky to have one happen within starship range.

Having dipped below the critical threshold of nuclear fusion, this star, which has been burning for billions of years, will, in only a few short hours, totally contract into itself—so rapid a contraction and the mass of the imploded star so great a gravitational force that no radiation—no light, radio waves, nothing—can escape. Phi Puma will disappear from all sensors, will cease to exist in any way we can measure. It will become a black hole in space.

It's good that we're a safe 100 A.U. away from Phi Puma. The waves of gamma rays and gravitational flux are staggering, even at this distance, but the *Kepler* is functioning excellently despite the barrage. A good thing too. No starship's warp power could negotiate the enormous deformations of the space-time structure, so warp drive is out of the question.

Wait a minute. Hold on. This is curious, let me check it out. Seems like the acceleration of the star's collapse has slowed down. This could be trouble. But there it is, acceleration decreasing. But that can't be, the mass of the star is too great for that to happen. Wait a minute. Computations from instantaneous sensor input call for a downward readjustment in mass rating of Phi Puma.

Acceleration drastically decreasing. There's no doubt about it . . . This star isn't going to make any black hole this stardate . . . Phi Puma's going to go supernova . . . It's going to blow in the biggest stellar explosion the Federation has ever felt . . . I wonder how it'll affect the nearby stars; it could set up a chain reaction of secondary novas!

But there's no question about how it'll affect the *Kepler*. We can't warp out of here. We can't budge against the gravity pull . . . In a few hours, the *Kepler* and all aboard will be vaporized.

FIRST VIOLATION OF PRIME DIRECTIVE
Captain relieved of command for preventing a world war.
2130

STARBASE 11, STAR FLEET STRATEGIC SPACE STATION
THADDEAU STONER, COMMODORE

Special Court Martial Log:

As President of this Star Fleet Special Court Martial, it is my duty to return the verdict in the indictment of James Smithson for violation of the Prime Directive. After hearing all testimony, and reaching after due deliberation the unanimous consent of the three-officer jury, this Court finds you guilty as charged.

I have never been called upon to pass a more difficult judgement in my thirty years in Star Fleet. Certainly this Court can appreciate the motives behind the Captain's actions. A world war is a horrible abomination, senselessly killing millions of innocents. In orbit around Vega Proxima, Captain Smithson held the technological capability to halt the first act of war, to give the planet one more chance to reconsider this violent choice. Without authority, he himself chose to harmlessly intercept and neutralize the nuclear missiles that would have doomed Vega Proxima. And none of the officers of this Court, including myself, is certain he would not have done the same.

But that is just why it is called the Prime Directive; it is the hardest as well as the highest order, and Captain Smithson's intentions do not mitigate the seriousness of his violation. Each world has its unique course of planetary evolution, the purpose of which is beyond this court's, or anyone's, understanding. If we are to make the exploration of new worlds a Federation goal, then its representatives must recognize and respect their limitations as uninformed outsiders. If those nuclear missiles had been aimed at a Hitler-figure who had been slaughtering millions genocidally, what seemed a benevolent action would have been heartless. We cannot know the historical and cultural complexities of a new planet.

And it is for that presumption of superiority that this Court finds you guilty, Captain Smithson. Our understanding your motives doesn't alter the fact that Vega Proxima's history has irreversibly altered by your personal decision, in direct violation of the Prime Directive you swore to uphold. Therefore, this Court relieves you of your command, your rank, and recommends you for dishonorable discharge from Star Fleet. This Court is adjourned.

LOGS

WORLDS IN EVOLUTION PROGRAM BEGINS
Educational excursion to Dinosaur World
2133

USS DEWEY, UNIVERSITY CLASS
CHUN JI, ARCHEOLOGY AND ANTHROPOLOGY OFFICER

The Federation's "Worlds in Evolution" Program has enabled students to visit planets in different stages of geological and/or evolutionary development. Begun with a modest five-planet itinerary, the program has continually added appropriate planets as they were discovered, until today there are seven different field routes, each encompassing eighteen varied worlds. The "Worlds in Evolution" Program is the most popular educational endeavor in Federation history and is always oversubscribed with students eager to learn from its unique vantage point.

Archeology and Anthropology Log:

Attention Students. The captain of the *Dewey* informs me we have entered standard orbit around Epsilon Reptus and can embark via shuttlecraft to the planet surface in approximately one hour. Let me remind you to check out your landing gear *before* reaching Reptus. The "buddy system" of paired students will keep the same safety twosomes as on Tan Tauri, and ask my permission before going off on any personal expeditions. Let's not have a repeat of the delay on Tauri when we wasted a full stardate searching for Kennedy and Peterson, all right?

Very well, then. This stardate's lesson concerns the Jurassic epoch of the Mesozoic Era: the Dinosaur Age. Roughly corresponding to Earth of 125 million years ago, Epsilon Reptus is inhabited with giant reptiles who represented the dominant life form on the planet at this time.

The land mass we've chosen to study has three reptiles of particular interest. If students would program their pocket videos to page 178, they could examine a holograph of the dinosaur whose Earth analog is the Allosaurus. This animal is approximately 2 m. long and 3 m. high and is noteworthy for his huge jaw that he can unhinge to swallow smaller beasts whole. On page 187, a cousin of the Brachiosaurus may be viewed. This is a huge reptile, a good 25 m. long and weighing 50,000 kg. Luckily, it is a plant-eater and poses no personal threat to us.

However, students should be especially wary of the Triceratops-like creature, page 201, a comparatively small 3 m. in length. But this reptile has a three-meter head and a brain mass of a full 2.1 kilograms, uncommon for this stage of development. The animal is ferocious and a meat-eater, so don't try feeding it or you'll end up as lunch.

All right. Get your gear in order. One hour till departure.

GALACTIC MYSTERY SOLVED
Exploding stars are found to lie on galaxy "fault."

DENEVA RESEARCH STATION
KHAN REVOX, ASTROPHYSICIST

2134

Science Log:

—Special Report to UFP Galactic Crisis Center—

The Special Task Force to Study the Mystery Novas of Sector 34.9 has reached some startling conclusions, conclusions which should clear up the mystery of the string of novas that has been besetting that sector but which will not be able to prescribe a cure.

While our galaxy experiences some twenty-five nova explosions per solar year, it is unprecedented that three such explosions should occur within one year, within one sector, and in an almost straight line through the three. There is no known galactic explanation for such a phenomenon; it's not caused by a supernova concussion and it appears to violate the law of averages.

Thanks to my colleague, Dr. Granville Webern, whose pioneering work in galactic techtonics is gaining widespread attention, I believe we have found a satisfactory explanation for the mystery. What these three novas illustrate and are caused by, is nothing less than a galactic "fault line" along the whole of the Omega finger of the Milky Way's Orion arm. Due to uneven stresses caused by the angular momentum of the rotating galaxy, and by local magnetic forces, it is becoming clear that a deformation in the space-time structure of certain neighborhoods can produce linear compression waves. These lines of extreme stress can extend through an entire finger, through an entire arm and theoretically, even through a whole galaxy, though none such can be viewed within our Milky Way. Stars located along these compression fronts are subjected to enormous pressures, and it is little wonder that some are unbalanced enough to go nova. This is what we believe is happening in Sector 34.9.

However, while that is the cause of the novas, we have absolutely no solution to suggest. The forces that are causing this fault are on the galactic level, a strength vastly greater than any counter-force the Federation could imagine. This Special Task Force recommends evacuation of the whole sector. We do not yet know how to predict which stars will succumb to the galactic compression pressures, so the whole sector must be considered an extremely dangerous region. Sector warnings should be posted immediately; another star may go nova while this is being read, and right now, there is nothing we can do about this galactic peril except avoid it.

TRANSPORTER THEORY HAS INITIAL BREAKTHROUGH

2135

DENEVA RESEARCH STATION
JANET HESTER, RESEARCH TEAM COORDINATOR

Science Log:

—Preliminary Summary of Deneva Research Team #4—

Exploring the possibilities of molecular reintegration, this research team wishes to report significant results with experiments involving single-cell protozoa.

Through the use of complex computer analysis and the latest advances in Abramson's transtator physics and warp-assisted energy transmission, this team had previously been able to structurally disintegrate a small inanimate object, transmit its encoded sequence signal through space (2.5 meters so far) and recombine the object with excellent molecular integrity. Just recently, however, we have had our first breakthrough with the transmission of organic life. A single-cell protozoa has been transported through space and survived, though all attempts at higher organisms have been consistent failures so far.

But the implications of these experiments are immense. If this transport system can be perfected, and life forms can also be transported, then ship-to-ship, surface-orbit, perhaps even interplanetary travel would be revolutionized. Men and materials would be able to beam down to a planet and back, wherever they chose, at the speed of light. Conclusion: Preliminary results very encouraging. This research team will petition the Deneva Science Review Board to allow the expansion of these experiments to include more complex lifeforms. No theoretical or practical objection to the transport of animate life is valid any longer. All experiments will of course proceed following the most conservative protocol through the evolutionary scale, if the results so warrant.

HARDING RICHARDSON, M.D.
CHIEF MEDICAL OFFICER

Medical Log:

I have just read the preliminary report of Research Team #4, and I feel it is my sacred obligation as a Doctor of Medicine to register my adamant opposition to their request to experiment on complex lifeforms.

I have been a practicing physician for forty-six solar years in every quadrant of the galaxy, and the one thing I can safely say I've learned is that science will never explain the nature of life. This research team sees no objection to dabbling with higher life, when they themselves admit imperfections in the replication mechanics. It doesn't take an old sawbones like myself to see the weakness in their argument, and I trust the Science Review Board will see the same.

Centuries of effort haven't been able to fit the soul of man into an equation. There are limits to progress, and for one, think we've gone far enough with this whole transporter nonsense. Man will never be transported.

UFP AND ROMULAN EMPIRE TENSE OVER INTERPLANETARY WAR
Conflict in Neutral Zone causes concern
2138

USS ALERT, CASTOR CLASS
LIAM O'NEILL, ADMIRAL

Admiral's Log:

We know the Romulans are out there. They know we're here. And I'm fairly sure they won't start anything. Our long-range sensors show six Romulan craft to our fleet of ten cruisers and destroyers, and those numbers aren't going to encourage them to cross the Neutral Zone. No, they're just sitting on their side, watching. And waiting.

Blast these stupid little wars. The third planet in Beta Cersus has claimed the fourth as its sovereign territory. The fifth planet insists it belongs to them. The fourth planet happens to be a lifeless, resource-barren rock, but no matter. It's enough to fight over, so fight they will. Just this stardate, our long-range sensors have picked up a "major" battle in which each side lost three ships. For a worthless chunk of matter.

Now, I frankly wouldn't care if these imbeciles wiped each other out; it would reduce the number of warring worlds by two as far as I'm concerned. But unfortunately, Beta Cersus is smack in the middle of the Romulan-Federation Neutral Zone, and I know the Romulans are just itching for any pretext to start a real war. Their vulture ships are just biding their time over there, waiting for any excuse to cry foul and start shooting.

But it won't happen as long as I'm in charge of this sector's security. At the start of this interplanetary war, I called the opposing commanders together and read them the Riot Act. You want to kill each other? Fine, I told them, the Prime Directive says you're free to. But outside your star system is neutral territory, and there will be *No* hostilities in that region. None. If you want to fight, I told them, keep it in your own home.

And they have. They're blasting away at each other within the neat limits I spelled out to them. And the Romulans haven't made any move to step in and help one side or another. They better not, either. Violation of the Neutral Zone is classified as an act of war, and I will respond accordingly. There will be no more *Patton* ambushes. We're ready for the Romulans.

INTELLIGENT FLYING CREATURES FOUND ON ALPHA VIRGINIS
2141

USS ICARUS II, PLACIDO CLASS
JAN OONLARGER, CAPTAIN

Captain's Log:

I'm entering in the log, an Official Notification of a New Lifeform Encounter. In the Alpha Virginis System, we've met an evolved and very intelligent species who call themselves Canaris. And they are, as far as I know, the first instance of a planet's dominant lifeform being winged humanoids.

In fact, our meeting with the Canaris took place in the air. The sensor scan of the planet registered some odd shifting lifeform readings, so a shuttlecraft was dispatched to the surface for closer investigation. Before we made it to the surface, however, we were met by a full hundred flying creatures who encircled the hovering craft. It seems the Canaris had mistaken the ship for some type of alien flying creature and had come to welcome it to their world. It took quite some sign language to convince them that we gravity-shackled, wingless humans were in fact the living masters of the shuttlecraft, for there are no evolved lifeforms found on the seismically shifting Alpha Virginis II's surface. Once the misunderstanding was cleared up, the Canaris extended their friendship to us and the UFP.

JOSE FREITAG, M.D., MEDICAL OFFICER

Medical Log:

The Canaris species is an anomaly among the advanced lifeforms encountered thus far in the galaxy. They are intelligent, flying humanoids and the most evolved species on their planet. Their head and torso resemble humans, the latter being thickly feathered. Also, their eyes are not sunk into the cranial cavity but extend out from the face to provide better peripheral vision. About where the human shoulder blades are located, the Canaris have astounding wing structures, accordion-closing struts connected by a translucent membrane of featherless skin. There are no developed legs to speak of, simply a pair of claws extending from the bottom of the trunk. Their long arms also terminate in sharp, tree-grabbing claws.

The evolution of the Canaris seems plausible considering their planet's light gravity and thick atmosphere. Nesting in the high tree tops, this species does not have any great natural enemies and consequently have no innate fear response. The Canaris have developed an extremely expressive language and interpersonal culture, and they exhibit all the "human" emotions of love, gratitude, compassion and kindness, without the negative counterparts of hate, aggression, or scorn of indifference. The Canaris are truly a race at peace with themselves.

INTERSTELLAR SPACESHIP'S BIG SUCCESS
Monthly service to Federation planets booked full.

2144

USS KING CHARLES, STELLARFORD CLASS
FARNSWORTH DILLINGHAM, CORRESPONDENT

Personal Log:

This stardate finds your roving reporter enjoying the pampered life aboard the luxury starliner USS *King Charles,* courtesy of my editor's expense account. Since every credit spent boils his Scottish blood, I have spared myself no extravagance offered on the maiden voyage of this elegant interstellar ship, reputed to be the finest in the Federation, to Andor, nearly a solar year away.

Not that the *King Charles* is overwhelming in its opulence. It's still a spaceship, and like all spaceships to date, hasn't completely solved the problem of artificial gravity and environment. Try as they might to freshen the air with odor-eating microbes and space scents, it still tastes like the canned air it is. And the ship's gravity keeps things in place, but just barely. Morning course corrections are still likely to clear desk tops and spill change out of the pockets of the unwary traveller's trousers.

One area the *King Charles* has leaped heads and tentacles above its predecessors is food. A complete kitchen, a well-stocked larder, and its own Cordon Rouge chef make dining on the *King Charles* a true gourmet experience. No freeze-dried protein packets on this cruise: it's Fettucini Alfredo znd Coq au Vin all the way. I've gained two kilograms already.

I should, of course, mention the other amenities the *King Charles* offers. There are complete recreational facilities to work off the cuising and to maintain full-gravity muscle-tone. Null-gravity squash courts, galactic-sized pool, and multi-environment sauna are all available. In addition, there are two nightclubs, with sphere-room dancing and a stock of Saurian brandy and old-fashioned Scotch whiskey this reporter has scarcely made a dent in, though not for lace of effort. Forward and rear observation decks provide stellar vistas for those curious souls who want to see where they've come from, or where they're going. For myself, I don't give a credit's worth if I never get wherever it is I'm supposed to be going. This ship is as close to heaven as I'll probably ever get.

Mr. Editor, please forward my paycredit, care of the USS *King Charles.* Till next time, or as they would say at our Andorian destination, "Thiptho lapth."

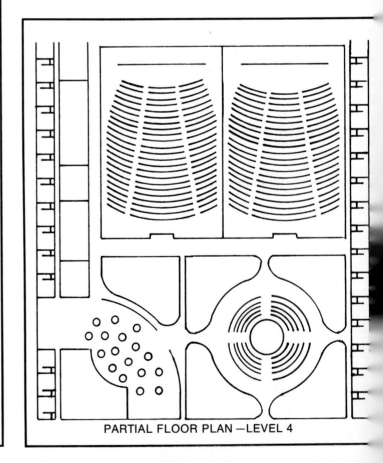

PARTIAL FLOOR PLAN —LEVEL 4

NEW TRICORDER HALTS WORST PLANET PLAGUE IN FEDERATION HISTORY

2147

USS CLARA BARTON, CASTOR CLASS
HARAS KEOLAR, M.D., MEDICAL OFFICER

Medical Log:

Thanks to the tricorder, the cause of this mysterious plague on Rigel II has been identified, and with the first shipment of serum being prepared to the tricorder's specifications, the scourge which has decimated a quarter of the planet should soon be obliterated.

I hate to think how many more Rigellians would have died before a pre-tricorder diagnosis could have been offered. There used to be rather severe limits on the research capabilities of a starship, and landing parties had it even worse. They had to make do with an only slightly updated version of the doctor's black bag. Without the tricorder, the more complex data analysis of blood samples, environmental parameters, and the like, would have had to have been transmitted via subspace radio to a research outpost for analysis and recommendations. Thousands could have died in the delay. I shudder at the idea, as anyone would who had seen just one plague victim slowly die in agony, as I have hundreds.

But these tricorders. Don't ask me how they do it, but these hand-held beauties apparently hold the whole of current Federation knowledge. They can read external and internal life signs, analyze systems malfunctioning and tissue health, and output a working diagnosis. I'm impressed. Who knows how long it would have taken me to associate this plague with Kassaba Fever; it's a strain I've never encountered and has some confusingly different symptons. The tricorder was not confused, though. Blocking serum is being manufactured aboard the *Clara Barton* and within the week, the planet plague of Rigel II will be a thing of the past.

UFP LAUNCHES 3RD GENERATION WARP SHIPS
Short lived class proves to be an "Edsel"

2148

USS TRITIUM, TRITIUM CLASS
REX OPPERMAN, CHIEF ENGINEER

Engineering Log:

What a fabulous idea! Three nacelles! A third more power than those old-fashioned ships. Greater acceleration. Faster warp engagement. Warp 4 capability. Looks great on the drawing board. A marvelous new generation of starships, ten years in the designing and making. Only one problem. They don't work.

Perhaps if they were absolutely perfect, the three-nacelle design might work, might do all the great things claimed for it. But nothing made by man is perfect, and in this case, nothing less than perfect will do. You would have thought the designers would have realized this. The symmetry of the matter/antimatter reaction and the balanced duality of the warp principle are fundamental principles of warp mechanics. Two self-adjusting nacelles have proven a very efficient engine design, the slight discrepancies between nacelle construction averaging out.

But to throw a third nacelle between the two? Instead of removing the descrepancies, the third nacelle accentuates them, its power peaks corresponding to the points of highest warp field fluctuation. As a result, the ship steers almost as bad as a Star Fleet tug. And the warp vibrations set up by the third nacelle's negative reinforcement mean this ship can't be sailed above warp 3 without practically shaking itself to pieces. The *Tritium* is a real Lemarian lemon, if there ever was one. Or to use a phrase my great-grandfather liked to describe a fiasco: this one's an Edsel.

OVERVIEW

This era continued the Pax Federationis, the Federation Peace, that had prevailed for almost half a century. But like all times, there were tragedies and atrocities to counterbalance the ever-expanding exploration and technological breakthroughs. It seems an unyielding principle that as much as mankind grows in scope and dominion, so too the dangers grow to threaten the hard-won progress.

Two dangers in particular arose to confront man during this period, one external and one internal. It was too much to expect the Romulans to be the only aggressive major power abroad in the galaxy. But even their cunning ferocity was scant preparation for the unparalleled bestiality of the Klingon Empire. Though hostilities were just barely avoided in the first confrontation with the Klingons, subsequent bloody ambushes have placed the Federation on notice that there is a deadly powerful enemy ready to conquer and pillage at the first opportunity.

The other danger sprang up in conjunction with man's bicentennial of spaceflight in 2157. This was the famous "Back-to-Earth" movement of the late twenty-second century. This surprisingly popular movement was filled with those who felt the present space expansion had gone far enough, further, they claimed, than the Earth could possibly control. This sentiment gained momentum throughout this period, finally coming to a head in the next era at the strife-torn Babel Conference of 2177.

Other crises were more quickly mastered. For instance, one of the renowned FLYING FORTRESSES, the armored starships used to transport the galaxy's most precious commodities among planets, was plundered of a new, experimental deflector prototype by the Klingons. If they had succeeded in getting clearly away, the balance of power in the galaxy might be quite different than it presently is. Luckily, the superior warp speeds of the Federation starships of that time ran down the Klingons, who were forced to jettison the deflector prototype and scramble back to the safety of their bellicose empire.

Also, the aftershock of the Phi Puma super nova that claimed the KEPLER continued to be felt, as it sent its star-jarring concussion in all directions at the speed of light. One heavily populated world, Bayard's Planet, had to be completely evacuated before its star exploded in a chain reaction nova.

Luckily, a new breakthrough in spaceflight capability had been achieved prior to the crisis. The mammoth warp superconvoys were developed to transport the vast amounts of raw materials needed for the Federation's industrial plant. Powered by linked configurations of warp tugs, these superconvoys could carry a hundred freighter containers and more at warp speeds. This capacity was stretched to the limit in the evacuation of Bayard's Planet. With an emergency refitting for life-support transport, superconvoys managed to remove ten million inhabitants from the doomed planet before it blew apart from concussive shock. Today, these superconvoys have grown even greater, with warp speeds of four an nore and the capacity to dismantle and ransport whole planets. No one can soon orget the sight of these immense super-onvoys, with their string of freighters trailng off to the vanishing point.

xploration was not neglected during this ra, though the loss of the KEPLER had parked renewed interest in the utility of nmanned probes. In fact, a whole new eries of probes, the "KEPLER Series," was onstructed to investigate the black hole henomenon, one of the most mysterious stronomical entities and the original focus f the KEPLER's tragic research effort. Telmetry readouts have provided convincing roof that these black holes distort the pace-time fabric sufficiently to create a gate" between our universe and parallel niverses. This is a subject of ongoing reearch to this stardate.

nfortunately, this era had its own starship agedy. The USS VALIANT, the second inerstellar ship to bear that name and which as likewise lost, vanished from the galaxy in e vicinity of Vendikar. Space was and still is led with unknown, deadly dangers.

nd indescribably natural wonders. The ater World of Hydra II was discovered in is time, a world completely covered by cean. And beneath the unbroken waters as found one of the pinnacles of civilized lture: the incomparably beautiful Water llet of Hydra II. Up to a thousand trained ncers swim exquisite, patterned epics of nmemorial antiquity, and to watch a per-

formance of such a timeless epic is truly an unforgettable experience.

Finally, two technological innovations took place during this era, one leading synergistically to the other. In 2171, the Earth physicist, Daystrom, introduced the revolutionary concept of duotronics into computer applications, and the already astounding potential of modern computers was multiplied a thousandfold more. With this new capability, the seemingly insurmountable technical problems that had stymied efforts to transport humans could be overcome. The transporter was perfected, man was beamed through space, and now this piece of equipment is standard on all modern starships.

Technological breakthroughs and tragedy, new enemies and new wonders, this period was filled with conflicting forces pulling it first forward with future promises and then backwards with age-old enmity. These forces would continue into the next era, producing the gravest crisis the UFP has ever faced and also producing the most advanced starships the Federation has ever known, the Constitution Class ships—the just pride of the Star Fleet.

A CONCISE LOOK AT SHIPS AND EVENTS
SPACEFLIGHT CHRONOLOGY

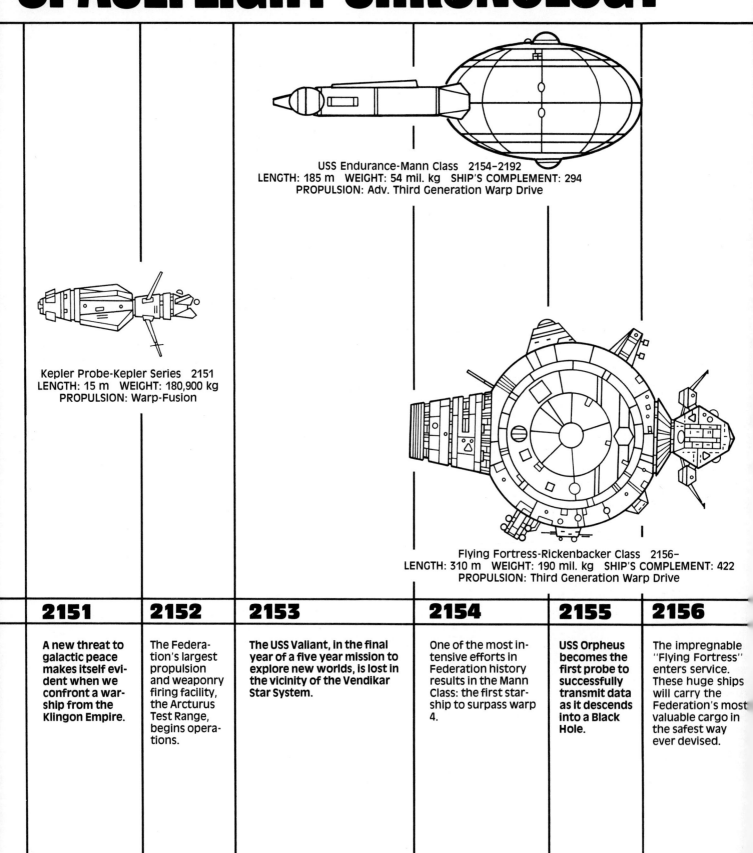

USS Endurance-Mann Class   2154–2192
LENGTH: 185 m   WEIGHT: 54 mil. kg   SHIP'S COMPLEMENT: 294
PROPULSION: Adv. Third Generation Warp Drive

Kepler Probe-Kepler Series   2151
LENGTH: 15 m   WEIGHT: 180,900 kg
PROPULSION: Warp-Fusion

Flying Fortress-Rickenbacker Class   2156–
LENGTH: 310 m   WEIGHT: 190 mil. kg   SHIP'S COMPLEMENT: 422
PROPULSION: Third Generation Warp Drive

2151	2152	2153	2154	2155	2156
A new threat to galactic peace makes itself evident when we confront a warship from the Klingon Empire.	The Federation's largest propulsion and weaponry firing facility, the Arcturus Test Range, begins operations.	The USS Valiant, in the final year of a five year mission to explore new worlds, is lost in the vicinity of the Vendikar Star System.	One of the most intensive efforts in Federation history results in the Mann Class: the first starship to surpass warp 4.	USS Orpheus becomes the first probe to successfully transmit data as it descends into a Black Hole.	The impregnable "Flying Fortress" enters service. These huge ships will carry the Federation's most valuable cargo in the safest way ever devised.

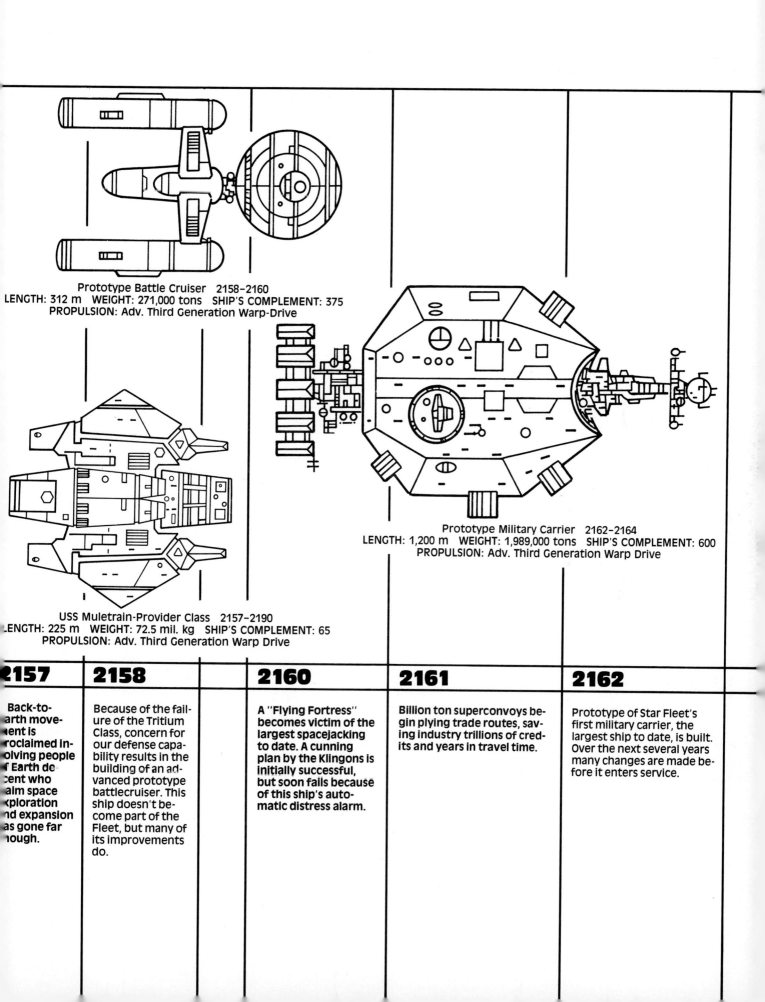

Prototype Battle Cruiser   2158–2160
LENGTH: 312 m   WEIGHT: 271,000 tons   SHIP'S COMPLEMENT: 375
PROPULSION: Adv. Third Generation Warp-Drive

USS Muletrain-Provider Class   2157–2190
LENGTH: 225 m   WEIGHT: 72.5 mil. kg   SHIP'S COMPLEMENT: 65
PROPULSION: Adv. Third Generation Warp Drive

Prototype Military Carrier   2162–2164
LENGTH: 1,200 m   WEIGHT: 1,989,000 tons   SHIP'S COMPLEMENT: 600
PROPULSION: Adv. Third Generation Warp Drive

2157	2158		2160	2161	2162
Back-to-Earth movement is proclaimed involving people of Earth descent who claim space exploration and expansion has gone far enough.	Because of the failure of the Tritium Class, concern for our defense capability results in the building of an advanced prototype battlecruiser. This ship doesn't become part of the Fleet, but many of its improvements do.		A "Flying Fortress" becomes victim of the largest spacejacking to date. A cunning plan by the Klingons is initially successful, but soon fails because of this ship's automatic distress alarm.	Billion ton superconvoys begin plying trade routes, saving industry trillions of credits and years in travel time.	Prototype of Star Fleet's first military carrier, the largest ship to date, is built. Over the next several years many changes are made before it enters service.

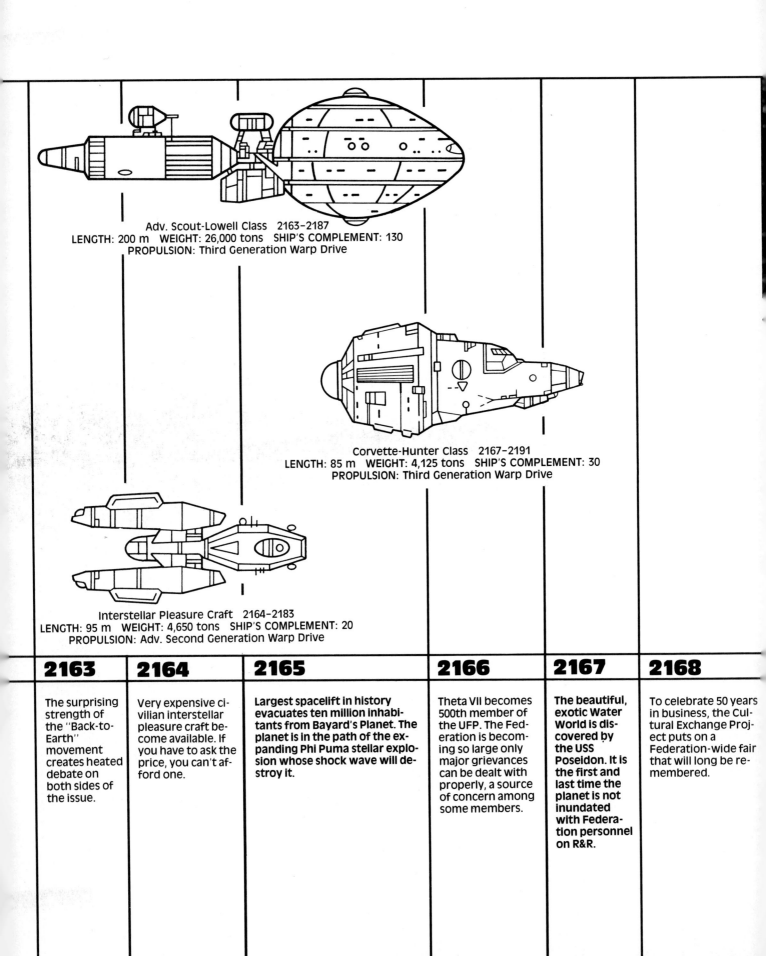

Adv. Scout-Lowell Class   2163–2187
LENGTH: 200 m   WEIGHT: 26,000 tons   SHIP'S COMPLEMENT: 130
PROPULSION: Third Generation Warp Drive

Corvette-Hunter Class   2167–2191
LENGTH: 85 m   WEIGHT: 4,125 tons   SHIP'S COMPLEMENT: 30
PROPULSION: Third Generation Warp Drive

Interstellar Pleasure Craft   2164–2183
LENGTH: 95 m   WEIGHT: 4,650 tons   SHIP'S COMPLEMENT: 20
PROPULSION: Adv. Second Generation Warp Drive

2163	2164	2165	2166	2167	2168
The surprising strength of the "Back-to-Earth" movement creates heated debate on both sides of the issue.	Very expensive civilian interstellar pleasure craft become available. If you have to ask the price, you can't afford one.	Largest spacelift in history evacuates ten million inhabitants from Bayard's Planet. The planet is in the path of the expanding Phi Puma stellar explosion whose shock wave will destroy it.	Theta VII becomes 500th member of the UFP. The Federation is becoming so large only major grievances can be dealt with properly, a source of concern among some members.	The beautiful, exotic Water World is discovered by the USS Poseidon. It is the first and last time the planet is not inundated with Federation personnel on R&R.	To celebrate 50 years in business, the Cultural Exchange Project puts on a Federation-wide fair that will long be remembered.

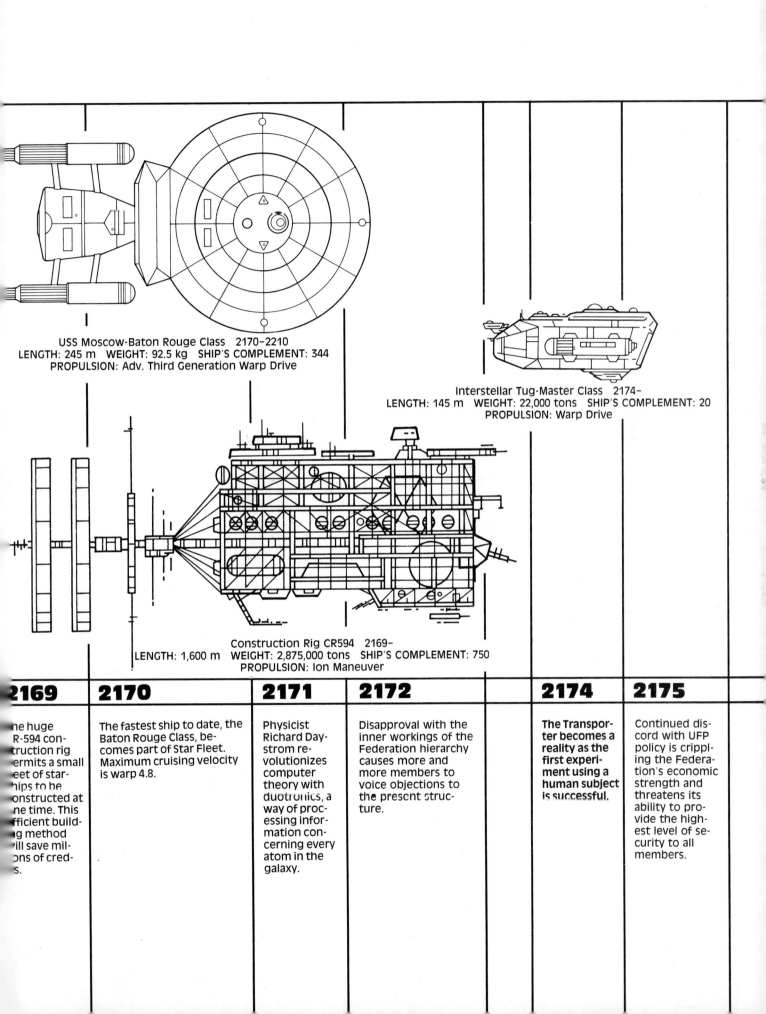

USS Moscow-Baton Rouge Class   2170–2210
LENGTH: 245 m   WEIGHT: 92.5 kg   SHIP'S COMPLEMENT: 344
PROPULSION: Adv. Third Generation Warp Drive

Interstellar Tug-Master Class   2174–
LENGTH: 145 m   WEIGHT: 22,000 tons   SHIP'S COMPLEMENT: 20
PROPULSION: Warp Drive

Construction Rig CR594   2169–
LENGTH: 1,600 m   WEIGHT: 2,875,000 tons   SHIP'S COMPLEMENT: 750
PROPULSION: Ion Maneuver

2169	2170	2171	2172		2174	2175
The huge CR-594 construction rig permits a small fleet of starships to be constructed at one time. This efficient building method will save millions of creds.	The fastest ship to date, the Baton Rouge Class, becomes part of Star Fleet. Maximum cruising velocity is warp 4.8.	Physicist Richard Daystrom revolutionizes computer theory with duotronics, a way of processing information concerning every atom in the galaxy.	Disapproval with the inner workings of the Federation hierarchy causes more and more members to voice objections to the present structure.		**The Transporter becomes a reality as the first experiment using a human subject is successful.**	Continued discord with UFP policy is crippling the Federation's economic strength and threatens its ability to provide the highest level of security to all members.

USS ENDURANCE
MANN CLASS

2154-2192

The Mann class was employed primarily for strategic purposes by Star Fleet Command, providing defense and security within the ever-growing Federation jurisdiction. Using advanced 3rd generation propulsion, these ships used pure matter/antimatter annihilation and were the first to warp. The *Endurance* supervised the largest spacelift in Federation history, where the over ten million residents of Bayard's Planet were successfully evacuated.

Specifications

Length	185 m
Beam	101.7 m
Draught	40 m
Mass:	54 million kg
Nacelles	length: 85 m
	diameter: 11.6 m
Living Ellipsoid	diameter: 101.7 m
	diameter: 40 m
Command Dome	diameter: 15.5 m
	height: 9 m

Ship's Complement

Officers — (Captain, Lieutenant, Science, Engineering, Medical (3), Navigation, Communication, Security, Ensigns (4)	14
Crew	280
Standard Ship's Complement	294

Performance

Range	Standard 1000 light-years
	Maximum 4000 light-years
Cruising Velocity	Warp 4 (64c)
Maximum Velocity	Warp 4.5 (91.1c)

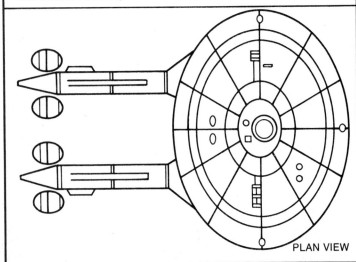

PLAN VIEW

Typical Voyage Duration	8 yrs @ st. comp.
Acceleration:	0 - .99c—3.4 min
	.99c - warp engage—1.2 min
	Warp 1 - 2—19.8 sec
	Warp 2 - 4—14.4 sec
	Warp 4 - 4.5—31.1 sec

Systems Overview

Navigation	Warp celestial guidance
Communication	Subspace Radio
Weapons	4 Laser Banks
	4 Particle Beam Cannons
	22 Photon Torpedoes
Life Support: Gravity	.2 - 1.2 g
Atmosphere	20% O_2; 11% humidity
Sustenance Duration	Up to 13.2 years if outfitted for long-duration exploration

Engineering and Science

- Engines — Advanced third generation warp drive
- Fuel — 1:1 matter to antimatter
- S.S exhaust radiator
- Turbo-lift elevator for easy on board access among decks and sections
- Intercooler fins

Improvements and Innovations

- First ship to surpass warp 4
- Equal matter to antimatter mix
- Waste heat management superior to previous class
- Omni directional antennae
- Can turn exterior hull of ship into very sensitive sensing skin for sensors
- Refitted over commissioned life to keep pace with 22nd century technological advances (transporter, duotronics, etc.)

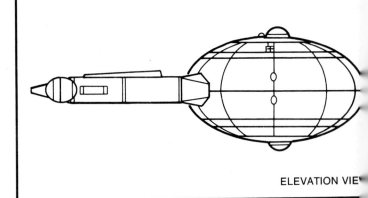

ELEVATION VIEW

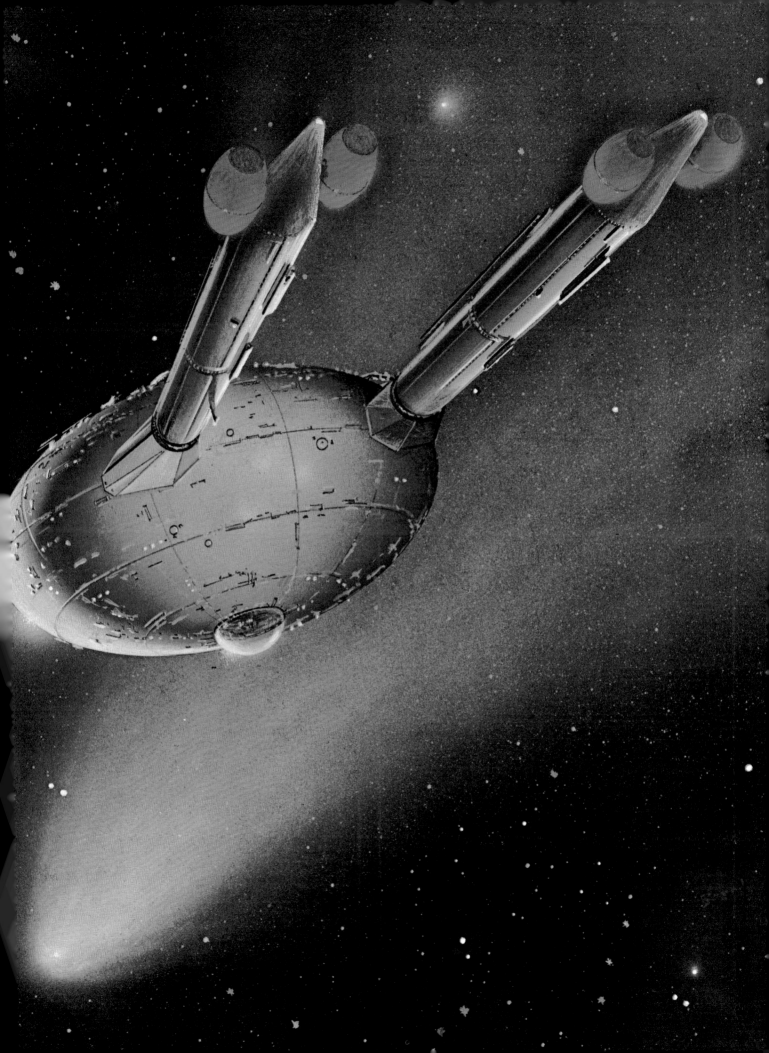

WARP 4.8 CRUISER

USS MOSCOW
BATON ROUGE CLASS — 2170-2210

The USS *Moscow* was the first ship equipped with transporter capability and the last without dilithium. The immediated predecessor to the Constitution Class, the Baton Rouge Class exhibited the distinct separated living disc and engine modules so familiar now. Uprated in the 2190's, these ships have only recently completed their commissioned usefulness as interstellar carriers.

Specifications

Length	245 m
Beam	153 m
Draught	64.6 m
Mass	92.5 million kg

Ship's Complement

Officers (Captain, Lieutenant, Science, Engineering, Medical (3), Navigation, Communication, Security, Ensigns (9))	19
Crew	325
Standard Ship's Complement	**344**

Performance

Range: Standard	1500 light-years
Maximum	5000 light-years
Cruising Velocity	Warp 4.5 (91.1c)
Maximum Velocity	Warp 4.8 (110.6c)
Typical Voyage Duration	4 yrs @ st. comp.

Systems Overview

Navigation	Warp celestial guidance
Communication	Subspace Radio
Computers	Duotronic capability (after 2171)
Weapons	4 Laser Banks 2 Particle Beam Cannons 250 Photon Torpedoes
Life Support: Gravity	.2 - 1.2 g
Atmosphere	20% O_2; 11% humidity
Sustenance Duration	Up to 16.1 years if outfitted for long-duration exploration

Engineering and Science

Engines	Advanced third generation warp drive
Fuel	1:1 matter to antimatter

- Separate living and engineering sections
- Uprated with Duotronic computers (after 2171)

Improvements and Innovations

- First ship equipped with transporters
- Modular design allows for greater engine performance

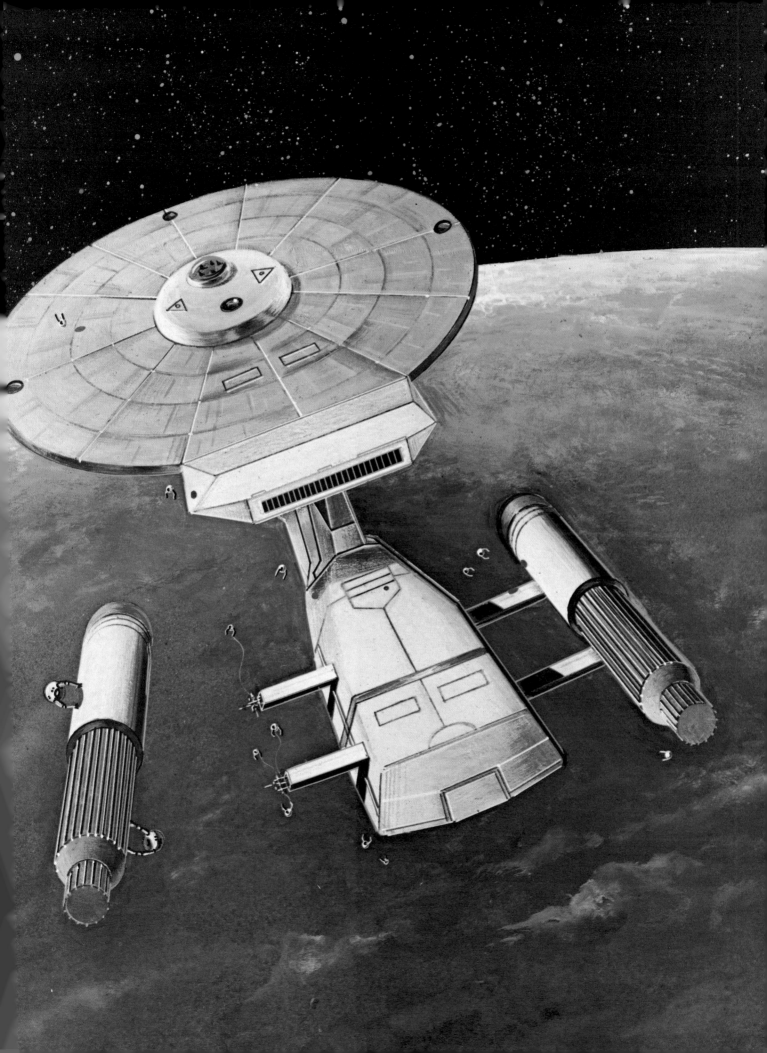

FLYING FORTRESS
RICKENBACKER CLASS   2154-

With one notorious exception, the Flying Fortresses have enjoyed a remarkably flawless security record for their precious cargoes. From multi-trillion currency shipments to classified military packages to the rarest materials in the galaxy (dilithium, Saurian brandy), these heavily armored and gunned vessels have provided safe passage throughout the Federation for decades. Even today, Flying Fortresses may be found in certain sectors of space.

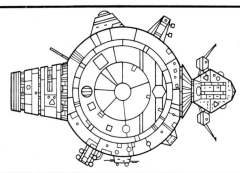

Specifications

Diameter	310 m
Draught	185.7 m
Mass	190 million kg
Command Pod	49 m x 38.8 m x 116 m (to antennae tips)
Security Saucer	195 m diameter

Ship's Complement

Officers — (Captain, Lieutenant, Engineering, Navigation, Communications, Medical, Recreation, Security Supervisor, 9 Ensigns)	17
Crew	405
Standard Ship's Complement	422

Performance

Range	2000 light-years
Cruising Velocity	Warp 4
Maximum Velocity	Warp 4.5
Engines	Advanced 3rd Generation Warp Drive
Fuel	1:1 matter to antimatter
Weaponry	Maximum circumferential Shielding (no unprotected flank) Secondary Shielding 10 laser banks (converted to phasers in 2002) 10 Energy Projectors 12 photon torpedo tubes Docking Bays for support and tender craft to keep Flying Fortress totally self-sufficient

USS MULETRAIN
PROVIDER CLASS   2157-2190

This was the lead ship for the warp superconvoys, the 100-kilometer cargo carriers that revolutionized interstellar industrial transport. Configured in 8-ship linked octogons at the head of the convoy, with 4-ship squares of booster tugs after each 10-container segment, and all controls subspace-radio synchronized, these superconvoys transported billions of kilograms per superconvoy.

Specifications

Length	225 m
Beam	220 m
Draught	45.6 m
Mass	72.5 million kg

Ship's Complement

Officers — (Captain, Lieutenant, Engineering, Navigation, Communication)	5
Crew	61
Standard Ship's Complement	66

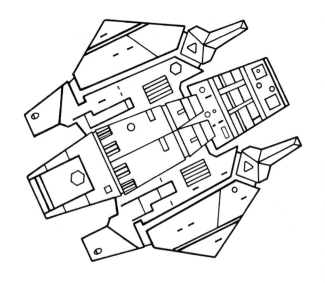

Performance

Range	2000 light-years
Cruising Speed	Empty - Warp 3.5 Loaded - Warp 2
Engines	Advanced 3rd Generation Warp Drive
Fuel	1:1 matter to antimatter
Tractor Beam coupling for cargo containers	
Most powerful thrust in starship history	

STELLAR EXPLORATIONS

Hydra II

Another example of lifeform evolution in different physical environments can be found on Hydra II, the "Water World." A very advanced aquatic civilization has developed on this world that is completely enveloped by warm oceans. The affable and graceful Hydrans have produced one of the most beautiful examples of culture to be found in the galaxy: the Hydran Water Ballet, in which a thousand and more swimming performers enact hours-long ballets of exquisite complexity.

Hydra contains five planets: one habitable (H); one potential (P); three uninhabitable

	Dist. from star (×10⁸km)	Diameter (km)	Revolution (Solar days & years)	Average surface temp (°c)
II(H)	1.45	12,756	2.15 yrs	28°
III(P)	1.72	7,745	2.89 yrs	17°

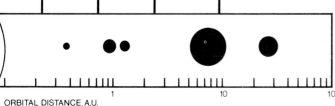

ORBITAL DISTANCE, A.U.

Warp 4+ capability opens new stellar frontiers.

As membership in the UFP continued to grow, so did the need for starships capable of spanning ever increasing distances between star systems.

The Mann Class, introduced in 2154, was the first to surpass warp 4 as it continued to expand the stellar frontiers, regularly exploring beyond Federation limits.

It was this quickness which enabled many from the class to participate in the Bayard's Planet evacuation, arriving in time from distances many lightyears beyond the capability of slower ships.

Toward the end of the era, the even quicker Baton Rouge Class debuted with an increase in range as well. But even this capability would be no match for what was about to revolutionize spaceflight; dilithium focused warp engines.

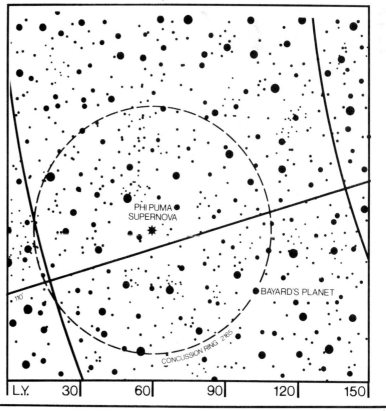

FIRST ENCOUNTER WITH KLINGON EMPIRE
Hostile alliance of worlds found beyond our frontier.

2151

USS SENTRY, ADVANCE CLASS
FRANCIS BENOIT, CAPTAIN

On the outskirts of Gamma Demetrius, the *Sentry* intercepted a distress call from a small warp shuttlecraft of unknown markings. The craft contained a family who asked for immunity from the Klingons, whom the *Sentry*'s captain had never heard of. He heard of them soon enough, as this Log records in this, the first confrontation between the Federation and the Klingon Empire.

Captain's Channel Log:

Sentry: This is the *USS Sentry*, Captain Benoit commanding. We represent the United Federation of Planets, whose territory you have entered. Please identify yourself and state your purpose.

Devisor: We want the family.

Sentry: Please identify yourself.

Devisor: Return the family or we'll blow you out of the quadrant.

Sentry: The *Sentry* is a fully equipped battlecruiser with more than enough firepower to answer any hostile act. Please identify yourself.

Devisor: This is the *Devisor*. I am Korall, Captain. The scum you are harboring are declared criminals of the Klingon Empire, and I demand their immediate delivery.

Sentry: What crime are they accused of, may I ask?

Devisor: They are enemies of the Empire. Inquire no further. I demand immediate receipt of the scum, so that their death sentence may be carried out.

Sentry: Captain Korall, you are in no position to demand anything. You are trespassing into Federation territory and you are greatly outgunned. The family we have on board have requested political asylum, and according to Star Fleet regulations, I am obligated to turn the matter over to a UFP Court for a decision whether to grant it. The Klingon Empire is of course, invited to state their side of the question before a verdict may . . .

Devisor: Verdicts, courts, asylum. What sort of weak-spined empire do you pretend to be? Justice belongs to the strong. We'll be back, to get the family, to get you, to crush your pathetic Federation. No one defies the Klingon Empire. We will destroy you utterly.

KLINGON SHUTTLECRAFT

USS VALIANT DISAPPEARS
Galactic Exploration Outreach Program now in doubt.

2153

STAR FLEET COMMAND

Star Fleet Alert:

Subspace radio contact has been lost with the United Federation of Planets Cruiser USS *Valiant*, NCC 1102.

At last report, the *Valiant* was heading at warp 3 along celestial warp coordinates 30° mark 175° mark 210°, and had entered Sector 4 of Quadrant III. The only system in the stellar vicinity is Vendikar III, which is thought to be uninhabited and an unlikely destination of the *Valiant*. Star Fleet Command believes the ship was embarked on an unknown exploratory goal further out in the sector.

The USS *Valiant* is part of the UFP's Galactic Exploration Outreach Program and was in the final year of a five-year mission to explore new worlds.

The *Valiant* has missed three consecutive reporting periods and is now officially classified as Missing in Action. All Federation ships are put on notice to be on sensor lookout for the *Valiant*, to monitor all subspace radio channels for distress signals, and to watch for hard evidence of its loss (ion trails, space flotsam, etc.).

Repeat–Star Fleet Alert–

Subspace radio contact lost with USS *Valiant*. Be on alert for starship, distress signals, or wreckage.

BLACK HOLE EXPLORED
Data indicates presence of alternate universe.

2155

USS ORPHEUS
KEPLER SERIES TELEMETRY PROBE

With the tragic loss of the *USS Kepler* in the supernova explosion of Phi Puma, the use of extremely sophisticated unmanned science probes was given a higher priority. In the case of black holes, those voids in space caused by the collapse of giant stars, these automated probes proved expedient, since any object committed to the star-swallowing gravitational field would be inexorably sucked into the hole and likewise "disappear" from our universe. The *USS Orpheus* was just such a probe, and this readout is the last received before it vanished into the black hole.

Telemetry Log:

Data Parameters:

Distance from Black Hole (BH):	1 A.U. (1.495 x 10^8 km.)
Velocity:	79,181 km./sec.
Acceleration due to gravitation:	2.305 x 10 km./sec.²
Committment to BH Descent:	Irreversible

Systems Report:

All warp engines off-line.
Warp power entirely diverted to telemetry transmission
Sensors still functional—error correction necessary for space-time deformation.

Quantitative Analysis:

Estimated Mass of BH, based on gravitational acceleration: 3.8 times Sol System sun
Estimated radius of BH, based on Field flux triangulation: 543 meters

—ATTENTION—ATTENTION—
Calibration sensors partially damaged by flux fields.
Damage Strategy: Revert to Qualitative Analysis.

Qualitative Analysis:

BH rotating on its axis at rapid rate approaching speed of light angular velocity.
BH pulsating at rate approaching speed of light: Cause Unknown. Virtual particle detector/analyzer reveals presence of particles from matter/antimatter annihilation. No source of antimatter could come from this universe. Preliminary data indicate possible presence of alternate universe gate at center of BH.
. . . . Repeating sequence

Data Parameters:

Distance from Black Hole (BH): .48 A.U. (7.176 x 10^7 km)
Velocity: 94,340 km/sec.
Acceleration due to . . . . End Readout

BACK-TO-EARTH MOVEMENT PROCLAIMED
Growing numbers throughout the galaxy want to return "home."

2157

BENECIA COLONY, TERRARETURN LEAGUE

While the expanding exploration of space continued each year with the consent of the majority of mankind, there were, inevitably, counterforces opposing this trend. The Back-to-Earth movement began with this Proclamation by the Terrareturn League, of the then relatively undeveloped Benecia Colony and spread with surprising force throughout the inhabited galaxy. This movement was a prime cause of the crisis that almost toppled the United Federation of Planets at the Babel Conference of 2177. But like all movements that lack true popular support, this eventually splintered and dissolved.

Proclamation Log:

For two hundred years mankind has been exploring space. For two hundred years we have been looking ever outward. For two hundred years we have been pretending the problems inherent in the human condition would somehow find a miraculous solution in the heavens somewhere, the next planet we find, the next galactic wonder we meet, somewhere. Anywhere but where they only can be found: in the hearts and souls of struggling, imperfect man.

Well, on this bicentennial of spaceflight, we would like to speak for millions of fellow space citizens when we cry, Enough! Enough senseless expansion. Enough running from ourselves. What purpose is served exploring new worlds when the world within ourselves yet remains a mystery? Enough, we cry. For all our sakes.

Descendents of Earth, it's time for us to return to our roots, to discover our own world. Back to Earth is our clarion call. Let us go back to a simpler time, a simpler life. For what have we found in the galaxy that we really needed, but new problems. Are not all the best things in life to be found back home?

Home. What does it mean to each of us? Is home Starbase 6, or Benecia, or a Rigel outpost? No, we may throw our lives away in distant sectors of space, but home to us all is and has always been but one place: Earth. Yet, instead of using our human potential to make Earth the strongest and most humane planet in the galaxy, we squander our irreplaceable resources on a thousand foreign worlds. This is madness. This is suicide.

Look to your own house, mankind. It needs you. Back to your roots, back to your home. Back to Earth!

SPACEJACKING OF FLYING FORTRESS BIGGEST EVER

2160

USS LEONIDES, MANN CLASS
PYOTR MIRABELLA, CAPTAIN

Captain's Log:

We have recovered the stolen booty from the greatest spacejacking in Federation history: the punctured remains of the *Flying Fortress*, over ten billion credits, and most importantly, the new deflector prototype being transported to Sector 15A for testing. The perpetrators turned out to be Klingon pirates, which should surprise no one familiar with the stories circulated about those barbaric and ferocious aliens. And if the safety of the prototype hadn't been of the highest priority, we would have continued the chase and taken the murderers prisoner before they could retreat back behind the borders of their empire.

The impregnable *Flying Fortress*, it was billed as. Totally invincible against any possible attack. For years they have coasted on their reputation, and not a single attempt had been made on their precious cargo vaults. Well, now they're 0 for 1. The Klingons figured out the one weak link in the armored ship's defenses: the humans at the helm.

I must admit their plan showed more cunning than I would have given the Klingons credit for. They established a "ship in distress" decoy that broadcast urgent appeals for assistance with seriously wounded, an old ploy that the Klingons improved on by camouflaging a Klingon spaceship as an exact replica of a Star Fleet Scoutship. The "Scoutship" then approached the *Flying Fortress*, radioing ahead that they were suspicious of the distress call and recommend the *Fortress* sail behind the "Scout," with full aft and flanking shields.

Unsuspectingly, the *Flying Fortress* fell into formation behind the "Scout." No sooner had they dropped their forward screens than a hidden Klingon laser discharged point-blank into the unprotected command module. The Klingons then boarded the perforated ship and slaughtered all hands, and ten billion credits and the top secret deflector prototype were diverted into their bloody hands. They towed the crippled *Flying Fortress* behind them and would have made safely away were it not for the automatic distress alarm that sounded at Starbase 2, when the power to the alarm was severed.

At once, a Federation Piracy Strike Fleet was dispatched at emergency warp speed. We quickly picked up the ion trail and soon caught up with the towing Klingon battle cruiser. At the sight of five approaching Federation star ships, the Klingon craft released their tractor beam on the *Flying Fortress* and sped back toward the borders of their empire. Once we established the deflector prototype was in our hands, we gave up chase, as per direct orders from Star Fleet Command. I don't believe that the Klingons knew the value of their plunder, for I can't believe they would have given it up without a fierce struggle. So the secret of the prototype is safe, and the greatest spacejacking case in history has been closed.

SUPERCONVOYS OPEN NEW ERA OF TRADE
Billion ton ships are boon to industry.
2161

USS MULETRAIN, PROVIDER CLASS
ALBERTO SABELLA, CHIEF ENGINEERING OFFICER

Engineering Log:

It's working! Warp effect is being engaged, and this superconvoy is rolling! Next stop—Centauri Spaceworks.

I'll let the boys upstairs take the glory, but the truth is old greasemonkey Sabella down here in the Engine Room is who straightened this whole mess out, I must admit in all humility.

Problem: how to transport raw materials from whistle-stop asteroid belts in the boondock sectors to the space factories of the UFP? And I'm not talking a freighter or two here. I'm talking about the billions and billions of metric tonnage needed each stardate to feed the Federation's ravening industrial plant. Star Fleet is stymied.

Solution: Sabella to the rescue. It's elementary, I patiently explain, what we need are warp convoys of a hundred freighters and more. It can't be done, sneer the design baboons. No ship could produce a warp effect that great. Who said anything about one ship? I reply.

So I spelled it out for them. At the head of the convoy, assemble a configuration of heavy warp-drive tugs, say eight of them in an octagon. Lock their controls together and use the whole pile as the inertial driver. Next, string out a dozen or so of those new kilometer-long cargo cans, coupling them with tractor beams. Then—and here my brilliance staggers even my own modest self—plug in another configuration of warp tugs, four should do it, and knit the rest of the convoy with the same pattern, synchronize it all with subspace radio so that all warp engines engage simultaneously, and ride into the sky!

It can't be done, cry the designers.

An interesting conjecture, muses Star Fleet.

It can be done, admit the designers in wonderment. Maybe only warp 2 or so, but this would save years of travel time, and trillions of credits.

Trillions? asks Star Fleet. Maybe we'll consider it. They considered it, they did it, it's done.

Merely brilliant, Sabella, I say. Merely brilliant.

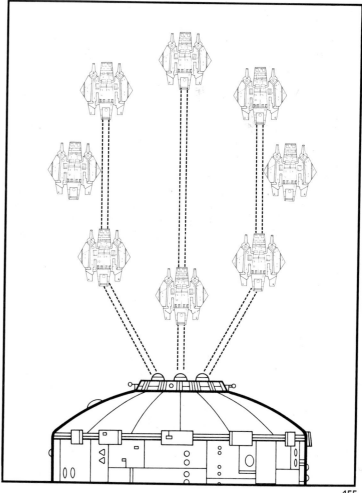

LARGEST SPACELIFT EVACUATES DOOMED PLANET

2165

USS ENDURANCE, MANN CLASS
OKURU NELSON, ADMIRAL

Admiral's Log:

Our flagship *Endurance* has run a final sensor scan of Bayard's Planet, and I can report with certainty that not a single inhabitant has been missed by this, the largest spacelift in history. None too soon either. The shock wave from the supernova explosion that destroyed the *Kepler* will reach this system's sun in less than three star-dates, and it is 100 percent probable that it will initiate a chain reaction nova.

And the nova will destroy all life in the star system. All oceans will boil away; the gamma ray bombardment will scorch the surface; the planet itself may undergo an internal disruption and blow apart. It was imperative that Bayard's Planet be evacuated. But how to evacuate ten million inhabitants? With the biggest spacelift ever.

Every starship within a fifty light-year radius was pressed into the effort by special request of the UFP. And I am just amazed by the response. Cruisers, destroyers, scoutships, corvettes, all rendezvoused. Also trading clippers, low-warp tugs, even pleasure crafts of every type all rallied to the cause.

But all these valiant volunteers twice over could not have removed ten million people in time. Then an engineer in Star Fleet Merchant Marine named Sabella came up with the novel idea of refitting those new super-convoys with life support and jury-rigged decks. And that turned the corner for us. Starbase 5 renovated two superconvoys to accommodate passengers in an amazingly short time, and after weeks of impossible logistics and unmeetable timetables, we have succeeded in evacuating the entire planet. The galaxy has never seen an operation of this scope before. And I for one fervently hope it never has to again.

WATER WORLD DISCOVERED
One of the galaxy's most beautiful planets becomes Federation haven.

2167

USS POSEIDON, MANN CLASS
STEPHAN STEPHOWSKY, RECREATION OFFICER

Recreation Log:

Our shore leave to the newly discovered Water World of Hydra II in Sector 16C, has been one of the most profoundly beautiful experiences of my life. Entirely covered by ocean, the planet itself is one of the natural wonders of the galaxy, but nothing in the unbroken vista of sea gives a hint at the wonders lying beneath.

Beneath the waves are the towering, kilometer-high underwater cities of Hydra II, seascrapers of sculpted coral connected by bridges draped in multi-colored seaweed. Among the spires swim the friendly Hydrans, who have been unfailingly hospitable to us, even inviting us to witness their most sacred social ritual, the Hydran Water Ballet.

And I'll never be the same for having seen it. Composed of a thousand and more swimming performers, the water ballet moves through graceful dances of incredible complexity, weaving hours of unrepeated patterns into an epic of exquisite beauty and power. We were overwhelmed, though the Hydrans dismissed the performance as a short piece of fluff. Some of the epics last days. I can't imagine it.

The Hydrans are eager to have more Federation visitors, and I cannot recommend this planet highly enough. Theirs is surely one of the greatest cultural achievements in the galaxy. The Hydran Water Ballet is an unforgettable experience.

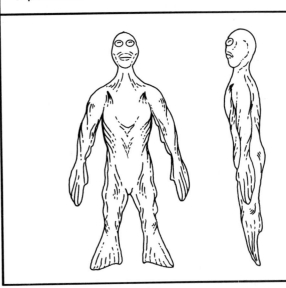

DAYSTROM INTRODUCES DUOTRONICS
Great advance in computer capability forseen

2171

STARBASE 6
DR. RICHARD DAYSTROM, RESEARCH PHYSICIST

Science Log:

I'm introducing in this Log what I believe to be a revolutionary new concept in computer theory. I have termed it duotronics and have applied to the UFP Patent Office for a Galactic Patent.

Previous computers have relied on essentially binary process: Yes/No=On/Off. No matter how sophisticated the microcircuitry, data storage has been built on pathways of Yes/No information bits. But the growth of galactic knowledge has been outstripping the capacity of standard processing; even at the speed of light there is a limit to how much can be done in a linear pathway.

I believe I've found the answer to this problem. Instead of a binary, Yes/No information bit, I propose a basic bit that is Yes or No *or* all the gradations of maybe in between these dualities. It is Yes *and* No in a calculated ratio, and the number of possible ratios is theoretically infinite, though processing materials will place a limit to the duotronic capabilities of a single bit.

But that limit is just for a single information bit. A pathway of two bits squares the number of possibilities; a three-way pathway cubes them, etc. Now a typical program may involve millions of bits in sequence. With the duotronic bit of d gradations, a million bit program would have possibilities of:

$$(d \times 10^6)^{d \times 10^6} \text{ or } (d^{d \times 10^6} \times 10^{6d}) = 10^{36!}$$

Since 10^{36} alone is a literally astronomical number, and a million-bit program relatively modest nowadays, duotronics has the eventual theoretical possibility of processing information concerning every atom in the galaxy.

Of course, duotronics would only be a mathematician's pipe dream were there no material available to realize this duotronic potential. But certain of the new generation of space-made, super-density synthetic crystals have internal structures that would be excellent duotronic conductors in the properly designed computer configuration. Such configurations, along with the mathematical theory behind duotronics, can be found in the patent application that follows as an ancillary transmission to the log. (Deleted: Ed.)

FIRST HUMAN TRANSPORTED
"Impossible" theory becomes reality.

2174

USS MOSCOW, BATON ROUGE CLASS
HENRY WINTHROP, CAPTAIN

Captain's Log:

I have been designated by Star Fleet Command as Official Observer to the Verification Test of the Transporter Demonstration Project. This project will attempt to provide conclusive evidence that the transporter can in fact discorporate a human being, beam a transmission containing his encoded molecular structure to another location, and reassemble him with absolute fidelity.

For this test, Science Officer Winslow has volunteered to act as Transporter Test Subject, and I can attest that he is presently standing on the transporter unit. As an additional control, Medical Officer, Dr. Covey, has taken an independently certified tricorder reading of Mr. Winslow's unique brain wave pattern and his vital signs. These will be correlated with a tricorder reading to be taken of Mr. Winslow when he reappears on the USS *Tehran*.

Chief Engineering Officer Chu is at the transporter console and will energize at my command. Now, Mr. Chu.

Mr. Winslow is beginning to shimmer, and flashing bits of light are replacing his fading form. With flickering intensity, these flashing lights are likewise fading. And now Mr. Winslow has entirely disappeared. I hope this works. I don't want to lose a good officer.

USS TEHRAN, BATON ROUGE CLASS
LUIGI PIRELLI, CAPTAIN

Captain's Log:

As designated Official Observer in the Transporter Demonstration Project's Verification Test, I await the expected arival of the *Moscow's* Science Officer. Dr. O'Leary is with me to take a certified tricorder reading of the transported officer.

Wait, there's something happening. A tube of glittering light has appeared in the test area center. It's assuming a man-sized contour and is becoming an opaque human being. The transmission is completed, and the Test Subject has stepped off the target. Dr. O'Leary takes his tricorder reading, and he signals to me that they correspond exactly to those taken on the *Moscow*. The Verification Test has been concluded successfully. Man has been transported.

OVERVIEW

This era closed the turbulent, expansive twenty-second century, a century that began in war and almost ended in anarchy, as outlined below. In between, hundreds of new worlds were explored, dozens of races befriended, and scientific and technological breakthroughs forever changed the shape of galactic history.

The supernova explosion of the past era that claimed the KEPLER had repercussions that extended into this period, as the shock wave of the Phi Puma cataclysm spread outward into the galaxy at the speed of light. Space sectors in the path of the expanding aftermath were issued periodic warnings, so that no more planet-wide emergency evacuations were necessary and so the affected residents could prepare for the possible destructive effects.

The century's major political crisis occurred in 2177, at the UFP's periodic Babel Conference. This turned out to be a most perilous affair, when different pressures that had been building for some time all came to a head, almost bringing about the dissolution of the Federation. One such tension was the swelling ''Back-to-Earth'' movement, filled with those who called for a halt in space expansion and a return to an Earth-centered society. Another came from Federation members who resented the UFP's authority and called for a severe curtailing of its powers and responsibilities. Conversely, the weaker member planets clamored for more defense, insisting the Federation's protection still left them prey to all sorts of space marauders.

All of these pressures blew up at Babel after a tragic (and to this stardate, unsolved) act of violence. On his way to the Conference, the Chief of Staff of Star Fleet Command was assassinated. Amid the gloom following this brutal event, recriminations, threats, and non-negotiable demands flew across the conference table. And at the height of the acrimony, a resolution was introduced to dissolve the United Federation of Planets. It was the darkest stardate in Federation history.

This crisis was averted largely through the skillful and unflagging efforts of two men, one military and one civilian. The military man was Admiral Shepherd, who ascended to Star Fleet Command to fill the tragic vacancy. He outlined a revised plan for Federation defense which increased Star Fleet patrols in sensitive sectors and provided suitable guarantees for galactic security without being overly intrusive in planetary affairs.

The civilian was the famous businessman and philanthropist, Carter Winston, then a young man in the first bloom of personal success. He spoke with great eloquence about the promise and potential of space, about how individuals exercising their initiative and own genius could still control their destiny. He also argued for greater planetary and individual input into Federation affairs. The galaxy's future, Winston declared, would be decided by the people, not governments. The resolutions he drafted and got adopted by this Babel Conference are largely responsible for the continuing openness and freedom that characterized the UFP.

n an historical irony, this whole political crisis took place while the most ambitious starships ever, the Constitution Class, were being designed. Utilizing the most recent advances in technology, such as duotronic computers and the transporter, these interstellar starships have become the vanguard of Federation security and exploration.

major innovation that occurred in this era was also included in the design of these Constitution Class starships. This, of course, was the discovery of dilithium's potential, accidentally discovered by a young mining engineer. Dilithium crystals align the matter/antimatter energy release along a coherent cylinder of flow, enabling warp engines to operate at twice their previous efficiencies. By now, dilithium crystals are an absolutely vital component for warp drive, deflectors and the maintenance of ships' energy production.

Constitution Class starships were initially equipped with advanced laser weaponry. On-going research and development made available, just before the century's conclusion, a new form of weaponry known as phasers. Combining the principles of particle-beam and laser weaponry, this new instrument has been used for hand guns as well as ship-sized phaser systems. All ships in this class were refitted to accommodate this advancement.

These amazing new starships extended mankind's exploration of space further than had even been dreamed of a few decades before. Along the way, new astronomical mysteries were opened up, such as the time gate stumbled through by the USS WELLS. The transition through this still unexplained hole in time nearly destroyed the ship, which managed to just limp home after a three solar-year journey, only to find it had been gone a mere month. Expansion had truly frightening consequences, like the encounter with the Talos Star System, which until recently, was declared off-limits to all Federation members on penalty of death. There were also incredible encounters with new races. However, like most forward steps, this new generation suffered a tragic step back. The dilithium equipped USS AJAX inexplicably blew apart, its disintegrated remains forming the mini-comet that bears its name.

Another space catastrophe was narrowly avoided with the rescue of the six hundred marooned passengers aboard a starliner that had been lost for twenty stardates. Through the sacrifice of its captain, who blew up the starliner to provide a traceable sign to searchers, all but five aboard were safely recovered having suffered with little more than minor cases of protein and vitamin deficiencies, and of course the psychological trauma of extended life-threatening anxiety. It was the largest deep-space rescue in history.

With the Babel Conference resolved and the Constitution class starships launched, the twenty-second century ended on a note of optimism and forward momentum. Mankind and his galactic peers were ready to face the challenges of the twenty-third century, stronger and more confident than ever before in history.

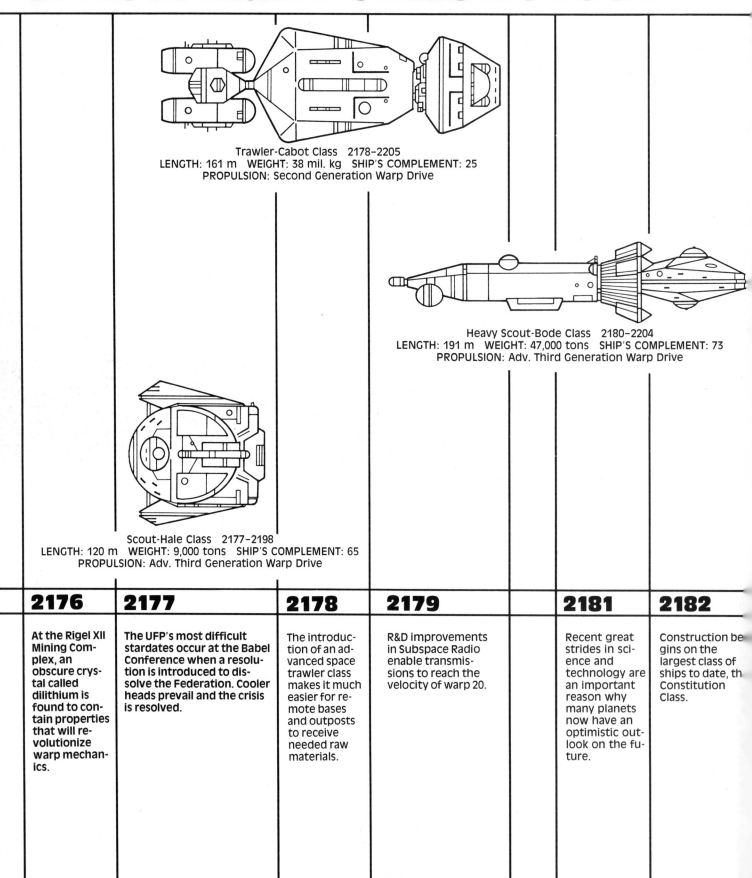

Trawler-Cabot Class   2178–2205
LENGTH: 161 m   WEIGHT: 38 mil. kg   SHIP'S COMPLEMENT: 25
PROPULSION: Second Generation Warp Drive

Heavy Scout-Bode Class   2180–2204
LENGTH: 191 m   WEIGHT: 47,000 tons   SHIP'S COMPLEMENT: 73
PROPULSION: Adv. Third Generation Warp Drive

Scout-Hale Class   2177–2198
LENGTH: 120 m   WEIGHT: 9,000 tons   SHIP'S COMPLEMENT: 65
PROPULSION: Adv. Third Generation Warp Drive

2176	2177	2178	2179		2181	2182
At the Rigel XII Mining Complex, an obscure crystal called dilithium is found to contain properties that will revolutionize warp mechanics.	The UFP's most difficult stardates occur at the Babel Conference when a resolution is introduced to dissolve the Federation. Cooler heads prevail and the crisis is resolved.	The introduction of an advanced space trawler class makes it much easier for remote bases and outposts to receive needed raw materials.	R&D improvements in Subspace Radio enable transmissions to reach the velocity of warp 20.		Recent great strides in science and technology are an important reason why many planets now have an optimistic outlook on the future.	Construction begins on the largest class of ships to date, th Constitution Class.

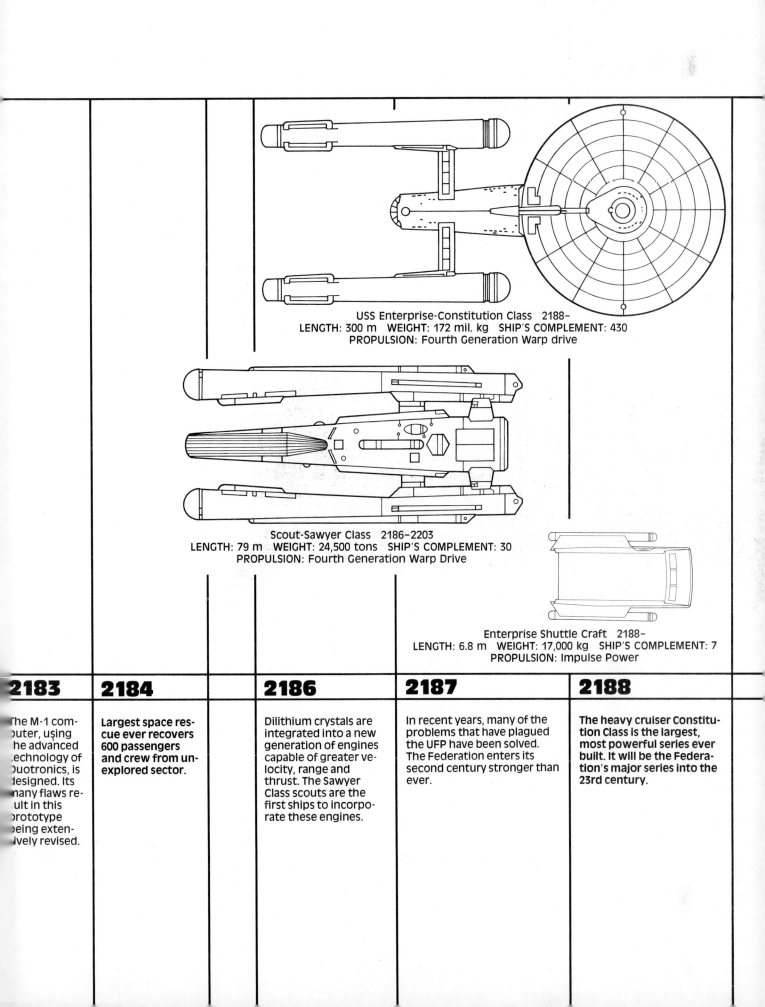

USS Enterprise-Constitution Class 2188–
LENGTH: 300 m WEIGHT: 172 mil. kg SHIP'S COMPLEMENT: 430
PROPULSION: Fourth Generation Warp drive

Scout-Sawyer Class 2186–2203
LENGTH: 79 m WEIGHT: 24,500 tons SHIP'S COMPLEMENT: 30
PROPULSION: Fourth Generation Warp Drive

Enterprise Shuttle Craft 2188–
LENGTH: 6.8 m WEIGHT: 17,000 kg SHIP'S COMPLEMENT: 7
PROPULSION: Impulse Power

2183	2184		2186	2187	2188
The M-1 computer, using the advanced technology of Duotronics, is designed. Its many flaws result in this prototype being extensively revised.	Largest space rescue ever recovers 600 passengers and crew from unexplored sector.		Dilithium crystals are integrated into a new generation of engines capable of greater velocity, range and thrust. The Sawyer Class scouts are the first ships to incorporate these engines.	In recent years, many of the problems that have plagued the UFP have been solved. The Federation enters its second century stronger than ever.	The heavy cruiser Constitution Class is the largest, most powerful series ever built. It will be the Federation's major series into the 23rd century.

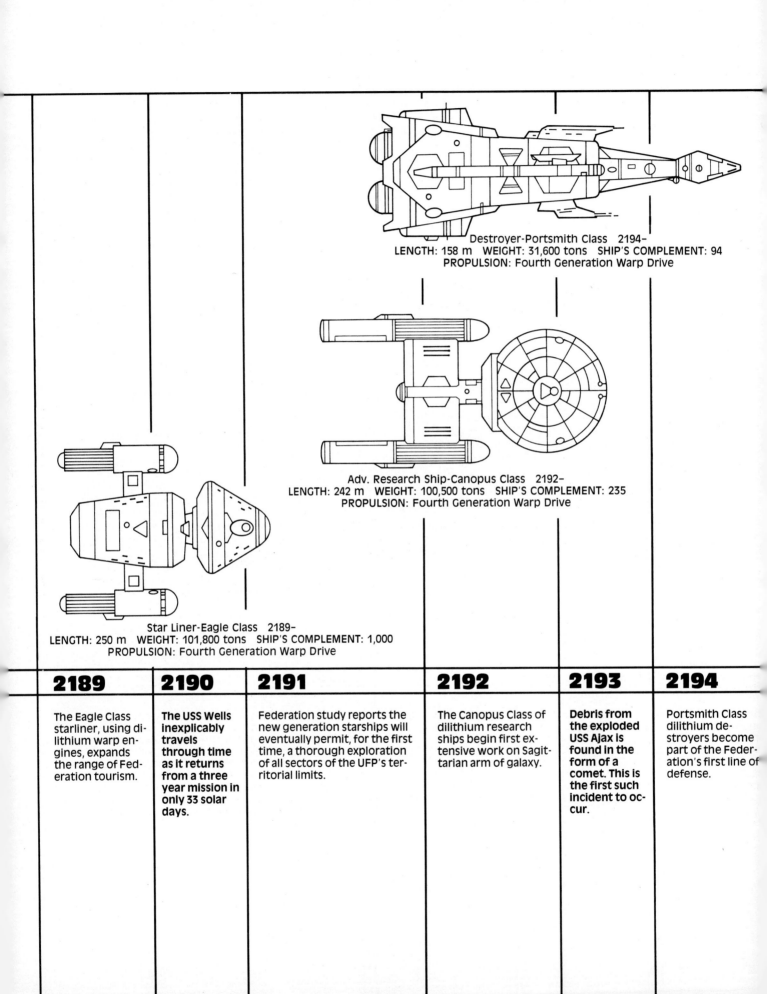

Destroyer-Portsmith Class   2194–
LENGTH: 158 m   WEIGHT: 31,600 tons   SHIP'S COMPLEMENT: 94
PROPULSION: Fourth Generation Warp Drive

Adv. Research Ship-Canopus Class   2192–
LENGTH: 242 m   WEIGHT: 100,500 tons   SHIP'S COMPLEMENT: 235
PROPULSION: Fourth Generation Warp Drive

Star Liner-Eagle Class   2189–
LENGTH: 250 m   WEIGHT: 101,800 tons   SHIP'S COMPLEMENT: 1,000
PROPULSION: Fourth Generation Warp Drive

2189	**2190**	**2191**	**2192**	**2193**	**2194**
The Eagle Class starliner, using dilithium warp engines, expands the range of Federation tourism.	**The USS Wells inexplicably travels through time as it returns from a three year mission in only 33 solar days.**	Federation study reports the new generation starships will eventually permit, for the first time, a thorough exploration of all sectors of the UFP's territorial limits.	The Canopus Class of dilithium research ships begin first extensive work on Sagittarian arm of galaxy.	**Debris from the exploded USS Ajax is found in the form of a comet. This is the first such incident to occur.**	Portsmith Class dilithium destroyers become part of the Federation's first line of defense.

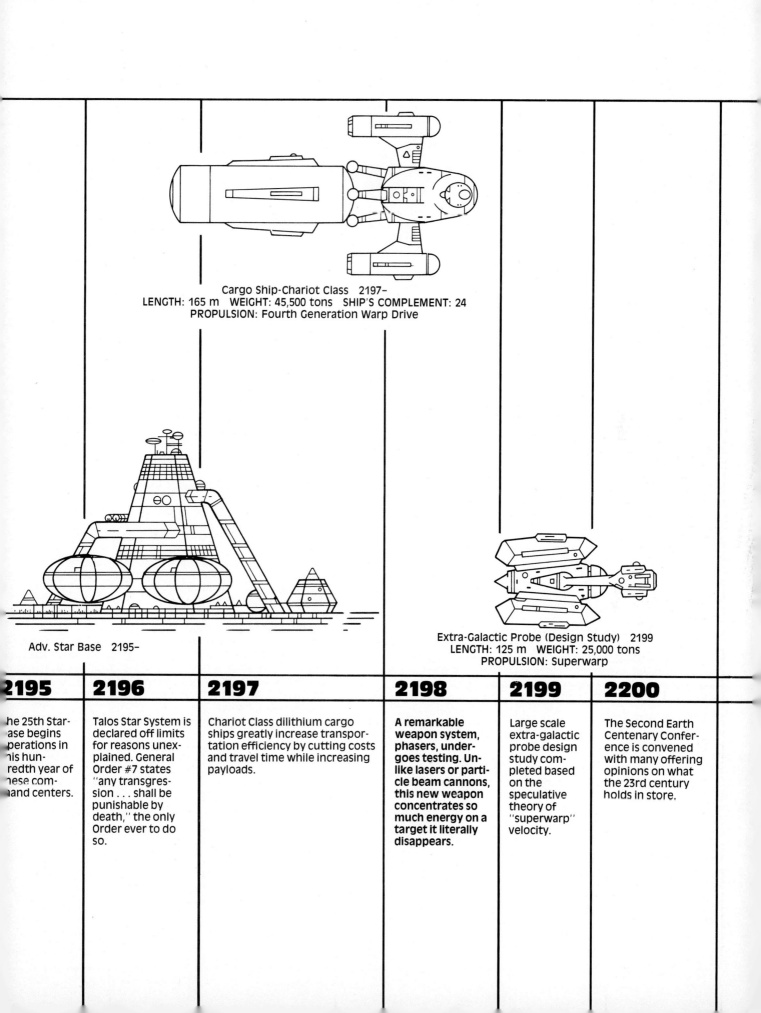

Cargo Ship-Chariot Class   2197–
LENGTH: 165 m   WEIGHT: 45,500 tons   SHIP'S COMPLEMENT: 24
PROPULSION: Fourth Generation Warp Drive

Adv. Star Base   2195–

Extra-Galactic Probe (Design Study)   2199
LENGTH: 125 m   WEIGHT: 25,000 tons
PROPULSION: Superwarp

2195	2196	2197	2198	2199	2200
he 25th Star- ase begins perations in his hun- redth year of ese com- and centers.	Talos Star System is declared off limits for reasons unex- plained. General Order #7 states "any transgres- sion . . . shall be punishable by death," the only Order ever to do so.	Chariot Class dilithium cargo ships greatly increase transpor- tation efficiency by cutting costs and travel time while increasing payloads.	A remarkable weapon system, phasers, under- goes testing. Un- like lasers or parti- cle beam cannons, this new weapon concentrates so much energy on a target it literally disappears.	Large scale extra-galactic probe design study com- pleted based on the speculative theory of "superwarp" velocity.	The Second Earth Centenary Confer- ence is convened with many offering opinions on what the 23rd century holds in store.

USS ENTERPRISE CONSTITUTION CLASS

2188-

The flagships of the UFP's exploration program, the famous *Enterprise* has been involved in the discovery of many new worlds and lifeforms. Integrating all the technological advances of the late 22nd century (dilithium, duotronics, transporter, etc.), these fourth generation warp starships have additionally provided strategic reinforcement for Federation defense. Recently the *Enterprise* was significantly refitted for a mission of supreme importance to the galaxy.

Specifications

Length	300 m
Beam	127.1 m
Draught	72.6 m
Mass	172 million kg
Engineering Section	length 103.6 m
	diameter: 34.1 m
Command/Living Saucer	diameter: 127.1 m
	draught: 32.3 m
Nacelles	length 153.6 m
	diameter: 17.3 m

Ship's complement

Officers	43
Crew	387
Standard Ship's Complement	430

Performance

Range: Standard	5000 light-years
Maximum	7500 light-years
Cruising Velocity	Warp 6 (216c)
Maximum Velocity	Warp 8 (512c)

Typical Voyage Duration	5 yrs @ st comp.
Acceleration	0 - .99c—35 sec
	.99c - warp engage—4.5 sec
	Warp 1 - 3—3.5 sec
	Warp 3 - 6—2.75 sec
	Warp 6 - 8—5.6 sec

Systems Overview

Navigation	Warp celestial guidance
Communication	Subspace Radio
Computers	Duotronic
Weapons	3 Laser Banks (uprated to Phaser in 2200)
	400 Photon Torpedoes
Life Support: Gravity	.2 - 1.2 g
Atmosphere	20% O_2; 11% humidity
Sustenance Duration	Up to 20 years if outfitted for long-duration exploration

Engineering and Science

- Engines —————— Fourth generation warp drive
- Fuel: Dilithium Focus, 1:1 matter to antimatter
- On board Duotronic computer memory stored galaxy's knowledge
- Transporter for ship/surface and ship/ship transfer
- Dilithium focus matter/antimatter warp drive
- Separate living, command, engineering and nacelles for very efficient warp drive

Improvements and Innovations

- Constitution Class ships contain all recent advances in
- Federation technology: Duotronic computers, transporter, dilithium focus warp drive, phasers, improved shielding, miniature Tricorders, advanced hull design, turbo lifts

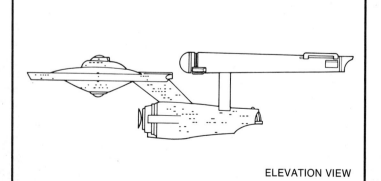

ELEVATION VIEW

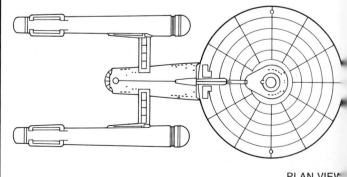

PLAN VIEW

TRAWLER CABOT CLASS 2178-2205

This trawler functioned as a portable refinery, traveling among remote star systems and bases to process a wide range of raw materials, from ore to oil, diamonds to dilithium. With low-warp capability and itineraries extending to the furthest reaches of the known galaxy, the crews of these trawlers would not see home for up to a decade at a time.

Specifications

Length	161 m
Beam	67.3 m
Draught	43.5 m
Mass	38 million kg
Command/Living Section	46 m x 36.7 m x 20.4 m
Refining Section	70.4 m x 49 m x 40 m
Side Shuttle Bays	27.5 m x 10 m diameter
Engine Nacelles	46 m x 12.4 m diameter

Ship's Complement

Officers	(Captain, Lieutenant, Engineering)	3
Crew		22
	Standard Ship's Complement	25

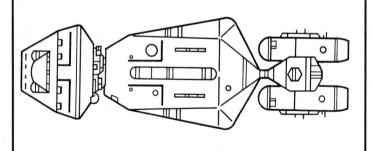

Performance

Range	Up to 1500 light-years
Cruising Velocity	Warp 3.5 Empty
	Warp 2.5 Loaded
Engines	Advanced 3rd Generation
	Warp Drive
Fuel	1:1 matter to antimatter
Sample Refining Capability	oil distillation
	condritic separation
	Antimatter extraction
	Dilithium refining
	Atmospheric purification

ENTERPRISE SHUTTLECRAFT 2188-

At least two of these intra-solar craft are carried in the Enterprises's Shuttlecraft bay. With a seven-person capacity, these useful vessels can be employed for both exterior repair work and for excursions beyond standard transportation range. This Shuttlecraft design represents a great improvement in life support capabilities over previous series, and they are still being ordered and manufactured.

Specifications

Length	6.8 m
Beam	4.1 m
Draught	2.3 m
Mass	17,000 kg
Propulsion nacelles	Length: 5.1 m
	Diameter: 0.4 m
Life Support Interior	4.5 x 2.2 m x 1.4 m
Passenger Capacity	7

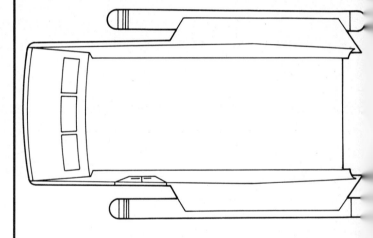

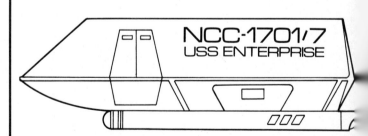

Performance

Range	Interplanetary
Landing/Takeoff Velocity	300 knots
Atmosphere Cruising Velocity	Mach 12 (14,200 km/hr)
Interplanetary Cruising Velocity	350 million km/h
Engines	Advanced Impulse Power

STELLAR EXPLORATIONS

Talos IV

Talos IV is one of the eleven planets in the Talos Star Group. A binary star, Talos has but one planet which is inhabited and until recently declared off-limits by General Order #7, a proscription so unequivocal its breach called for the death penalty. The Talosians, a genetically weakened race with extremely strong psionic powers of suggestion unscrupulously sought more vigorous species to use as breeding stock to maintain their world.

Talos contains eleven planets: one habitable; ten un-inhabitable

	Dist. from star (×10⁸km)	Diameter (km)	Revolution (Solar days & years)	Average surface temp (°c)
IV	1.29	10,974	295 d	35°

ORBITAL DISTANCE, A.U.

The impact of dilithium.

Today, many still vividly remember the revolution that occured when dilithium crystals were integrated into warp engines. Within a few years velocity and range doubled! And just as fast, pre-dilithium ships were dated, creating a small mutiny among Star Fleet crews that were assigned to these much slower, less spaceworthy vessels.

In the following decade, though, ships of every description were built with the new engines, as exploration, tourism and trade took a tremendous leap forward toward the thriving, galactic community we live in today.

EXPLORATION ROUTES –·–·–·–·–·–

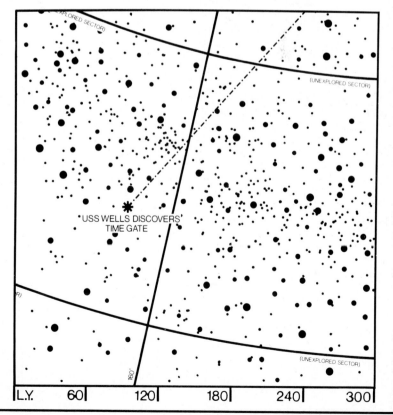

"USS WELLS DISCOVERS" TIME GATE

(UNEXPLORED SECTOR)

DILITHIUM PROPERTIES DISCOVERED
Obscure crystal is potentially tremendous energy source.

2176

RIGEL XII MINING COMPLEX
WENDELL HERZOG, GEOPHYSICIST

Science Log:

I am entering into the Log, for validation and follow-up by Federation societies, a discovery that I believe will revolutionize warp mechanics: dilithium crystals.

Until now, there's been a seemingly unbreachable limit to the amount of warp drive to be attained from matter/antimatter annihilation. No matter how efficient the mixing, how clean the waste products, a maximum of about 4.8 warp was all that could be coaxed out of the process. No longer. If my calculations are valid, then warps of 8 or 9, or perhaps even higher, may soon be within the reach of spaceflight technology.

What I've discovered, after extensive research, are some unique properties of dilithium, an obscure crystal till now known only for its use in jewelry. While experimenting with antimatter in my laboratory, I noticed the dilithium in my bracelet begin to glow softly, apparently absorbing some radiation from the process. Fascinated, I removed the crystal from the bracelet and began subjecting it to a wide array of physical and chemical tests. I quickly discovered that dilithium is what the jewelrymakers claim, the hardest and most rigid material known. But it was when I placed the crystal in close proximity to a partially shielded matter/antimatter reaction that I observed a startling effect. When I increased the exposure, to what turns out to be dilithium's critical discharge threshold, the crystal emitted an energy beam from one facet that bored through the thick steel workbench, the floor, and as I measured later, twelve meters of surface rock.

Subsequent experiments have shown that the reddish-gold octahedron acts as a storage conduit and focus for the matter/antimatter reaction. The crystal aligns the random radiation along a coherent cylinder of energy that doubles the efficiency of the process. Incorporated into warp engines, velocities previously thought impossible can be attained, and I fully expect dilithium crystals will be an integral, even vital, component in the starships of the future. It is an amazing substance.

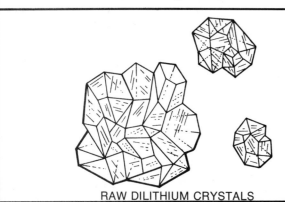

RAW DILITHIUM CRYSTALS

CRISIS AT BABEL RESOLVED
Members reject resolution to dissolve UFP.

2177

BABEL INTERPLANETARY CONFERENCE
ADMIRAL SHEPHERD, CHIEF, STAR FLEET COMMAND

Conference Log:

There have been many objections raised at this Conference about the UFP's present functioning and future utility. About the latter, I have little to contribute. Of the present functioning, however, I can speak with some authority. With your permission, I would like to demonstrate the responsiveness and vigor of Star Fleet.

Complaints have been voiced about unnecessary intrusion into a star system's space. In response, I am issuing new guidelines to starship commanders prohibiting entry into a friendly planet's territory without planet approval. Exceptions will be made for matters of overriding Federation security, and I believe this represents an equitable solution to this problem.

Several sectors have had the opposite complaint: not enough Star Fleet patrol. To address their needs, a revised deployment of starships will double the number of patrols and firepower available.

Star Fleet is not an unresponsive monolith, callously disregarding the needs and wishes of member planets. I will always be available for questions, reservations, suggestions and criticisms at any time. But there is no alternative to Star Fleet. I needn't remind delegates that we are surrounded by two possibly deadly enemies, the Romulans and Klingons. Star Fleet will answer their threats to Federation security, as I will answer your dictates.

CARTER WINSTON, BUSINESSMAN

I feel a little out of place at this Babel Conference. For I have no complaints at all. I've made my fortune already. So why am I here?

Well, I guess it's all this talk I've been hearing about limits, and suffocating bureaucracy, and the need to "return to our roots" and such. And I frankly don't recognize the Federation and galaxy I know anywhere in this talk. My great-grandparents were born on Earth, and I have a great fondness for the old place, but it isn't home to me any more than is Deneva, where I was raised. My home is the stars, and my success was won there, with hard, hard work, and little of this Federation interference I hear tell. The galaxy is too vast and too rich for any political body to control with such authority. Not to belittle this great organization, but I cannot ever envision the galaxy being contained within its strict oversight.

Let us hear no more about limits, when the whole galaxy beckons us outwards. Let us put down roots where we will and make that place ours. And we must remember, the United Federation is what we make it; it is ours to fashion into our best image. If we complain about the UFP, we are only complaining about ourselves.

The future is not bleak or constrained. It is filled with promise and mystery, and it can be ours for the choosing. I for one vote for the future.

SUPERNOVA AFTERMATH STILL GALACTIC HAZARD

2179

UFP CENTRAL HEALTH AUTHORITY

The Phi Puma supernova that vaporized the Kepler had repercussions that persisted for decades as the radiation concussion spread in all directions at the speed of light. While Bayard's Planet was the only world that had to be entirely evacuated, systems further away still felt strong effects from this largest stellar cataclysm in Federation history. So periodically, the UFP would issue warnings to all systems who were to experience the stellar shock in the near future and even today, certain seismically unstable systems are still alerted to the supernova's dangerous afteraffects.

Federation Health Notice:

Notice to All Planets in Sector 3.G4; Quadrant II

The effects of the Phi Puma supernova will pass through this sector in the coming solar year. All inhabited regions are hereby cautioned to:

- Monitor all solar and/or seismic upheavals very carefully. No chain reaction novas are expected in this sector, but existing structural faults are likely to be severely stressed.
- Expect disruption of electromagnetic transmission and increased sunspot activity.
- Recalibrate all programmed trajectories of all orbiting bodies to compensate for the stellar concussion.

Furthermore, on the days of peak radiation barrage, sector inhabitants are warned to:

- Remain indoors if possible. There will be alpha radiation included in the barrage, and it cannot penetrate interiors.
- Never under any circumstances look directly toward the supernova. Serious eye injury or even blindness may result.
- Suspend all magnetohydrodynamic (MHD) processes to protect equipment from damage.
- Avoid interplanetary travel. Navigational sensors will be affected unpredictably, and other ship systems will suffer similar unknowable stresses.
- Have a stock of radiation blocking doses on hand in case of accidental overexposure.

The supernova concussion is an extremely serious galactic health hazard, and every possible precaution should be taken to prepare for its arrival. Are you ready?

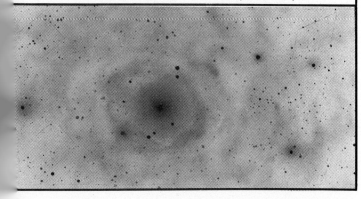

LARGEST SPACE RESCUE IN HISTORY
600 safely recovered from interstellar void

2184

USS DEERSLAYER, VOYAGER CLASS
ROGER TRAUTMANN, CAPTAIN

Captain's Log:

The greatest space rescue operation has come to a successful conclusion. After twenty stardates of unrelenting search with the combined Rescue Fleet of fifteen Federation vessels, I can finally report we've located and secured the lifeships from the Starliner *Juliana,* with all passengers and all but five crew members alive. While there has been some cases of dehydration and vitamin deficiencies, the survivors are generally in good health and spirits considering what they have gone through.

The man most responsible for our success is one of the casualties, the skipper of the *Juliana* Captain Demetrius Kovanas. We're still piecing together the specific details of the *Juliana*'s breakdown, but it appears that some unexpected local discontinuity in the warp fabric violently transported the large cruise ship to a totally unfamiliar sector of space, well off their flight itinerary. The disruption also shattered the dilithium assembly, killing all crew on the Engineering Deck and causing a rapid and complete power loss aboard ship. The order was given to abandon ship.

Captain Kovanas was obviously faced with a desperate situation. His ship was wrecked in an unknown sector of space, and he had no power to radio a distress call. How would rescuers possibly find the stranded passengers? The solution he arrived at, and for which he sacrificed his own life, was to blow up the *Juliana.* When the lifeships had gotten far enough away, the captain fabricated an explosive device within the by now lifeless hulk, believing he had enough time to safely leave the ship. The subsequent fallout of radioactive ship fragments might provide an easily located marker.

And in fact that was what happened. After the *Juliana* was late in reporting its weekly check-in, our Rescue Fleet was dispatched along the ship's flight route. We could find no trace whatsoever of the starliner, and our search spread out further and further looking for any possible clues. At last, random long-range scanning detected a smear of radioactive debris, we investigated, and soon the survivors of the largest space wreck were found.

In light of his sacrifice and dedication to the welfare of his passengers, I recommend Captain Demetrius Kovanas for the posthumous Federation Medal of Honor.

CONSTITUTION CLASS LAUNCHED
Enterprise to be flagship of
4th generation warp fleet

2188

USS ENTERPRISE, CONSTITUTION CLASS
ROBERT APRIL, CAPTAIN
Captain's Log:

As we approach Starbase 4 at the conclusion of this shakedown cruise of the *Enterprise,* I'd like to report each Officer's impressions concerning the ship's systems functioning, beginning with myself. Straight out, this is simply the best starship I have ever sailed. From my command station at the center of the bridge, I have had the pleasure of commanding the *Enterprise* through stardates of complex stress tests and emergency simulations, and the maneuverability, responsiveness and overall spaceworthiness of the vessel are staggering. Everything is better—helm handling, warp capability, shielding, phaser power, even the food. While I've let my Officers evaluate their respective systems, I think I can speak for the whole crew when I state my conviction that the *Enterprise* and its fellow Constitution Class vessels will become the cutting edge of a great leap forward in galactic security and exploration.

CHARLES FOURRIER, CHIEF ENGINEERING OFFICER
Engineering Log:

Since the engineering on the *Enterprise* differs from all previous starships on account of the integration of dilithium into the warp engines, I cannot make substantive comparisons with older systems. It is safe to say, however, that the *Enterprise*'s engineering is vastly superior to any predecessor's. The dilithium convertor assembly allows for cruising speeds of up to warp 6, and stress tests have achieved warp 8.5 without serious breakdown, though a flow sensor did malfunction at that speed. The two-nacelle design delivers symmetrical matter/antimatter field flux, and the warp engagement delay and warp acceleration are substantially better than I've ever known. In disaster simulation, the auxiliary impulse unit delivered as much lifesaving power and sub-warp maneuverability as I could expect. In sum, the *Enterprise*'s engines are better designed, stronger and faster than any previous starship in Federation history. They are beautiful.

KAREN VAN FLEET, COMMUNICATIONS OFFICER
Communications Log:

Communications on board the *Enterprise* is excellent. Subspace radio transmission of warp 30 is now possible, due to the increased warp power designated for communications. Telemetry encoding has been flawless; even communications three day's travel away, 221.7 light-years, are transmitted and received without error, in sharp contrast to the garbled messages previous ships would on occasion receive at a quarter the distance. Space noise damping is -90 decibels, and frequency response on all hailing and sideband channels is accurate to 10^{-9} MHz. I would rate *Enterprise* communications as excellent, bordering on superb.

LUIS FERARRA, HELMSMAN
Helmsman's Log:

The *Enterprise* is a joy to steer. Its turning radius is sharper than you would expect in such a large craft, and the helm's response is quicker than any I've ever sat behind. I'm not crazy about having the Captain's chair directly behind mine, since it's hard to shake the feeling he's looking over my shoulder all the time, but the time delay between the giving of a command and its execution is that much faster. The *Enterprise*'s weaponry is a marked improvement over previous systems. The forward and rear laser banks can discharge stronger and faster than anything I've ever fired. But I would be less than honest if I didn't say this remarkably innovative ship is using weaponry first developed a century ago. Even still, I sure wouldn't want to cross this ship.

GREGOR ALLINSKY, SCIENCE OFFICER
Science Log:

Some significant improvements have been designed into the Science Console, notably, a much greater sensor capability. The warp-assisted long-range sensors, both tight focused and wide scan, can sweep fore and aft ships to distances up to 30 light-years, while the capability of close-range sensors is simply unbelievable, as they can detect individual molecules in the interstellar void.

But the most extraordinary science innovation is the amazing new on-board computer. With the duotronic circuits installed, the *Enterprise*'s computer contains practically the whole of present galactic knowledge, making my task as Science Officer immeasurably easier. My duty tour aboard the *Enterprise* will be a pleasure.

SARAH APRIL, M.D., MEDICAL OFFICER
Medical Log:

I am on the whole satisfied with the Sick Bay and auxiliary medical facilities available on the *Enterprise*. Landing party tricorders are more powerful and have a much greater diagnostic range because of the duotronic-assisted transtator circuits. The Sick Bay's Metabolic Analyzer is excellent, as is most surgical and post-operative equipment.

However, the *Enterprise* has a much, much greater range than any previous starship. It is going to go farther and run into more kinds of trouble than any previous ship, and I have my doubts that the Sick Bay is capable of responding to all the demands that will inevitably be placed on it. I am going to continue examining this situation, and I'm confident that some significant improvements can be made in this area.

FIRST TIME GATE FOUND BY USS WELLS

2190

STARBASE 20
GREGORY TREE, COMMODORE

Commodore's Log:

I have impossible news to report, the circumstances of which I can positively confirm, but which are, well, impossible. The USS *Wells* embarked from Starbase 20 thirty-three solar days ago on a five-year exploratory mission to several unknown sectors of space. Yesterday, the ship returned, limping in on impulse power, its warp engines badly damaged. However, when the Captain reported to me, as per star Fleet protocol, he stated that the *Wells* had been gone over three solar years. This is impossible.

It is also clearly irrefutable. Not only do the crew of the *Wells* swear to it unanimously, but the computer-kept Ship's Log verifies it, and the engineering tests reveal metal stress and other operating deterioration that could only have occurred over years of interstellar travel. Clearly, the *Wells* has somehow traveled back in time.

And it nearly destroyed them. The *Wells* captain knows exactly when this time-jump happened. His ship was traveling through an empty sector when ship sensors began picking up inexplicable starboard drag on the warp engines. First, of course, he suspected engine malfunction, but his Science Officer reported that it was the local space-time geometry itself that was creating the effect, and its power was issuing from a particular point in empty space.

Investigating this phenomenon closer, the *Wells* approached the mysterious point, until the entire ship felt a violent wrenching. Several shuddering waves passed through the vessel, damaging the dilithium assembly. Afterwards, everything seemed the same, except the damaged warp engines dictated an early return from their mission. They almost didn't make it back either. Power levels on the ship had dipped dangerously low by the time they returned, not even able to initiate warp drive by the end.

But at the end, they and we discovered that this unexplained wrenching sent them back in time several years. There is no possibility of fraud, and no acceptable explanation according to known laws of physics. What that time gate is, and how it reverses the time flow, is a subject I'll leave to the scientists, but I'll verify the actual event: the *Wells* traveled through time.

COMET IS CREATED AFTER WARP CRUISER EXPLODES

Incredible incident is first of its kind.

2193

USS BRAHE, CONSTITUTION CLASS
PETER SULLIVAN, CAPTAIN

Captain's Log:

I'm reporting that we've located the remains of the USS *Ajax*, recently reported missing. It just seems like most every new generation of starship is hailed as the most spectacular achievement of modern technology, and every new generation has its own terrible disaster, its own sacrifice at the cost of progress. Some are lost in collision; others disappear. And some, like the *Ajax*, blow up.

Initial playbacks of the *Ajax*'s final Log receptions are unrevealing, but at some point, approximately three stardates ago, to judge by the scatter velocity of the remains, the *Ajax* underwent an enormous on-ship explosion great enough to disintegrate the warp cruiser.

Though the boys from the Star Fleet Safety Board are good enough to pull explanations almost literally out of thin air, we might never know the cause of the accident. Well, I may not be an expert, but it seems obvious that the only force that could have caused the unforseen, cataclysmic explosion is matter/antimatter annihilation. And, if you ask me, it had something to do with that new dilithium convertor assembly. That's such a critical component in new starship design, and one that should have been tested more, that, well, I'm afraid we haven't seen the end of trouble from this "miracle" crystal.

Whatever the cause, the aftereffects of the ship's explosion have produced what looks like, and for all purposes is, in fact, a comet. The dust has frozen into a single cluster, whose head had been heated to glowing luminosity by the nearby star and whose tail extends out behind it a full hundred kilometers. I don't believe there has ever been an artificial comet produced before; I'm only sorry it was such a tragedy that caused this one.

In memory of the lost *Ajax* and its crew, I recommend that this new mini-comet be named after the ship.

TALOS STAR GROUP DECLARED OFF-LIMITS

2196

Star Fleet Command

There were some interstellar dangers encountered in space exploration that were, for one reason or another, simply too terrible a menace to reveal. The Talos Star System posed just such a threat, and General Order #7 was issued banning any contact whatsoever with the unknown peril, a peril so awesome that this Order carried with it, a sentence of death for breaking it, the only Order in Federation history to do so.

It was more than a decade later that the galactic danger posed by Talos was revealed. The Talosians were a race who had developed extraordinary psionic powers of illusion-making, but at the expense of their genetic vitality. No longer able to reproduce, they desperately needed breedable species to inhabit their planet, and with such psionic abilities, could have enslaved millions under the spell of their illusion. Moreover, on first contact, the Talosians seemed quite ready to do so, hence, General Order #7.

GENERAL ORDER #7

Notice is hereby given to all United Federation of Planets' ships, of every class and mission, that the Talos Star System and all space within ten light-years has been declared OFF-LIMITS.

No ship or person shall trespass into this proscribed region for any purpose whatsoever. There are *NO* exceptions to this Prohibition.

Any transgression of General Order #7 shall be punishable by DEATH.

Repeat: The Talos Star System has been declared OFF-LIMITS.

FEDERATION DEVELOPS ITS ULTIMATE WEAPON: THE PHASER

2198

ARCTURUS TEST RANGE
BRUNO WILHELM, SCIENCE OFFICER
Science Log:

—TOP SECRET—
Confidential Report to Star Fleet Command

Declassified Stardate: 2827.8

Contained herein is my preliminary report on the development of the new phaser weaponry.

We have had excellent results with the melding of two separate weapons systems, lasers and particle-beam cannons. Lasers had the penetration but not the impact force of particle beams, and similarly particle-beams delivered a big punch, but couldn't penetrate shielding the way lasers can.

It looks like we've been able to combine both into a single device. The hardest part was aligning the frequencies of the separate systems so that they would complement one another, instead of interfering. With wide-band frequency sampling and multi-core ejection nozzle, the phaser can fire a blast that will cut through all present shielding with devastating force.

Consequently, a direct hit produces a whole different type of destructive effect than lasers or particle beams. So much energy is concentrated on a single target, that the inter-molecular cohesion is ruptured: the object literally disintegrates. Anyone who watched as we vaporized a drone ship would know that this is a whole new level of weaponry.

While we've only been experimenting with large-scale systems here at Arcturus Firing Range, calculations I've been making on the side seem to indicate that the phaser can be constructed as small as a handgun. Its power would be much less, of course, but with transtator physics, there doesn't seem to be any theoretical objection to such a design. In addition, this less severe setting can be modified so that the target would not be destroyed but, rather, organic processes would be temporarily stunned. This would make the hand-held phaser a much more humane defensive instrument than currently available.

Firing and analysis will continue, but I think we've got the main problems licked. I wouldn't be surprised if phasers don't become standard equipment on starships in a few solar years.

23rd
CENTURY

(INCLUDES DECLASSIFIED MATERIAL)

OVERVIEW

The first fifteen years of the twenty-third century have been filled with exploration, encounters with extra-galactics, and startling evidence of time warps and parallel universes. There were starship dramas, political crises, and meetings with a large number of new lifeforms from hostile Gorns to lovable Tribbles. It appears that the Federation's activities are growing so rapidly that a decade now contains as much significant activity as did a quarter-century before.

While this era's Babel Conference wasn't nearly as tumultuous as its predecessor, it too had its own high level of drama. The entry of Coridan, a dilithium-rich planet, into the Federation was the most controversial topic, and an assassination attempt and a plot to blow up a delegate-laden starship was made to stymie the election. To no avail: Coridan is now a full member of the UFP.

Dr. Daystrom, the inventor of duotronics, tried to forge another revolution in computer theory, the M-5 computer. Engrammed with human personality traits to supplement its independent-thought circuits, the M-5 proved tragically flawed, destroying several starships during a war-games exercise. The M-5 turned out to be anything but the "ultimate computer" its designer claimed it to be.

Perhaps the most important political event of the decade was the Treaty of Organia, establishing an uneasy peace between the Federation and the always-hostile Klingon Empire. Organia was thought to be a placid but backwards world that both the UFP and the Klingons were trying to bring under their sphere of influence (Klingon influence, of course, means total domination by their mpire). However, it turned out that the Or-anians were creatures with unimaginable sionic powers of such magnitude that their herest thought could have obliterated a tarship. Faced with such unquestionable uperiority, the two combating alliances greed to galactic neutrality, a neutrality hat is often tested, but not yet violated.

he meeting of new worlds and races con-nues at an ever-growing rate, but it is in e field of theoretical astronomy that the ost startling encounters have been taking ace this past decade. Federation starships ave, on several occasions, entered into ackwards time warps, placing them cen-ries or even millennia in the past. In addi-on, the existence of several, perhaps many, arallel universes accessible to our own rough time gates or local space-time de-

formations, opens up a broad field of scientific speculation. There seems to be substantial limitations on the scope of our present scientific theories, and it is very possible that in the near future, another Daystrom or Einstein will come along and outline an entirely new universe-picture. Nothing short will explain the scientific enigma that has been occurring with increasing frequency. As the twenty-third century progresses, it appears that more questions are going to be raised than answered. And so we forge into the future, learning ever more, learning more and more what remains to be known.

USS ENTERPRISE CONSTITUTION II CLASS

2215

After completing three years of its last five year mission, the much-used *Enterprise* was returned to Earth dry dock, where it has recently completed extensive refitting and uprating. From one-third better engine performance to warp-powered phasers, from improved medical facilities to faster turbo-lifts, the refitted *Enterprise* has solidified its position as flagship for the UFP Star Fleet

Specifications

Length	304.7 m
Beam	146.2 m
Draught	67 m
Mass	190 million kg
Engineering Section	length: 112 m
	diameter: 32 m
Command/Living Saucer	diameter: 146.2 m
	draught: 32 m
Nacelles	length: 154.6 m
	diameter: 12.4 m

Ship's Complement

Officers	47
Crew	438
Standard Ship's Complement	485

Performance

Range: Standard	6,500 light-years
Maximum	10,000 light-years
Cruising Velocity	Warp 8 (512c)
Maximum Velocity	Warp 12 (1728c)
Typical Voyage Duration	5 yrs @ st. comp. (est)
Acceleration	0 - .99c—19 sec
	.99c - warp engage—1.1 sec
	Warp 1 - 4—.78 sec
	Warp 4 - 8—.67 sec
	Warp 8 - 12—2.13 sec

Systems Overview

Navigation	Warp celestial guidance
Communication	Subspace Radio
Computers	Duotronic II
Weapons	9 Phaser Banks
	200 Matter/Antimatter Magnetirap Photon Torpedoes
Life Support: Gravity	.2 - 1.2 g
Atmosphere	20% O$_2$; 11% humidity
Sustenance Duration	Up to 22 years if outfitted for long-duration exploration

Engineering and Science

Engines	Advanced fourth generation warp drive

- Fuel: Dilithium Focus, 1:1 matter to antimatter
- Duotronic II computer capability
- Matter/Antimatter mixing chambers in fins to nacelles for more efficient energy conversion (pulsed warp drive)
- Cumulative radiation exposure shields installed in upgraded transporter room
- Matter/Antimatter mixing chambers to also fuel adjacent
- Impulse engine, to guarantee propulsion in case of warp engine failure

Improvements and Innovations

- Pulsed warp drive provides much more efficient propulsion
- Phasers tied directly into matter/antimatter engine for much more powerful delivery
- Enlarged cargo deck
- Improved sick bay
- Expanded recreation facilities
- Additional docking ports added

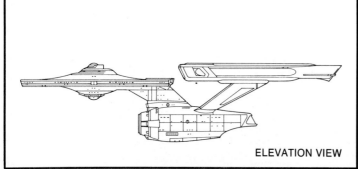

ELEVATION VIEW

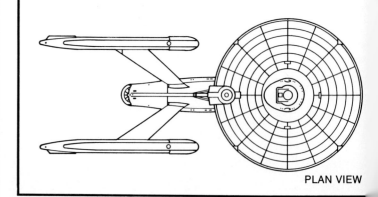

PLAN VIEW

SPECULATIONS

Introduction:

The purpose of this Chronology is to give a concise history of spaceflight so that our present capabilities and resources may be better understood. However, this knowledge has little cogency until it's applied to the future, and it is the future of spaceflight that this section examines.

Star Fleet Command recently commissioned a blue-ribbon panel of experts to ponder the future, and offer their speculations on the future of spaceflight as it relates to their specific discipline. Now, an expert's opinion is just as likely as not to be too conservative, too grandiose, or just plain wrong (see Chapter 5: 2100 Conference). But these speculations should provide a framework for personal future-thinking. Who knows, perhaps there is an Einstein out there who will read this book and forever alter our lives by some revolutionary breakthrough sparked in whatever small way, by the Chronology.

STELLAR ENGINEERING: IF YOU DON'T LIKE A PLANET'S CLIMATE, MOVE IT!

The energy-boosting properties of dilithium have been incorporated into starship construction, but these revolutionary crystals haven't yet filtered down to the industrial level. When they do, we will have the most powerful tool at hand in history. What's more, intensive research is discovering more efficient configurations of dilithium faceting, coupled with the synergistic advantages of multiple engine coordination, will mean man can soon move mountains and more.

Preliminary calculations indicate that we will soon be able to provide enough thrust to move a planet the size of the Earth's moon out of its orbit and to another location as far away as we wish. The possibilities of terraforming new worlds to accomodate all intelligent lifeforms will be greatly expanded, and the occasional disasters caused by worlds colliding will now be prevented. There is speculation that a warp-generated field may some stardate be strong enough to deflect a whole star from its position; we may be able to move whole stars around the galaxy. We are nowhere near the capability yet, but there is nothing theoretically impossible in the scheme. And possibly, it will be a reality in our lifetimes.

PSIONICS: DO YOU KNOW WHAT I'M THINKING? YOU PROBABLY DO.

The United Federation of Planets contains lifeforms of extremely advanced intelligence, capable of exploring the galaxy and other modern marvels. However, in the course of these explorations, Federation starships have again and again encountered lifeforms unimaginably superior to our own. And this superiority almost invariably takes the form of psionic abilities. Whether it is the Platonian ability to move objects or the awesome power of Organians, psionic aptitude seems to be the evolutionary path all we lifeforms are pursuing.

Perhaps this speculation has no place among the other practical suggestions in this chapter, but neurophysiologists tell us there are no inherent limitations in our brain structure prohibiting the development of advanced psionic abilities in humans. In fact, all the equipment seems already to be in place; we only lack the knowledge or wisdom to be able to tap this amazing potential within ourselves.

So this is perhaps where the real face of the future will be determined. If mankind evolves sufficiently to be able to harness his psionic potential, then all the technological wonders in the galaxy will be as children's tiny steps to this gigantic leap in progress. As sages have told us throughout recorded history, the future is within ourselves.

SUPERWARP: NEXT STOP, THE NEXT GALAXY.

There have been numerous experiences in recent Federation history with alternative universes, different dimension of space-time. Ships have been lost to parallel universes, and the forward momentum of time does not appear to be irreversible. Clearly, our present laws of physics and chemistry are incomplete. Until we can arrive at a new theory that can account for these "impossible" events, we must make the best with our admittedly inadequate universe-view.

However, there has been some mathematical speculation done into this question of different dimensions. There is no mathematical barrier to conceptualizing higher dimensions, and in fact the mathematical computations have already been worked out for the next dimension of space-time after warp. This dimension, called superwarp, operated on what the mathematicians inform us is the integrated metrical tangent to the warp curve.

Simply put, this means that instead of cubing the speed of light (warp 3 $=3^3c$. or 27 times the speed of light), superwarp will produce phenomena at the fourth power. Therefore superwarp 3 will be eighty-one times the speed of light; warp 7 will be 2401 times c., etc. No one yet knows how to achieve this superwarp effect, but the mathematics are in place. It will no doubt only be a matter of time before the technology catches up, and then

SPECULATIONS

spaceflight will undergo a quantum leap comparable or perhaps even greater (extra-galactic travel?) than that which accompanied warp drive.

SPACEFLIGHT EXPLORATION: WHERE DO WE GO NEXT?

Up till now, the United Federation of Planets has, understandably, directed the thrust of its exploration program to new worlds in neighboring sectors of space. This has yielded invaluable new contacts and knowledge and will be continued. But there are two other directions that future spaceflights will explore.

The first is inward, toward the galactic center. Approaching the middle of the Milky Way, the number of stars and their proximity grows ever greater, until all space is lit by the fires of a billion close suns, and the gravitational forces are stronger than any we can imagine, stronger at least than a million black holes. All the known laws of physics will be distorted in unknown ways, and explorations in this direction should generate some startling new insights into the scientific picture of reality.

The other direction, of course, is outward, to neighboring galaxies. At 48 kiloparsecs, the Large Magellanic Cloud is our nearest neighbor, and this distance seems unreachably distant. However, if the speculation about the superwarp speeds produces a new quantum leap in spaceflight range, then a speed of superwarp 10 would reach the LMC in approximately fifteen years. Some stardate, travel to galaxies will take only as long as travel among stars now consumes.

EDUCATIONAL TIME TRAVEL: HOW TO VISIT THE GOOD OLD DAYS.

It's well known that the most popular educational program of modern times has been the "Worlds in Evolution" course that permits students to travel to planets in different stages of development in order to experience firsthand the drama and mystery of lifeform evolution.

The next, probably inevitable step is to visit, not other worlds, but other times. The capacity to travel back through time is nearly within our control. Numerous starships have slipped through time gates into previous eras, and a concerted research program could locate those areas in space where the space/time fabric opens in a threshold to the past.

The educational benefits would be incalculable. What better demonstration of starships tactics could there be than to witness the Battle of Cheron being fought? Or imagine the excitement of watching the legendary Wright brothers make the first-manned flight at Kitty Hawk? Time travel will no doubt be the most important step forward education has ever taken.

Educational Time Travel—Minority Opinion
"I Live For Today."

A very optimistic picture can be painted about the benefits and excitement of educational time travel, to really be at the scene of history in the making. But this glowing vision neglects one vital and probably unsolvable problem. How do we twenty-third-century time tourists keep from interfering with the course of events? How do we prevent ourselves from altering the course of history, with incalculable consequences?

The answer is quite simply we can't. Our presence is almost guaranteed to enter into the flow of events. A man we might talk to on the street might be so distracted by our foreignness that he steps in front of an automobile five minutes later, and his son who will now never be born was to have been the person to discover a new vaccine that would have saved millions of lives, among whom are the forebearers of billions of galactic citizens, etc.

And this scenario is not only plausible, it is inevitable. I cannot believe that adequate safeguards separating time travelers from the times they visit can be designed, much less perfectly implemented. Time travel, for educational or any other reason, represents a terrible menace and should by all means be forever prohibited.

MEDICAL SPECULATIONS: MAYBE IT'S TIME FOR A BETTER YOU.

The most promising field in medicine right now is the reexamination of a concept that had been proposed as early as the twentieth century, but had lost popularity. This is the idea of the cyborg, the adaptation of the human body to exist naturally in environments otherwise inimical to mankind. This may take several forms. The first is the introduction of exogenous compounds, chemical and electrochemical devices, into the body and connected with the regulating homeostatic system humans already use to keep themselves functioning. This could include artificial lungs, which could extract usable oxygen from an atmosphere otherwise deadly, or perhaps artificial digestion organs can be implanted to use available but presently indigestible indigenous foods. Another plan calls for a metallic exoskeleton, connected to the central nervous system for control, which would multiply man's strength enormously. Other cyborgnetic concepts can be easily imagined.

The number of new worlds we are finding has created unlimited potential for human settlement, if only humans could adapt to the particular ecological characteristics of each planet. The cyborg concept will permit just such a useful adaptation.

Medical Speculations—Minority Opinion
"I like the way I am!"

The Minority Opinion takes vehement exception to the casual endorsement of the cyborg concept. It seems that its proponents have unfortunately short historical memories.

The last great conflict that divided mankind concerned eugenic engineering, the manipulation of genes to produce "superior" humans. Well, the superior humans turned out to be meglomaniac oppressors, and the subsequent genetic studies have shown that a diversified gene pool is absolutely vital to the successful evolution of the species. We don't know what dangers await us in the future, and the versatility of genes to adapt may some stardate ensure the survival of the species.

The Minority Opinion can easily envision the same schism in the human race developing between regular people and cyborgs. Though their capabilities cannot be genetically transferred, the tendency to equate superiority with cybrinetically increased strength or more adaptable breathing or eating ... s, we believe, considerable and even inevitable.

Superior strength or superior genes; neither adds up to a superior human being. The Minority Opinion feels that research should be aimed not at adapting man to environment but environment to man. At any cost, let us try and avoid any discordant fragmentation of the species. Mankind is divided enough without this additional splitting.

WE HAVE INSTANT EVERYTHING, SO WHY NOT INSTANT COMMUNICATIONS?

Subspace radio is one of the crowning technical achievements of our time. Communication of warp 30 and higher speeds messages across the Federation at an incredibly swift rate. But not swift enough. The frontiers of exploration are expanding at a rate faster than subspace radio can keep up with, and communications can sometimes take weeks before reaching a Star Base.

There is a theory gaining currency that will clear up this time lag, will in fact, produce communications that will be practically simultaneous. Subspace radio now uses encoded particles that are sent down the warp curve and retrieved and decoded at their destination. If instead, an energized light wave can penetrate the warp curve into the warp dimension and then emerge back into our space, the time this process would take is negligible. Since it would bypass the time curve of warp, this superspace radio will be nigh on instantaneous.

Presently, there is no known technology that can energize a light wave transmission sufficiently to penetrate this theoretical warp curve exterior. But that certainly doesn't mean it won't be found and that we won't some stardate be able to call among star systems as quickly as we could call around the corner.

WEAPONRY: THE UNBELIEVABLE IS YET TO COME.

On the graphic boards at Star Fleet Command is a new system of

detention inspired by the confrontation with the Tholians. This consists of a self-spinning energy web of contracting tractor beams. An intruding ship is torpedoed by a web matrix that rapidly spins itself around the ship, completely immobilizing it. Deflector shields are useless against this human binder, since the shields themselves are also wrapped within the shrinking energy shell. So without violence, these webs can incapacitate an enemy, leaving surrender as the only alternative.

A more radical and destructive weapons systems is also being contemplated. Since we can send our own starships and our subspace radio into another dimension, theoreticians are working on a weapons system that, when fired at an enemy ship, will deform the space-time fabric around the vessel sufficiently to send it into another dimension. The ship would simply disappear forever from our universe. Whether this awesome final weapon can or will be built is a subject of intense debate currently within Star Fleet Command.

WHAT WILL THEY THINK OF NEXT? STARSHIPS THAT CHANGE THEIR SHAPE!

As dilithium and future technological innovations become operational, starship design will naturally be adapted to accomodate the breakthroughs. A Ship Page in this chapter gives a picture of what coming starships might ressemble.

However, there is discussion and research going on that would produce an unlimited number of ship designs, for this idea concerns the exterior sheathing that defines starship lines. Because of warp stresses and galactic parameters, starship hulls are presently made of thick layers of trititanium, the hardest shipbuilding material known.

But there is an equivalence between matter and energy, and there is no reason why hulls can't be manufactured from energy fields of varied density and strength. A future ship's computer can calculate the optimum contour for a particular mission, and a field-energizing generator (perhaps like the one discussed in the "Weaponry" speculation of this chapter that would

produce a Tholian-like detention web) would simply create the field. It could be opaque or transparent, as large or small as needed, any shape, and exit ports located anywhere they're programmed to be. With the breakthroughs happening every stardate in computer capacity and energy generation, this still visionary scheme may become a reality sooner than might be thought.

SHIPS

Declassified SF 101SW

As a result of breakthroughs in advanced warp theory and starship construction, the Constitution II Class ships will, in the near future, be superseded by an impressive new generation of ships. No longer tied to the rigid specification of metal alloys, new starship hulls will consist of variable magnetic matrix sheathing which can be computer-conformed to each particular mission's needs.

Specifications

Length	638 m
Beam	380 m
Draught	166.7 m
Mass	80 million kg

Ship's Complement

Officers	52
Crew	540
Standard Ship's Complement	592

Performance

Range	Standard 50,000 ly
	Maximum 200,000 ly
Cruising Velocity	SuperWarp 6 (1,296c)
Maximum Velocity	SuperWarp 8 (4,096c)

Systems Overview

Navigation	SuperWarp galactic guidance
Communication	Superspace Radio
Weapons	10 Phaser Banks
	500 Magnetirap Photon Torpedoes
	Field disruption prevention generator

Life Support

Gravity:	.2-1.2 g
Atmosphere:	20% O_2; 11% Humidity

Engineering and Science

Engines	First generation SuperWarp drive
Exterior Sheathing	A conformable magnetic matrix instead of traditional metallic alloys

Improvements and Innovations

- Largest starship in Federation history
- First to be equipped with SuperWarp capability
- Superspace Radio communication using same breakthrough in warp theory
- Ship capable of traveling to Small Magellanic Cloud

(ELEVATION VIEW)

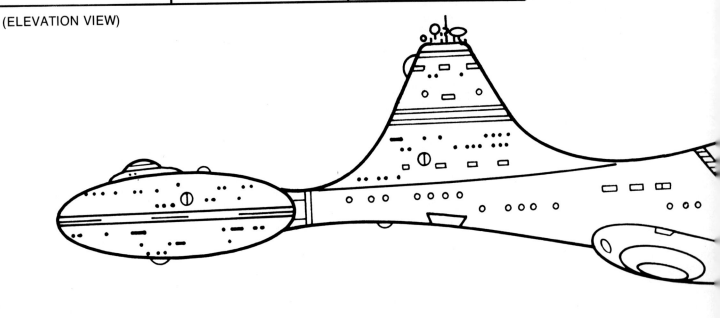

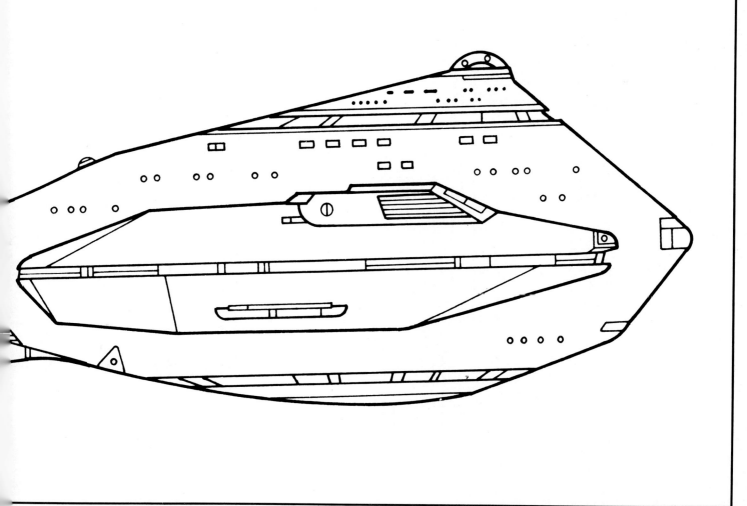

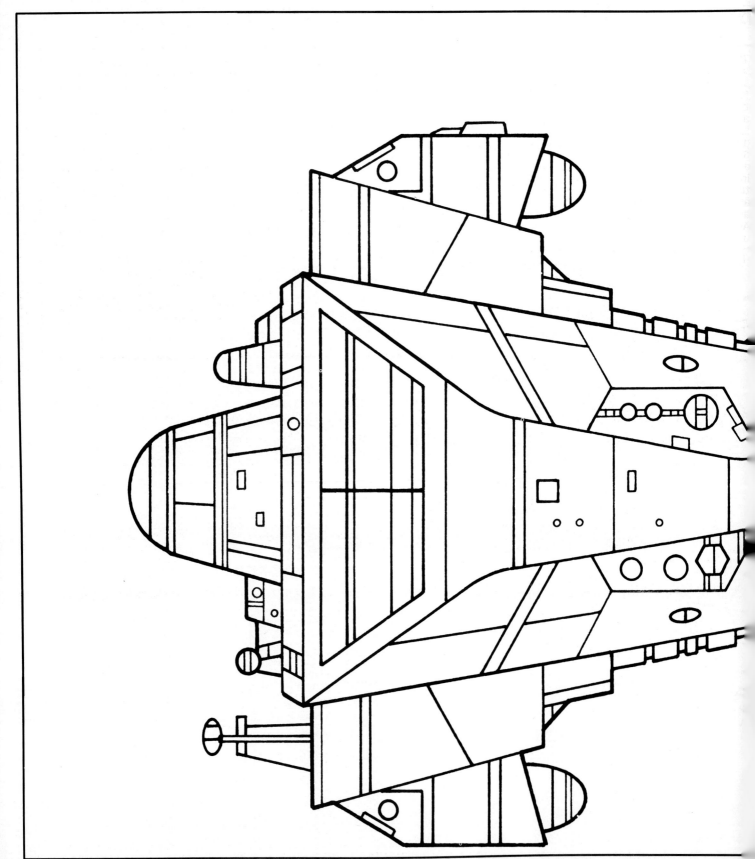

Declassified SF 102SW

This proposed SuperWarp vessel is intended to be the stellar workhorse of the future. Because of a new breakthrough in warp theory, a whole new power of warp speed, SuperWarp, has been added (SW 2 equals $2^4 = 16c$; SW 3 equals $3^4 = 81c$; etc.). As a result of this quantum leap in starship capability, voyages to the galactic center, Small and Large Magellanic Clouds and perhaps even to the Andromeda galaxy may soon be possible.

(PLAN VIEW)

Specifications

Length	524 m
Beam	193 m
Draught	85 m
Mass	57.5 million kg

Ship's Complement

Officers	58
Crew	427
Standard Ship's Complement	485

Performance

Range	Standard 75,000 ly Maximum 225,000 ly
Cruising Velocity	SuperWarp 7 (2400c)
Maximum Velocity	SuperWarp 9 (6500c)

Systems Overview

Navigation	SuperWarp galactic guidance
Communication	Superspace Radio
Weapons	6 Phaser Banks 250 Magnetirap Photon Torpedoes Field disruption prevention generator
Life Support	Gravity: .2-1.2 g Atmosphere: 20% O_2; 11% Humidity

Engineering and Science

Engines	First generation SuperWarp drive Intercooler flank fins Separable command con
Exterior Sheathing	A comformable magnetic matrix instead of traditional metallic alloys

Improvements and Innovations

- Wedge planned to be new workhorse of galactic transportation
- Equipped with SuperWarp propulsion and Superspace Radio

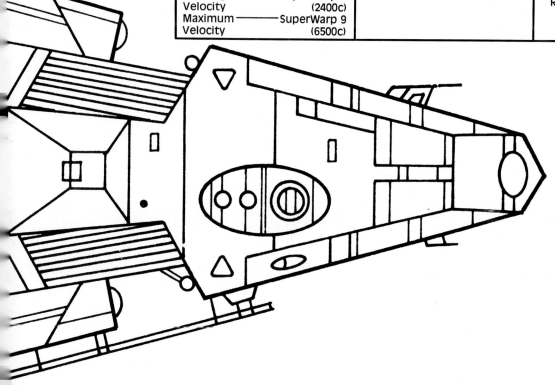

SHIP SUMMARY

SHIP	LENGTH	MASS	SHIP'S COMPLEMENT CREW AND PASSENGERS	PROPULSION	RANGE	CRUISING VELOCITY	IMPROVEMENTS AND INNOVATIONS
Copernicus	100m	2.72 mil.kg	22	Chemical/ Fission	900M km	55,000 km/hr	First mass produced circumlunar ships
Lewis and Clark	125m	2.81 mil.kg	109	Fission	150 mil. km	700,550 km/hr	Clean fission engines doubled the efficiency of early-fission power packs
Wheeler	145m	4.17 mil.kg	36	Advanced Fission	600 mil. km	135,000 km/hr	First class of ships to be equipped with elementary independent thought computers
Tycho Brahe	300m	.5 bil.kg	98	Fusion	800 mil. km	200mil. km/hr	First class of ship with elementary interstellar celestial navigation
Icarus	120m	8.6 mil.kg	40	Advanced Fusion	5.75 bil. km	.75c (800mil. km/hr)	First class of ship with onboard shuttle craft for extra-vehicular excursion
Bonaventure	206m	19.4 mil.kg	45	Warp Drive	25 Light-years	Warp 2 (8c)	First class of ship with warp drive
Amity	236m	25 mil.kg	112	Advanced 1st generation warp drive	35 Light-years	Warp 2.5 (15.6c)	Separate warp engines provide more efficient warp drive
Pollux	258m	27.7 mil.kg	93	2nd advanced 1st generation warp drive	50 Light-years	Warp 2.75 (20.8C)	First class of ship equipped with warp communication capability
Horizon	280m	38.5 mil.kg	224	2nd generation warp drive	150 Light-years	Warp 3 (27c)	First UFP-sponsored starship class

SHIP	LENGTH	MASS	SHIP'S COMPLEMENT CREW AND PASSENGERS	PROPULSION	RANGE	CRUISING VELOCITY	IMPROVEMENTS AND INNOVATIONS
Patton	225m	22.7 mil.kg	157	Advanced 2nd generation warp drive	300 Light years	Warp 3.5 (45.5c)	First class of ships equipped with warp-generated defensive shielding
Enterprise (Starliner)	300m	52.7 mil. kg	950	Advanced 2nd generation warp drive	350 Light-years	Warp 3.2 (36.5c)	First class of ship equipped with subspace radio
King Charles	264m	34 mil. kg	2000	Advanced 2nd gen. warp drive	400 Light-years	Warp 3.5 (45.5c)	Largest capacity starship in Federation history
Tritium	202m	47.6 mil.kg	250	3rd gen. warp drive	(Est) 800 Light-years	Warp 4 (64c)	First starship with third generation warp drive engines. First starship equipped with tricorder.
Endurance	185m	54 mil.kg	294	Advanced 3rd gen. warp drive	1000 Light-years	Warp 4 (64c)	First starship to surpass warp 4
Moscow	245m	92.5 mil.kg	344	Advanced 3rd gen. warp drive	1500 Light-years	Warp 4.5 (91.1c)	First starship equipped with transporter
Enterprise	300m	172 mil.kg	430	4th gen. warp drive	5000 light-years	Warp 6 (216c)	This class contains all recent advances in Federation technology
Enterprise (Uprated)	304.7m	190 mil.kg	485	Advanced 4th gen. warp drive	6500 light-years	Warp 8 (512c)	Pulsed warp drive provides much more efficient propulsion

GLOSSARY

ANTIMATTER—identical but exactly opposite to matter found in our universe; when matter becomes antimatter, both are completely transformed into energy.

ANTIMATTER NACELLES—rear fuel tubes containing antimatter for warp engines.

ANTIMATTER UNIVERSE—universe with exactly opposite space-time matrix than ours (see space-time matrix).

ASTROTELEMETRY—the science which specializes in communications over interplanetary and astronomical distances.

ASTRONOMICAL UNIT—unit of measurement based on distance between Earth and the Sun.

BLACK HOLE—site of a dying giant star's irreversible collapse; the gravitational attraction is so great no light or any other radiation can escape.

BORON-STEEL—extremely hard metal alloy used in early starship construction.

CARTOGRAPHY—the science of map-making.

CEPHEID VARIABLE—star whose luminosity changes over time, brightening and darkening over (usually) periodic intervals.

COCHRANE DECELERATION MANEUVER—textbook starship maneuver first deployed with great success during the Romulan War.

CONDRITIC ROCK—deep space rocks, particularly common in the Sol System asteroid belt, containing many different elements (iron, nickel, silicon, traces of titanium).

CONTROLLED-GROWTH MICROORGANISMS—organic crops of space farms that can be processed into a full range of foodstuffs.

DILITHIUM CRYSTALS—crystalline mineral used to focus matter-antimatter energy for warp drive.

DUOTRONICS—theoretical computer breakthrough conceived by Earth scientist Richard Daystrom; found in starships from Baton Rouge Class ships onward.

EARTH APPROACHING ASTEROID—Wanderers from the Sol System asteroid belt. There are two classes:
  a) Apollo Asteroids have orbit that intersects Earth
  b) Amor Asteroids have orbit outside Earth, but inside Mars.

ELLIPTICAL TRAJECTORY—flight path using planet fly-by for "slingshot effect" acceleration.

GAMMA RAYS—high energy, ionizing electromagnetic radiation (also known as X-rays).

GENERAL THEORY OF RELATIVITY—descriptio of geometry of four-dimensional space by twentieth century Earth physicist Einstein (see unified field equations).

GEON HOLES—discontinuities in the "walls" o geodynamometric space-time; utilized in warp communication.

GIGAWATT—one billion watts.

HODGKINS' LAW OF PARALLEL PLANET DEVELOPMENT—principle of cultural evolution stating similar planets develop similar cultures.

HOLOGRAPH—three dimensional picture created by programmed lasers.

HYPERSPACE—space outside walls of geodynamometric space-time matrix.

IMPULSE POWER—main propulsion for smal sub-warp craft; also back-up power on war drive starships.

LIBRATION POINTS—gravitational balance points between orbiting bodies, such as Earth and Moon, resulting in weightlessnes

LOCAL SPACE-TIME GEOMETRY—mathematic laws describing physical conditions of surrounding space-time matrix.

NULL GRAVITY—a condition of natural or induced weightlessness.

OCTAHEDRON—an eight-sided structure, such as the eight-faceted dilithium crystal.

OH GROUP—hydroxyl group: one of the basic units of organic life, consisting of bonded oxygen and hydrogen.

PARALLEL UNIVERSES—universes coexistent with our own but in a different space-time matrix (see antimatter universe).

PARSEC—a standard unit of interstellar distance, equivalent to 3.26 light years.

PHASERS—Federation's most advanced weapons system using synergistic combination of lasers and particle-beam cannons.

PROJECT SETI—an early search for extra-terrestrial intelligence succeeding finally with the reception of the "Sagittarian signals" (see Chapter 3, Log 2).

PSIONIC POWER—generic term for extra-evolved mental powers, ranging from telepathy to telekinesis (mind moving matter) and beyond.

RADIO ASTRONOMY—the part of astronomy that studies electromagnetic signals in the radio wave bandwidth, which can be perceived to the limits of the known universe.

S-STARS—unusual class of stars (the Sun among them) containing significant quantities of radioactive technetium-99.

SOLAR YEAR—old-fashioned dating system based on the Earth's time of revolution around the Sun.

SOLID CRYSTAL RECORDINGS—psionically triggered records made from crystals encoded three-dimensionally along lattice structures.

SPACE-TIME MATRIX—a term referring to four-dimensional reality, derived from theoretical mathematics.

SPECIAL THEORY OF RELATIVITY—twentieth century Earth physicist Einstein's brilliant formulation stating that because of the constant speed of light, all physical frameworks are relative to one another.

STARDATE—relativistic dating system based on both chronology and location (see space-time matrix).

SUBSPACE RADIO—warp-speed communications whose signals travel via warp-accelerated, computer-encoded particles.

TECHNETIUM-99—unstable radioactive element created in the cores of certain types of stars (see S-Stars).

TIME GATE—local deformation of space-time matrix, allowing instantaneous entry to the past or, theoretically, the future.

TRANSTATOR PHYSICS—breakthrough in electromechanical physics that revolutionized technology; found in tricorders, transporters, etc.

TRITITANIUM—exceptionally hard metal alloy used in starship construction.

UNIFIED FIELD EQUATIONS—twenty-first century mathematical solutions to the General Theory of Relativity.

UNIVERSAL CUBE LAW—velocity principle underlying warp dynamics; warp $2 = 2^3c. = 8c$; warp $3 = 3^3c = 27c.$; etc.

WARP DRIVE—spaceship propulsion using controlled matter-antimatter annihilation to achieve faster-than-light speeds.

WARP PRINCIPLE—an integration of the normal space-time curve producing faster-than-light speeds (warp $2 = 2^3c. = 8c.$; warp $3 = 3^3c = 27c.$; etc.).

UNITED FEDERATION OF PLANETS